40
W.O.
8743

[*Notified*

G000122349

INSTRUCTIONS
FOR ARMOURERS
1931

By Command of the Army Council,

THE WAR OFFICE,
   30th September, 1931.

The Naval & Military Press Ltd

Published by

The Naval & Military Press Ltd

Unit 10 Ridgewood Industrial Park,
Uckfield, East Sussex,
TN22 5QE England

Tel: +44 (0) 1825 749494
Fax: +44 (0) 1825 765701

www.naval-military-press.com
www.military-genealogy.com

CONTENTS

PAGE

INTRODUCTION vii

PART I

DUTIES AND GENERAL INSTRUCTIONS

CHAPTER I

DUTIES 1

CHAPTER II

EXAMINATIONS AND INSPECTIONS

SEC.
1. Examination by Armourers of Small Arms, Machine-Guns, Mountings and Bicycles of Regular Units ... 3
2. Examination by Circuit Armourers 5
3. Inspections of Small Arms, Machine-Guns, Bicycles, etc., by the C.I.S.A. and R.A.O.C. 6

CHAPTER III

GENERAL INSTRUCTIONS 6

CHAPTER IV

PACKING AND STORAGE OF SMALL ARMS, MACHINE-GUNS, ETC.

1. Packing 10
2. Storage 12

PART II

SMALL ARMS

CHAPTER I

RIFLES

SEC.   PAGE
1. Stripping and Re-assembling   13
2. Cleaning and Lubricating of Rifles in use, and the
   Clearing of Obstructions from the Bore   20
3. Examination   22
4. Repairs, Modifications and Adjustments, etc.   ...   27
5. Re-browning and Re-blacking   46
6. Description and Use of Armourers' Gauges and certain
   Tools   47

CHAPTER II

BAYONETS AND SCABBARDS

Bayonets

1. Stripping and Assembling   51
2. Cleaning   52
3. Examination   52
4. Repairs, Modifications and Adjustments   53

Scabbards

1. Stripping and Assembling   54
2. Cleaning   54
3. Examination   55
4. Repairs, Modifications and Adjustments   55

CHAPTER III

PISTOLS

Pistols, Revolver, No. 1 ('455-in. Webley), Mks. III, IV,
      SEC.   V and VI
      1. Stripping and Assembling   58
      2. Cleaning   59
      3. Examination   60
      4. Repairs, Modifications and Adjustments   ...   61

					PAGE
Pistols, Signal, No. 1, Mk. III*	...	...	...	...	66
Horse-Killer, ·310-in., Mk. I	...	...	...	...	67
Cattle-Killer, ·455-in., Mk. I	...	...	...	...	69

CHAPTER IV

SWORDS AND SCABBARDS

SEC.
1. Stripping and Assembling 70
2. Examination 71
3. Repairs, Modifications and Adjustments 72

PART III

MACHINE-GUNS

CHAPTER I

GUNS, MACHINE, HOTCHKISS, ·303-IN., MKS. I and I*

1. General Information 74
2. Stripping and Assembling 77
3. Cleaning 79
4. Examination of the Gun, etc. 82
5. Repairs, Modifications and Adjustments 86
6. Re-browning and Re-painting 95
7. Description and Use of Tools and Gauges 96

CHAPTER II

GUNS, MACHINE, LEWIS, ·303-IN., MK. I

1. General Information 99
2. Stripping and Assembling 103
3. Cleaning, etc. 106
4. Examination of the Gun, etc. 107
5. Repairs, Modifications and Adjustments, etc. ... 111
6. Re-browning and Re-painting 126
7. Description and Use of Tools and Gauges 127

CHAPTER III

GUNS, MACHINE, VICKERS, ·303-IN., MK. I

SEC.   PAGE

1. General Information   129

2. Stripping and Assembling   134

3. Cleaning, etc.   138

4. Examination of the Gun, etc. 140

5. Repairs, Modifications and Adjustments, etc.   ... 148

6. Re-browning and Re-painting 169

CHAPTER IV

MOUNTINGS FOR VICKERS' ·303-IN. M.G'S.

Mounting, Tripod, ·303-in. M.G., Mk. IV

SEC.

   1. General Information   171

   2. Stripping and Assembling   172

   3. Examination   174

   4. Repairs, Modifications and Adjustments   ... 177

Mounting, Overbank M.G., Mk. I   183

Mounting, Trench, M.G., Mk. I   184

PART IV

BICYCLES

1. General Information   185

2. Stripping and Assembling Mks. IV and IV* Bicycles   187

3. Examination   192

4. Repairs and Adjustments   193

LIST OF APPENDICES

APPENDIX

   I. Browning Mixture and Process   202

   II. Painting of Machine-Guns, Mountings, etc.   ... 203

   III. Polishing of Mountings, tripod, ·303-in. M.G.
      Mk. IV   204

APPENDIX   PAGE

   IV. Instructions for Packing Small Arms in Chests
        Nos. 1 to 12   205

    V. List of Fittings in Chests S.A. Nos. 1 to 7   209

   VI. Plates, Screw, and Taps S.A.   210

  VII. Stocks and Dies, Bicycle   212

 VIII. Special Gauges, components special to examiners,
       and special tools (N.I.V.) supplied to commands
       at home and to authorized stations overseas for
       use of the R.A.O.C. in the examination of Small
       Arms and Machine-Guns in the hands of troops   213

   IX. List of General Drawings supplied apart from these
       instructions   219

INTRODUCTION

These Instructions are for the information and guidance of armourers in the repair and general maintenance of the weapons, etc., entrusted to their care.

They will *not* be taken as authorizing supply, issue or condemnation of stores. Such authority will be found in Equipment Regulations, R.A.O.S., or other relevant War Office regulations, and Instructions for Armourers will *not*, in any circumstances, be quoted as a supporting or superior authority.

For convenience, the general drawings referred to in Appendix IX, and also at the head of some of the chapters, and at the commencement of Part IV, are supplied apart from these instructions in a water-proof docket, and will be separately accounted for. Armourers must not allow these drawings to leave their possession.

INSTRUCTIONS FOR ARMOURERS

PART I

DUTIES AND GENERAL INSTRUCTIONS

CHAPTER I

DUTIES

1. The duties of armourers consist in the examination, re-browning, etc., where necessary, and execution of repairs, modifications, and adjustments, where authorized, of the small arms, machine-guns and mountings, accessories and tools employed with those weapons, bicycles, helmets and chains, and the metal work of accoutrements, saddlery and appointments.

They will also mark all Lewis machine-guns, small arms, bicycles, drums, bugles and trumpets, which may be supplied, in accordance with the instructions contained in Chapter III and as detailed in E.R., Pt. I.

2. In addition to the duties laid down in the foregoing paragraph, armourers will execute any trifling repairs, and also such other work within their capabilities as, under special authority, they may be called upon to perform.

3. Supervision of armourers' work will be carried out by the Assistant Inspectors of Armourers attached to commands or to Central Ordnance Depots.

4. Armourers posted to regular units or corps will be responsible to the C.O. for all repairs, etc., executed by them, and for drawing attention to any neglect of weapons, etc., which pass through their hands. They will also bring to the notice of the C.O. any failure to submit weapons, etc., for inspection at the regular intervals laid down in E.R., Pt. I.

When the duties of their own unit admit, their services will be available for similar duty with other units or corps without extra remuneration.

When posted to commands for duty at Army Ordnance Depots or for employment as circuit armourers, they will be under the immediate orders of the D.A.D.O.S. of the area in which they are stationed.

5. Circuit armourers will perform the work, as required, of all units not provided with armourers. They will also be called upon, as required, to carry out, under the direction of the A.I.A., the R.A.O.C. examination of small arms, machine-guns, mountings, etc., and bicycles, referred to in E.R., Pt. I, and perform any other duties to which they may be directed by the D.A.D.O.S.

6. Armourers are not allowed to make any charge to, nor accept payment from, soldiers for work performed within the scope of their ordinary duties. Repairs necessitated by carelessness or wilful damage on the part of troops are to be executed without addition to pay. Cases of carelessness or wilful damage must be immediately reported, and, except in emergency, repair in such cases is not to be carried out until authority to proceed is obtained.

7. Every endeavour must be made to maintain the weapons, mountings and other equipment in a serviceable condition, and to ensure that, whenever any work has been carried out, the article is serviceable in every respect before it is re-issued.

8. Due care must be exercised that no unnecessary expense to the State is incurred by careless workmanship or by the sentencing of parts as unserviceable which have an appreciable remaining life.

9. The inspection of the weapons, etc., must be carried out periodically, as laid down in E.R., Pt. I, and whenever it becomes necessary. The work must be promptly dealt with in order to avoid accumulation in the workshops, and the withholding of weapons, etc., from troops.

Examination of weapons, etc., taken over from another unit must be carried out as early as possible in order that their condition may be ascertained and reported ; failure to do this may involve the unit in charges for which it may not have been actually responsible.

10. Modifications or alterations to service stores must on no account be made unless authorized. L. of C. and A.C.Is. are published monthly, and should be closely watched for

matters which concern armourers' work. Armourers should keep a record of the paras. concerned.

11. The tools and gauges supplied, *vide* E.R., Pt. I, are to be kept in good repair and are not to be employed for private purposes. When worn out by fair wear, they will be replaced at public expense.

Where practicable, any special tools which may be required for service purposes are to be made or improvised by armourers as required. Material for small services of this nature will usually be available in regimental workshops, but failing that source of supply, an indent for the necessary material, accompanied by an explanation of the circumstances under which it is required, should be submitted. Should the work in hand necessitate the employment of special tools which, having regard to the expense and work involved, it is undesirable to make or improvise locally, application should be made through the A.I.A. who, if satisfied that the tools are essential, will make the necessary recommendations for issue on loan if available.

12. Whenever armourers are in doubt upon any technical details of their work, they will apply direct to the A.I.A. for instructions.

CHAPTER II

EXAMINATIONS AND INSPECTIONS

Section 1.—Examination by Armourers of Small Arms, Machine-Guns, Mountings and Bicycles of Regular Units

1. Examinations are to be carried out by armourers periodically as laid down in E.R., Pt. I. The following is for general guidance :—

Quarterly.—All rifles, bayonets and scabbards, swords and scabbards, pistols, machine-guns (including D.P.) with spare parts, mountings and accessories in use, and all bicycles on charge.

Annually.—All rifles, pistols, bayonets and swords with their scabbards, and bicycles in use, and all machine-guns, with their mountings and accessories, including those held for mobilization. In this examination, the machine-guns, rifles, pistols, and bicycles are to be thoroughly stripped, cleaned and re-oiled. The examination is to take place during the winter season at a time to be determined by the C.O., and, where possible, should coincide approximately with the dates when the quarterly examinations are due in order to avoid unnecessary duplication of work.

2. During the foregoing examinations, repairs are to be effected and defects remedied wherever possible, and the result entered on Army Form G.1048 in duplicate. One copy will be retained by the armourer for reference, and the other forwarded to the O.C. Company, Squadron, or detachment, etc., in the case of the quarterly examination and to the C.O. in the case of the annual examination.

The particulars entered on A.F.G.1048 should be placed under the following headings :

(*a*) Deficiencies, damages and repairs not due to fair wear (*vide* Chapter III).

(*b*) Repairs, due to fair wear, necessitating the exchange of a component.

(*c*) Articles of equipment not seen.

The serial and unit numbers of the weapons, etc., should be quoted in all cases, and the abbreviation " N.F.W." entered in red ink against each item under heading (*a*).

The armourer should then certify that all the equipment (naming the different classes of weapons, etc.) on charge, with the exception of those not seen, has been examined and, where necessary, repaired or adjusted and placed in a serviceable condition before re-issue.

He should then state the general condition of the equipment seen and mention any malpractices which are causing wear or damage to the equipment.

Any exceptional defects found during examination are to be brought to the notice of the A.I.A., who will take action as necessary.

3. The annual report is to present to the C.O. a full statement of the general condition of the weapons, etc., and bicycles on charge of the unit at the conclusion of the annual training.

4. A complete record of the daily work performed at the periodical examinations is to be recorded in Army Book 281 ;

this record is to be ready for the inspection of the A.I.A. at all times.

5. The A.I.A. will visit units in each command in those areas not due for current inspection by either the C.I.S.A. or R.A.O.C.—*see* Section 3—to ensure that authorized repairs are being carried out, and that any serious defects are being brought to notice.

Section 2.—Examination by Circuit Armourers

1. Small arms, machine-guns, etc., and bicycles of units without armourers, will be examined and repaired, etc., as required, by circuit armourers detailed by the D.A.D.O.S. of the area. At these visits the tools supplied to N.C.O. Instructors (*vide* E.R., Pt. I) will also be examined.

2. The circuit, and the dates of visits to the various units in the circuit will be arranged by the D.A.D.O.S.

3. Workshops indents—A.F. G.1045—which under normal circumstances will be supplied before a tour is to commence, should be carefully perused in order that any details which are not fully understood may be made clear before departure. Should it be found that any of the work could be more economically dealt with at the R.A.O.C. workshop or regimental depot, as the case may be, the matter should be brought to the notice of the D.A.D.O.S.

4. Small arm, machine-gun, and bicycle components, including tyres, estimated to be required for use in repair will be supplied in advance by the O.O. Lists of components expended with each unit, supported by the certificate of the C.O. and any unused balance must be produced, on completion of a tour, for accounting purposes, care being taken to ensure that the balance consists only of serviceable components as issued.

5. Circuit armourers attached to regimental depots will draw components, as required, from stock under the authority of the O.C.

6. When weapons, etc., or bicycles are found to be unserviceable, or require more extensive repair than can be executed on the spot, the circumstances will be reported to the D.A.D.O.S.

7. The result of the examination of the arms and bicycles of each unit will be entered on A.Fs. C.349, 350 and 351 and forwarded direct to the A.I.A.

Section 3.—Inspections of Small Arms, Machine-Guns, Bicycles, etc., by the C.I.S.A. and R.A.O.C.

Particulars of these inspections are given in Equipment Regulations, Part I. The special gauges and specially selected components, etc., supplied to commands and certain authorized establishments at home and abroad are detailed in Appendix VIII.

These gauges and components, etc., are to be forwarded to the C.I.S.A., Enfield Lock, Middlesex, annually for examination.

CHAPTER III

GENERAL INSTRUCTIONS

1. Before any examination or repair, etc., is performed on firearms, it must first be ascertained that the weapon is unloaded. Whenever live ammunition is found in a weapon, passed to an armourer for examination, etc., the fact must be immediately brought to the notice of the officer in charge, and the ammunition handed over personally to authorized custody.

On no account must live ammunition be taken into a workshop.

As an extra precaution, regular examination of dummy cartridges must be made before commencing each day's work to ensure that no live rounds are present.

Weapons must never be left cocked.

2. No repair work on small arms and machine-guns which have not recently been examined with gauges, and which, in itself, requires the use of gauges, is to be undertaken unless the gauges are available.

In accordance with this general rule, the repairs detailed in E.R., Pt. I, will not be undertaken in R.A.O.C. workshops by armourers with units nor by circuit armourers.

Repairs excluded by the rule, and not specified in the Appendix, will not be undertaken without reference to the C.I.S.A. through the A.I.A.

At home stations, in cases of doubt, small arms, machine-guns, etc., can be submitted to C.I.S.A.'s travelling examiners by special arrangement with the C.I.S.A. Whenever possible the A.I.A. should first be made acquainted with the facts of the case by the armourer, who should then await the A.I.A.'s instructions.

3. Those parts of machine-guns for which spares are provided for use of troops, and which must be, in consequence, strictly interchangeable, are not to be adjusted in any way which may adversely affect interchange.

Similar care is to be taken with other interchangeable parts of all weapons, etc., and bicycles.

4. Any weapons, mountings, etc., and bicycles, or parts of same, found to be unserviceable must be carefully segregated, and labelled where necessary, to avoid any possibility of their becoming mixed with those which are serviceable. For the same reason D.P. small arms and machine-guns should be kept apart from service weapons during examination and repair.

5. The annual allowances of components, etc., for the repair of small arms and machine-guns are detailed in Equipment Regulations. Armourers should make themselves acquainted with the paras. and appendices of Equipment Regulations, Part I, which concern their work. Circuit Armourers should be fully acquainted in addition with Equipment Regulations, Part III.

6. Spare parts accompanying machine-guns are not to be drawn upon until the component parts of the guns and the annual allowance of parts have been used up.

When parts are of necessity withdrawn from the gun spares, indents must be put forward immediately for their replacement. Similar action must be taken when any small arms, machine-guns, mountings, etc., or bicycles are out of action owing to unserviceable parts, when corresponding serviceable parts are not in possession.

Any unused materials for repair remaining at the end of the year are to be reported to the C.O. as in possession when the indent is forwarded for the next year's supply.

7. Where an ordnance depot is situated at the station of the unit, unserviceable articles, etc., will not be replaced until they have been returned to that depot.

Where such a depot does not exist at the station the unserviceable articles must be returned to store as soon as possible after receipt of the articles in replacement.

8. Any damaged weapons, etc., bicycles, or parts sentenced during inspections or by a board or court of inquiry for special examination by C.I.S.A. or other authority concerned, are to be clearly labelled accordingly before despatch, including a reference to the order under which they are sent.

9. When, on receipt of service stores in replacement of unserviceable peace equipment, it is found that they are in better condition or of later pattern than those held on mobilization charge, a recommendation as to turnover will be made to the C.O.

No change of mobilization equipment must be made unless authority is given.

10. Whenever authorized alterations or modifications to service equipment have been carried out, a report to this effect is to be rendered to the C.O.

11. In all reports relating to rifles, the number of the rifle, including the index letter where shown, and place of manufacture is to be stated. The numbers on pistols and machine-guns and bicycles are also to be quoted.

When any parts of weapons, etc., and bicycles form the subject of a special report, the number, if marked, or any other marking, which may be useful for identification purposes, should be quoted.

12. The gauges supplied to armourers will be verified by the A.I.A.'s annually with the reference gauges supplied, also at any intermediate time should the results of examination of the weapons, etc., indicate such a course to be desirable.

13. Suggestions for improvements in design of service stores may be submitted through the normal channels. Such suggestions should be accompanied, where possible, by sufficient data, including sketches, to enable them to be clearly understood, and should be signed by the individual responsible for the suggestion. Effect upon interchange with existing service stores should be borne in mind.

14. For repair work *not* to be undertaken in R.A.O.C. workshops, nor by armourers with units, nor by circuit armourers, reference should be made to Equipment Regulations, Part I.

15. The classification of small arms and machine-guns other than Service weapons is given in Equipment Regulations, Part I.

16. The marking of small arms, Lewis machine-guns, bicycles and certain musical instruments will be carried out

strictly in accordance with Equipment Regulations, Parts I and III. Any other form of marking is unauthorized and strictly forbidden.

17. The re-browning of small arms and machine-guns will be carried out in accordance with the instructions contained in Parts II and III, Appendix I, and Equipment Regulations, Part I.

18. The painting of machine-guns, etc., will be carried out in accordance with Appendix II, and Equipment Regulations, Part I.

19. Instructions as to materials and components and tools for the repair of bicycles are given in Equipment Regulations, Part I. Details are also given as to additional tools for repair of bicycles available on loan from the R.A.O.C. in peace.

20. Damages and repairs due to unfair wear (negligence or carelessness) will be reported and dealt with in accordance with Equipment Regulations, Part I.

21. Barrels of rifles found to be cord-worn, but not unserviceable, will be marked $\frac{*}{W}$ on the left side of the " knox " form at the rear end when the wear is at the breech, and at the front end when the wear is at the muzzle.

When any doubt exists, the following points will be observed when determining the serviceability or otherwise of cord-worn barrels :—

    (i) The barrel is unserviceable through cord-wear at the breech when the cartridge fired in it shows clear signs of having expanded into the grooves made by the cord.

    (ii) Before a barrel is sentenced as unserviceable through cord-wear at the muzzle, it will be, if possible, tested for accuracy by the unit.

For other markings, indicating damages to small arm and machine-gun barrels which do not render the barrels unserviceable, see Equipment Regulations, Part I.

CHAPTER IV

PACKING AND STORAGE OF SMALL ARMS, MACHINE-GUNS, ETC.

Section 1.—Packing

1. Small arms, and machine-guns with spare parts, etc., tools and accessories must be properly packed to avoid injury during transit.

For this purpose, approved patterns of chests and cases, as detailed in Sections B.3 and C.1 of Vocabulary of Army Ordnance Stores, are provided. Where not provided with metal hinges or fastenings, the lids are secured by screws.

2. Instructions for packing small arms in Chests Nos. 1 to 12 are given in Appendix IV.

3. A list of the fittings of small arms Chests Nos. 1 to 7, shewing those which are common to two or more of the chests and those which are special to a particular chest, is given in Appendix V.

4. On removal of the contents from chests and cases having loose fittings, the fittings must be properly replaced in position. Under no circumstances must the fittings be thrown in loosely.

5. Chests for Vickers or Lewis guns have fixed, or otherwise secured, fittings which must not be detached except for authorized modifications made locally. These chests are fitted to take either Vickers ·303-inch, Mk. I, or Lewis ·303-inch, Mk. I guns, the middle bottom hinged fitting, and the chock secured by a cord, being reversed as required for each type of gun respectively.

The Mk. I chest, of which few were made, differs from the Mk. II in that it is about one inch shallower.

The Mk. III differs only slightly from the Mk. II in that it has a steel strip in lieu of a basil strip on the lid to secure the edge of the canvas backing.

A number of chests were provided with additional fittings to take certain Lewis gun spares—*see* para. 19344 L. of C.—but in the case of units now provided with the canvas holdall, the fittings are not used, but one chest for every four guns—stencilled " Lewis Gun & S." is modified to take the screw jack on the barrel and contains also a No 1 wallet, piston rod and gas cylinder.

The chests are stencilled as required according to the

contents, *i.e.*, when containing a Vickers gun, they are stencilled " Vickers ·303 M.G.," for the Lewis gun " Lewis ·303 M.G."

The felt or other absorbent linings must be kept greased with red mineral jelly.

6. Chests are not supplied for inland transport of Mk. IV tripod mountings, but local arrangements will be made to pack them in crates or cases, as available. Care must be taken to protect the dial and joint pins from damage in transit by wrapping canvas, hessian, old blanket or other suitable material round them. The legs must be well clamped and securely tied together.

When issued overseas, the mountings are packed in chests or suitable strong packing-cases.

7. When packed for transmission, other than by sea, the exposed surfaces of steel of small arms and their parts and the unpainted surfaces of steel of machine-guns and their spare parts and tools will be covered with a thin coating of the mixture consisting of equal parts of G.S. lubricating oil (M/80) and red mineral jelly. Unpainted surfaces of steel parts of machine-guns and their spare parts and tools will be coated with red mineral jelly only. Thick coatings must not be applied, owing to the difficulty of removal. In cold weather, the mineral jelly must be heated until it becomes liquid.

When packed for shipment overseas, red mineral jelly only will be used for both small arms and machine-guns, and will be more freely applied.

The bores of rifle, pistol and machine-gun barrels will be similarly treated, the lubricant to be heated as necessary until it becomes thin, and then applied by means of a strip of flannelette well saturated with the lubricant and inserted in the eye of a rod made of twisted copper wire.

In the case of rifle and pistol barrels, the rod must be drawn through from muzzle to breech ; the flannelette should fit fairly tightly in the bore, and the ends be cut evenly, so that any excess of the lubricant may be squeezed out and prevented from reaching the chamber.

The size of the flannelette strip for ·303-inch barrels should be about 8 inches by $1\frac{1}{2}$ inches.

In the case of machine-gun barrels, the rod will be drawn through from both ends. The exterior will also be coated with the lubricant in a cooler condition.

The chamber of rifles and chambers of revolvers will be coated with the lubricant in an unheated condition by means of a strip of flannelette on a short length of bent wire, applied from the breech end.

All surfaces and parts must be thoroughly clean and dry before the lubricant is applied.

8. The barrel casing and steam tube of Vickers machine-guns must be quite free from water, and the screwed and cork plugs removed to prevent condensation on the barrel. The asbestos packing should be dried and oiled to prevent it from rusting the barrel and its bearings.

9. Wherever possible, grease-proof paper should be used when packing steel parts. The use of woollen, linen or cotton materials is strictly forbidden, as they absorb moisture and set up rust. Brown paper must never be in direct contact with steel parts.

Section 2.—Storage

1. Instructions for R.A.O.C. storage are contained in R.A.O.S., Pt. I; unit or mobilization storage in E.R., Pt. I. Special attention should be given by armourers to the care of chests and cases when in their charge, to the materials to be used for cleaning and preservation of the weapons, etc., in store, and the packing of assembled rifle bolts and revolver cylinders when stored separately from the arms.

They must also not fail to fill in and sign A.F. G.1090, posted in the storehouse, containing mobilization equipment, after they have carried out an inspection.

2. Machine-gun barrels for use on mobilization only are distinguished by a white band painted on them, under the orders of the C.I.S.A.

When under special authority such barrels are issued for peace use, the white band will be removed before issue.

PART II

SMALL ARMS

CHAPTER I

RIFLES

Drawing Nos. S.A.I.D. 2058; 2059; 2267; 2268; 2269.

Section 1.—Stripping and Re-assembling

1. *To strip Rifles No. 1, Mk. III & III*, and Rifles No. 2, Mk. IV*.*

Remove the nose-cap screws front and back, and nose-cap.
Remove the outer band screw, swivel, outer band and front handguard with cap and screws.

Remove the inner band screw and spring.

Remove the magazine.

Remove the screws, guard, front and back.

Remove the guard, trigger pin and trigger.

Raise the backsight leaf, and remove the handguard, rear.

*† Remove the fore-end, with stud and spring, and the protector with nut, and screw.

Remove the butt plate screws, butt plate, wad, stock bolt, and stock butt.

Remove the bolt from the body—*see* para. 2.

Remove the locking bolt spring screw, spring, and washer (or aperture sight), locking bolt, and safety catch.

Remove the sear spring.

Remove the sear screw, retaining spring and sear.

Remove the magazine catch pin and catch.

Remove the cut-off screw, and cut-off (rifles No. 1, Mk III, only).

Remove the sight leaf—*see* para. 5.

---

* Attention is drawn to the importance of removing the fore-end before attempting to unscrew the stock bolt.

† In No. I, Mk. III, rifles of early manufacture, fitted with long-range sights, raise the aperture sight and, when necessary, remove the dial sight screw washer and dial sight before removing the fore-end.

2. *To remove the bolt from the body :—*

Raise the knob with the right hand as far as it will go, draw back the bolt-head to the resisting shoulder, release the bolt-head with the forefinger of the right hand from the retaining spring, raise the bolt-head to the full extent, and draw back and remove the bolt.

3. *To strip the bolt of rifles No. 1 :—*

Remove the extractor spring, extractor screw and extractor.

Remove the striker screw ; see that the stud on the cocking-piece is in the short cam; unscrew the bolt-head ; unscrew the striker and remove the mainspring.

4. *To strip the bolt of rifles No. 2, Mk. IV* :—*

Follow the procedure as in para. 3, but remove the firing pin from the bolt-head after the latter has been unscrewed.

5. *To strip the backsight :—*

Remove the washer pin, washer, axis pin, and leaf.

Press the slide catch screw, and remove the slide from the leaf.

Unscrew the slide catch screw, and remove the spring and catch.

* Remove the fixing pin, windgauge screw head and spring.

* Unscrew the windgauge screw and remove the windgauge and spring.

Remove the screw and spring from the bed.

N.B.—The sight bed must not be removed from serviceable rifles.

6. *To strip magazines of rifles No. 1 :—*

No. 1 " A."—Turn the stop clip down to the front of the magazine. Depress the rear end of the platform and draw the platform forward ; the platform and spring may then be withdrawn from the case ; force off the auxiliary spring and, only when actually necessary, slightly raise the spring clips on the underside of the platform, and remove the spring.

No. 1 " B."—Depress the rear end of the platform as far as possible, at the same time holding up the front end ; then pull the front end towards the rear end of the case, passing it under the front side lips and forcing it between the inner forward ribs of the case. The front end of the platform should then rise up out of the case. Then tilt the rear end of the platform sideways—left side uppermost—and draw it forward out of the case.

---

* Does not apply to No. 1 " B " leaf, which has a fixed cap secured by a screw.

To re-assemble Rifles No. 1, Mks. III and III*, and Rifles No. 2, Mk IV*

1. *Magazine of rifles No. 1* :—

Where necessary replace the platform spring in the platform, and close down the clips.

Replace the auxiliary spring.

Replace the platform in the magazine, and turn the stop clip (No. 1 " A " magazine only) upwards to retain it.

2. *Backsight* :—

* Replace the windgauge, spring and screw.

Replace the spring and screw head, and, after ensuring that the positioning lines on the head and windgauge screw coincide, insert the fixing pin.

Replace the catch, spring and screw in the slide.

Replace the slide on the leaf.

Replace the sight leaf on the bed, and insert the axis pin from the left side.

Replace the washer and washer pin.

Replace the spring and screw in the bed.

3. *Locking bolt and safety catch* :—

Place the safety catch on the stem of the locking bolt so that the line marked across the face of the catch is parallel with the flat at the end of the locking bolt.

When the safety catch is screwed home, the top end should be in line with the rear end of the thumbpiece on the locking bolt.

4. *Bolt of rifles No. 1* :—

Replace the mainspring and striker in the bolt, then place the cocking-piece in position on the bolt, ensuring that the stud is in the long cam ; screw home the striker until the end is flush with the rear end of the cocking-piece and the keeper screw recess is in its correct position ; replace the keeper screw, and screw home the bolt head.

Turn the cocking-piece into the long cam, and gauge the height of the striker point from the face of the bolt-head.

Replace the extractor, screw and spring.

5. *Bolt of rifles No. 2, Mk. IV** :—

Proceed as in para. 4, but before assembling the bolt-head, see that the firing pin is inserted, that it is quite free, and that its rear end does not project beyond the end of the bolt-head tenon when the firing pin is in its most forward position.

---

* Not for No. 1 " B " leaf.

When gauging the height of the firing pin point, the bolt should be held vertically—firing pin upward. The projection should be the same as for No. 1 rifles.

6. *The rifles :—*

Replace the sight leaf.

Replace the magazine catch and pin.

Replace the sear, retaining spring, sear screw, and spring.

Replace the cut-off and screw (rifles No. 1, Mk. III only).

Replace the safety catch, locking bolt, washer or aperture sight, spring and screw.

Assemble the stock butt to the body, and screw home the stock bolt, seeing that the square end of the bolt protrudes through the face of the body within the limits of the gauge supplied, and that it is in the correct position for the keeper plate.

Replace the wad, butt plate and butt plate screws.

* Replace the protector, screw, and nut on the fore-end.

Replace the fore-end, taking care that the inner band and the fore-end stud and spring are in their correct position in recesses in the fore-end.

Replace the inner band spring and screw.

Replace the trigger, and trigger pin in the guard.

Replace the trigger guard, and screws, back and front.

Replace the magazine.

Replace the handguard, rear.

Replace the handguard, front (with cap and screw assembled).

Replace the outer band, swivel and screw.

Replace the nose-cap and screws, front and back.

Replace the bolt in the body—*see* para. 7.

7. *To replace the bolt :—*

See that the resisting lug and cocking-piece are in a straight line, and that the bolt-head is screwed home. Place the bolt in the body with the extractor upward, push forward the bolt till the head is clear of the resisting shoulder, turn the bolt-head down to the right, press it over the retaining spring, close the breech, and press the trigger.

To Strip Rifles No. 3

1. *Remove in following order :—*

Bolt.

Nose-cap screw, band screw, and swivel.

Magazine plate, spring, and platform.

---

* In rifles of early manufacture fitted with long-range sights, replace the dial sight fixing screw and washer also, if detached.

Screws trigger guard, back and front.

Trigger guard with magazine catch, and magazine case.

Nose-cap from the stock, and handguard, front.

Band and handguard, rear.

Barrel and body from the stock.

Sear axis pin, sear, with spring, and trigger.

Bolt stop screw, bolt stop, with spring and ejector, and aperture sight.

* Safety catch, locking bolt cover plate, locking bolt and spring.

† Backsight axis screw, nut and leaf.

Screw and spring from the backsight bed.

2. *To remove the bolt from the rifle :*—

Withdraw the bolt to its full extent ; pull outwards the thumb-piece of the bolt stop and draw the bolt out of the body.

3. *To strip the bolt :*—

Turn the extractor to the right until it covers the gas escape hole and the nib is clear of the cannelure, and push the extractor forward. With a piece of string round the stripping nib, or with the " Tool, stripping, bolt," if available, draw out the cocking-piece so that the tooth is clear of the rear end of the bolt, and then unscrew the bolt plug. Place the point of the striker on a piece of hard wood, press down the bolt plug until the rear end is clear of the cocking-piece, give the cocking-piece a quarter turn and lift it off the striker. Let the bolt plug rise slowly and remove it and the mainspring from the striker. Care should be taken not to let the bolt plug slip when the mainspring is compressed.

4. *To remove the block, band, foresight, from the barrel :*—

Drive out the fixing pin from right to left.

Remove the block by gently tapping it with a mallet towards the muzzle end of the barrel.

Take the key from the seating.

Note.—The block is never to be removed from the barrel except when it becomes necessary to exchange the nose-cap, or handguard ring.

5. *To remove the safety catch :*—

Turn the safety catch backward until the thumb-piece is

---

* The safety catch must be removed before removing the locking bolt cover plate in order to prevent the locking bolt from flying out of its housing. In " W " rifles of early manufacture, the cover plate is dovetailed into the body from the underside.

† The end of the axis screw is riveted over the nut ; when removing the nut, care must be taken to avoid breaking off the end of the screw.

in the lowest position and pull it outward, slightly oscillating the thumb-piece during withdrawal.

6. *To remove the magazine plate, spring and platform :—*

With the point of a bullet, depress the magazine catch and slide the bottom plate backward ; the three parts will then come out together. Slide the ends of the spring out of the recesses in the plate and platform, raising the bent ends to allow the spring to move backwards.

To Re-assemble Rifles No. 3

1. *To re-assemble the magazine platform and spring to the plate :—*

Slide the narrow end of the spring into the recess on the platform.

Slide the wide end of the spring into the recess on the bottom plate.

2. *To replace the magazine plate :—*

Insert the platform and spring into the magazine case, press the plate flat on the trigger guard and slide it forward, noting that the catch rises to engage and lock the plate in position.

3. *To re-assemble the locking bolt and safety catch :—*

Replace the locking bolt (with V-groove horizontal) and spring in the housing, and push forward as far as possible with a thin drift inserted through the hole at the rear of the housing. Hold the safety catch in a position which allows the flat of the half moon to lie horizontally, with the thumb-piece pointing downward (the half moon must pass over the drift) ; push the safety catch home and withdraw the drift smartly.

4. *To re-assemble the bolt :—*

Place the point of the striker on a piece of hard wood, replace the mainspring and slightly compress it. Place the bolt plug in position with the flattened sides of the hole in line with the flats on the striker. Force the bolt plug down as far as possible and grip it firmly. Place the cocking-piece in position with the flats inside the cylindrical portion in line with the flats on striker, push the cocking-piece down until its rear end is flush with the rear end of the striker. Give the cocking-piece a quarter turn, so that the tooth is in line with the slot in the bolt plug, which can then be allowed to rise.

Place the striker and mainspring inside the bolt and screw the bolt plug into the bolt, drawing back the cocking-piece clear of the rear end of the bolt with a piece of string or with the " Tool, stripping, bolt," if available, until the tooth is directly behind the short groove.

Slide on the extractor so that the undercut portion passes over the lugs on the ring.

Lift the retaining nib over the face of the bolt and into the cannelure (care being taken not to overstrain and set the extractor), and turn the extractor so that it lies over the solid lug on the right of the bolt.

5. *To replace the block, band, foresight on the barrel :*—

Replace the key in the seating, seeing that the pin groove coincides with the pin groove in the barrel.

Replace the block, and, if necessary, gently tap it with a mallet until the fixing pin hole coincides with the pin grooves in the barrel and key.

Insert the fixing pin from left to right, and gently tap it home into position.

During the operation of removing and replacing, care must be taken not to damage the key and pin.

Blocks are not interchangeable and are fitted to barrels on first assembly. It is therefore essential, when a block is removed from a barrel, that it should be re-assembled to the same barrel ; in order to ensure this, the block should be immediately replaced on the barrel, from which it was removed, even though the replacement of the nose-cap and handguard ring has to be carried out later.

6. *To assemble the rifle :*—

Replace in the following order :—

Spring and screw in the backsight bed.

Leaf, axis screw, and nut.

Locking bolt and spring ; safety catch and locking bolt cover plate.

Aperture sight, bolt stop spring *, ejector, bolt stop, and screw.

Trigger, sear spring, sear, and sear axis pin.

Barrel and body in the stock, lubricating with mineral jelly as required.

Rear handguard, lower band, front handguard, and nose-cap.

† Magazine case, trigger guard and screws front and back.

Magazine plate, spring, and platform.

---

* It is essential that the outer face at the front end of the bolt stop spring should be flush with the outer face of the bolt stop, and not below the latter, otherwise the front end bearing of the spring may be sheared during movement of the bolt stop, and the rifle rendered unusable.

† Care should be taken when assembling that the projection at the top front end of the magazine-case is correctly positioned in the recess under the body before the trigger guard is screwed up.

Lower band screw and swivel and nose-cap screw.
Bolt.

7. *To replace the bolt in the rifle :—*

See that the bolt plug is screwed home, that the tooth on the front end of the cocking-piece is engaged in the short groove on the end of the bolt, and that the extractor is in direct line with the solid lug on the right of the bolt. Insert the bolt in the body of the rifle, depress the platform and press the bolt home.

Section 2.—Cleaning and Lubricating of Rifles in use, and the Clearing of Obstructions from the Bore

Note.—The lubricating oil referred to in this section, and elsewhere as " G.S.," is termed M/80 in the V.A.O.S.

1. The rifles are to be kept in a clean condition, special attention being given to the interior of the barrel and the breech action.

Instructions for the care and cleaning of rifles by troops are contained in Small Arms Training, Vol. I, 1924, Chapter II, Sections 38–40. Armourers should make themselves thoroughly acquainted with these instructions in addition to the instructions given hereunder.

2. Oil, lubricating, G.S., only is to be used for cleaning the action ; the use of abrasive substances, such as emery and emery cloth, is forbidden.

3. To prevent water soaking into the stock, and at the same time to give the latter a polished appearance, it should be well rubbed with oil. French polish or varnish is on no account to be used. Red mineral jelly should be applied between stock, handguards, barrel and body as a protection against rust. At stations abroad, a mixture of two parts mineral jelly to one of beeswax will be employed.

4. *To clean the bore of ·303-inch barrels :—*

(i) Oil, lubricating, G.S., only is to be used, but mineral burning oil (paraffin) can be mixed with it, as necessary, when cleaning with brass wire and with jute and emery, as detailed below.

(ii) To clean a slightly rusty barrel with the double pullthrough, remove the bolt and nose-cap, drop the pullthrough weight through the barrel from the breech, clamp the muzzle guide on the muzzle of the barrel to prevent damage by the friction of the cord, well oil the gauze wire, and, with the necessary assistance, pull the gauze wire to and fro until the rust is removed. Care must be taken to draw the pull-through out of the barrel in line with the bore, as friction between the pullthrough cord and the wall of the chamber at the breech will cause the chamber to become oval and thus render the barrel unserviceable. When, in consequence of frequent use, the gauze wire ceases to fit the barrel tightly, narrow strips of the gauze, about ⅛-inch wide, or flannelette or paper, may be inserted under each side to increase its diameter.

(iii) To clean rusty barrels with brass wire, emery and jute, fill the eye of the No. 4 rod with from 50 to 60 strands of the hard brass wire, No. 26 W.G., supplied in 3-inch lengths, and press the ends well back along the rod. The rifles must then be held in a vice, and, after the nose cap has been removed, the wire, well oiled with a mixture of two parts of " Oil, lubricating, G.S.," to one part of paraffin oil, is inserted in the muzzle end of the barrel ; the muzzle guide * is then clamped on the muzzle and the rod worked up and down the bore to remove the rust. When a barrel is very rusty, it will be found easier to loosen the rust by plugging the muzzle of the barrel, pouring in paraffin oil from the breech end, and leaving it there for a few hours. After loosening the rust, wipe out the barrel with jute inserted in the No. 1 rod and examine (the jute should be cut in lengths of about 8 inches).

If a barrel is found to require further cleaning, coil the jute round so that it fits the bore tightly, sprinkle on a little flour emery, replace it in the barrel, and after clamping on the muzzle guide, work the rod well up and down until the barrel is clean.

A slightly pitted surface will usually remain ; this should be oiled with " Oil, lubricating, G.S."

To preserve the wire on the No. 4 rod when not in use, a cartridge-case cut short at the shoulder will be found useful as a cap. The length of the No. 4 rod is such as will ensure that the wire will not pass beyond the front end of the chamber and become jammed. The No. 1 rod, for jute, is of a suitable length to pass through the barrel from the breech end.

(iv) When rifles are received from store, and the bore of the barrel is thickly coated with mineral jelly, the latter must be removed and the bore lightly oiled with G.S. oil before the rifles are issued to troops.

5. *To clean the chamber of* ·303-*inch barrels :—*

Use only a piece of gauze wire, or a piece of oiled flannelette, as necessary, in the chamber cleaning stick. Care must be

---

* When a muzzle guide becomes badly worn in the cleaning rod guide hole, and no longer protects the bore of the barrel, it should be exchanged.

taken not to enlarge or damage the chamber by the use of unauthorized materials. A bright chamber is not to be insisted upon.

6. *To clean the bore of rifles No. 2, Mk. IV* (·22-inch) :—*

The No. 6 rod with leather washer, and the brass cleaner for flannelette, and the brush, which are made to screw on to the rod, are provided for the use of units in possession of these rifles. Oil, lubricating, G.S., only is to be used for cleaning purposes.

When proper care is taken by units to clean and oil the bore immediately after firing, the barrels can be kept in good condition. Armourers should draw the attention of the responsible officer concerned to the fact when the barrels are not kept in good order.

In the event of an obstruction, such as flannelette, etc., being found in the bore, great care must be taken not to put excessive pressure on the rod, as damage to the bore may thereby be caused. If the obstruction cannot readily be removed by the armourer, a report will be rendered in order that the matter may be investigated and the rifle sent to C.I.S.A. for special examination.

7. *To clear ·303-inch barrels when a pullthrough has broken and become jammed in the bore :—*

Screw the " tool plug " on the " rod," place it in the barrel at the end nearest the jammed flannelette and compress the flannelette and cord as much as possible. Withdraw the rod and plug, unscrew the plug, and screw on the bush and screw bit. Pass this into the barrel at the end nearest the jammed flannelette and turn it to the right, pressing it firmly against the jammed material until a good hold is obtained ; then pull strongly on the rod, causing the screw to grip tightly in the material by turning the rod whilst pulling.

Note.—Only the hardened steel rods issued are to be used for cleaning and clearing purposes. Rods of soft metal or wood must on no account be employed.

Section 3.—Examination

Rifles No. 1 and No. 2, Mk. IV*

The following instructions are for general guidance ; the sequence may be varied to meet special circumstances, *e.g.*, when a particular defect due to unfair wear or other cause is prevalent, or when a brief examination only is called for.

Reference should be made to Section 4 for Modifications,

Repairs and Adjustments and to Chapter III, Part I, for special markings.

1. *General.*—Examine the rifle to see that the number, and the series letter where marked, on the nose-cap, fore-end, sight leaf, barrel and bolt agree with the number on the body, and that the rifle is complete.

Record deficiencies, if any, and damage due to unfair wear for report.

2. *Barrels.*—(i) Examine the bore and chamber. Rust, bulges, bad cuts, cord-wear and bends should be looked for, and should be reported in the normal manner. Slight rust pitting in the chamber may be ignored except in cases where hard extraction has been reported.

When the gauges for bore and lead are available under the conditions laid down in E.R., Pt. I, and there is any doubt by the unit as to the accuracy of shooting, the barrel should be gauged as follows :—

·303-inch plug should run.

·307-inch plug should not run.

·308-inch plug should not enter the muzzle more than $\frac{1}{4}$ inch.

·310-inch plug should not enter the breech more than $\frac{1}{4}$ inch. $\begin{cases} i.e., \text{ the rear end of the} \\ \text{gauge should not pass} \\ \text{inside the barrel.} \end{cases}$

Note.—(*a*) Each limit gauge for the bore, also the lead gauge, independently determines the normal life of the barrel, but, should the rifle still be shooting accurately, the armourer will use his discretion before reporting the barrel as unserviceable.

(*b*) When a rifle shoots inaccurately, and the barrel is within the gauging limits, and the stocking correct, it will be reported for special examination by C.I.S.A.

(ii) Test the backsight bed and foresight band block for rigidity, and the foresight blade for security. Slight lateral movement in the bed and block, provided it is insufficient to affect sighting and accuracy, may be ignored.

Blades, foresight, known as Mk. II, introduced in India, having a base of ·03 inch wider than that of Mk. I foresights to enable them to be set to a maximum of ·045 inch off centre, may be met with in rifles brought home in the past by troops. Such foresights may remain until exchange for another height is necessary, when they will be replaced by the ordinary service No. 1 pattern.

The Mk. II sights are stamped with the figure 2 alongside the H N or L marking.

Barrels of rifles No. 2 (·*22-inch*)—Will be examined without gauges. Special attention will be paid to the muzzle in order

that wear resulting from careless use of the cleaning rod may
be detected, and to the chamber at the end of the extractor
way, where burrs are liable to be caused by the extractor. A
burr at this point may affect extraction, and should be removed
by means of a keen-edged scraper. Care must be taken to
avoid enlargement of or damage to the chamber. When a
·22-inch barrel is found on examination to be eroded or worn
to such an extent that accuracy may be affected, its condition
will be reported to the responsible officer concerned in order
that the rifle may be tested for accuracy. When a rifle fails
to group within the prescribed limits, it will be reported for
special examination by C.I.S.A. (*see* Small Arms Training).
If it appears that proper care is not being taken in the
cleaning and oiling of these rifles, a report will be rendered
to the responsible officer concerned to this effect, and a copy
of the report will be retained for future reference.

3. *Butt, fore-end and handguards.*—Examine for damage,
splits, warping, excessive dryness or rot, and, especially at sea-
coast stations, for salt deposit ; evidence of the latter will
usually be indicated by rust on the barrel. Where salt deposit
is distinctly in evidence, the fore-end and handguards should
be replaced.

See that the butt is firmly held in the body, and that the
correct stocking conditions are maintained ; where the parts
are patched, see that the patches are secure.

Note.—A split at the rear end of the fore-end, at the junction portion under the stock bolt plate, may be ignored, provided
the screwed wire has a firm hold.

If the stocking is satisfactory, lubricate, as required, with
red mineral jelly, or, at stations abroad, with a mixture of two
parts mineral jelly to one part beeswax.

4. *Action :—*

Bolt and bolt-head.—(i) Test the distance of the bolt from the
end of the chamber with gauges ·064-inch No. 1 and ·074-inch
No. 1 ; the bolt should close over the ·064, but not over the
·074 ; when using the latter gauge, light thumb-pressure only
should be applied to the knob. Also test to see that the wing
of the bolt-head does not lift off the rib of the body.

(ii) Examine the bolt for fracture and damage, especially
at the cocking cam and recoil shoulders. Test the striker
for free movement and fit in the cocking-piece ; gauge the
length and radius of the striker point ; examine the bents
and condition of the cam stud of the cocking-piece.

(iii) Test the fit of the bolt-head in the bolt, and examine
the face for erosion ; when erosion is excessive or the rib

turns beyond the rib of the bolt freely, fit a longer bolt-head and adjust to the ·064 gauge as necessary.

(iv) Examine the extractor at the hook and for fit on the screw, and test to see that the screw is secure. Weigh the spring from the hook with the trigger tester—not less than 6 lb. and not more than 9 lb. should be required to move it.

Note.—The bolts of rifles in use should be completely stripped at each annual examination and lubricated lightly with G.S. oil.

Body, etc.—Examine the body of No. 1 rifles for fracture, especially in the region of the recoil shoulders ; test the charger guide bridge for security—if oil exudes at the rivets, but no appreciable looseness is found, no action is necessary ; test to see that the retaining spring is held rigidly by the sear screw. Examine the sear and magazine catch for condition and free movement, and oil, as required.

Gauge the protrusion of the stock bolt and see that the squared end is correctly located for the keeper plate in the fore-end.

Locking bolt and safety catch.—Examine for fracture and wear, and test for functioning in both cocked and fired positions of the rifle ; see that the locking bolt spring is held firmly by the screw and that the screw is secured.

Pull-off, spring weights, etc., will be tested with the trigger tester as follows :—

	Limits	
	Minimum	*Maximum*
To release the bolt-head from the retaining spring	10 lb.	16 lb.
To draw back the cocking-piece against the mainspring—		
(*a*) in the fired position	7 ,,	9 ,,
(*b*) at full cock	14 ,,	16 ,,
Pull-off—(*a*) first pull	3 ,,	4 ,,
(*b*) second pull	5 ,,	6 ,,
To lift the butt trap at the nib	2 ,,	3 ,,

Both first and second pulls should be tested by hand to ensure that they are correct and smooth in operation. The safety of the engagement of the sear nose with the bent of the cocking-piece should be tested by forcing the bolt home as sharply as possible.

The engagement of the half-bent of the cocking-piece with the nose of the sear should be tested by only partially closing the bolt, so that on pulling the trigger, the stud of the cocking-piece will rest on the end of the cam stud of the bolt. Upon releasing the trigger and fully closing the bolt, the sear should securely engage in the half bent; it should not then be possible to disengage the sear by pressure on the trigger.

Cut-off of No. 1, *Mk. III rifles.*—Examine for damage, and test the action when the magazine is empty and when filled with dummy cartridges.

Where the cut-off is of an earlier pattern than No. 1 (*i.e.*, with the short stops at the rear end) and the end of the slot in the body is so worn as to render the stops ineffective, the cut-off should be exchanged for a No. 1.

Magazine of No. 1 *rifles.*—Examine for damage; see that the platform spring is securely held in the platform, and that the auxiliary spring is secure.

See that the case is securely held by the magazine catch, and then test the feed into the chamber when filled as above.

Note.—The magazine-case only, marked ·22 on the left side, is used in No. 2, Mk. IV* rifles.

Extraction and ejection.—These functions can be observed when testing the magazine; tests should be carried out also with fired cartridge-cases.

The action of the lug of the bolt on the extracting cam of the body should withdraw the bolt from ·08 to ·10 inch. A rifle having this amount of draw should not fail to extract provided the action is otherwise correct. In case of failure to extract a tight cartridge-case under the normal conditions of operation, the following points should be looked for:—

- (i) play between bolt and bolt-head;
- (ii) play at extractor axis;
- (iii) excessive clearance between extractor hook and rim of cartridge.

Replacement of the part or parts found to be noticeably worn should be made as necessary to effect a remedy.

When ejection is unsatisfactory, examine the ejector screw and the lower corner of the extractor, and test the weight of the extractor spring; if the corner of the extractor is sharp, it should be slightly rounded off.

Note.—The foregoing applies more especially to No. 1 rifles. In the case of No. 2 rifles, the condition of the extractor hook and its engagement with the rim of fired cases should receive attention. See also that the extractor does not foul the edge of the extractor way of the barrel.

5. *Freedom of the muzzle of the barrel and fit of the bayonet.*— Insert a hard wood plug in the muzzle of the barrel and test to see that the barrel is free in the nose-cap and that it is pressed upward by the stud and spring. If the bayonet is

very slack on the nose-cap, exchange the bayonet for a closer-fitting one off another rifle on which the slack bayonet is a better fit, and then re-number the bayonets to the rifles.

6. *Securing screws.*—Before re-issue of rifles to troops, see that they are complete, and then expand the swivel screws and secure the front trigger-guard screw.

Note.—If complaint is made of misfires occurring in any No. 1 rifle, the point of impact of the striker on the fired cases should be examined ; when found badly eccentric, the rifle should be set aside for special gauging by the A.I.A. or C.I.S.A.'s Examiners at their next visit. Should, however, the rifle be urgently required, it can be sent to C.I.S.A. for special examination.

In the absence of fired cases, a dummy cartridge, with cap chamber filled with beeswax, will serve the purpose.

Rifles No. 3, Mk. I* (T) and Mk. I* (F)

These rifles will be examined on similar lines to those for Nos. 1 and 2 rifles, but special care must be taken with them, especially with Mk. I* (T) rifles fitted with telescopic sight, in view of the importance of the accuracy of shooting required for " sniping " and of the high standard of adjustment attained before the rifles are issued from the ordnance factory.

The instructions given in Sections 1, 2 and 4 contain the information necessary for general guidance when examining these rifles.

See also Section 6—Gauges ·064, No. 2 and ·074-inch No. 2 and application of plug and rod gauges to barrel.

Section 4.—Repairs, Modifications and Adjustments, etc.
Rifles No. 1, Mk. III and III*, and Rifles No. 2, Mk. IV*

1. *Misfires.*—When misfires have been reported with any rifle, the mainspring should be weighed and the protrusion of the striker gauged. It is also possible for the force of the striker blow to be reduced by an accumulation of oil in the spring chamber of the bolt.

If the impression made by the striker on the cap is notice-ably out of centre, the rifle should be placed on one side for special examination, as directed in Section 3.

2. *Fitting new ejector screw.*—When fitting a new ejector screw, see that the end of the screw just touches the bolt in its passage, but not sufficiently to cause appreciable friction.

3. *Fitting new striker.*—When fitting a new striker, care must be taken to adjust it for length to the gauge striker

point ; the point should be carefully rounded to the radius in the gauge ; a long or badly-rounded striker is liable to cause pierced caps.

4. *To tighten striker in cocking-piece.*—Take an unserviceable cocking-piece with the thread for the striker in good condition ; split it with the slitting saw down the centre ; tap with the plug tap No. 10 ; and harden and temper. Then screw in the loose striker until the rear end protrudes a little beyond the rear end of the cocking-piece ; grip the cocking-piece in the vice, and centre-punch the centre of the end of the striker, or otherwise expand the metal ; then unscrew the striker and remove any burr or superfluous metal from the end.

5. *Fitting new platform and spring to No. 1 " A " magazine of rifles No. 1.*—(Platforms and springs for No. 1 " B " magazines are not issued separately.) Insert the spring under the nibs of the platform with the raised stop on the spring between the nibs, and close the nibs down tightly on the spring, seeing that the spring is in line with the platform and held tightly.

In rifles of all patterns, work the spring and platform in the magazine until they raise the cartridges freely.

6. *To increase or decrease the weight of the pull-off and to produce and regulate the double pull.*—To reduce the weight, increase, with an oilstone, the angle made with the vertical by the face of the bent " A " (Fig. 1). To increase the weight, reduce the angle.

When fitting a new sear, trigger, or trigger guard, the double pull will be regulated, as necessary, in the following manner :—

Remove the fore-end from the rifle, insert the new sear in the body, the new trigger in the guard or the old trigger in the new guard, withdraw the front guard screw collar from the fore-end, assemble the guard with the collar in position under the guard and fully cock the rifle. " A " (Fig. 1) shows the correct position of the sear nose on the end of the cocking-piece at full cock. Upon pulling the trigger, the rib on the trigger at " B " coming in contact with the sear, draws the sear down to the position shewn at " C " ; the rib on the trigger at " D " then comes in contact with the sear and draws the sear off the cocking-piece. If the sear is drawn off the cocking-piece by the first action of the trigger, and there is no second pull, the height of the rib " B " should be reduced with oilstone or emery cloth until the sear assumes the correct position, as shewn at " C," care being taken to maintain the shape.

Note.—Before removing the front guard screw collar from the fore-end, see that the ends of the collar are flush with the fore-end ; if the collar is short, replace it, as otherwise a false result will be obtained for the pull-off.

7. *To fit new bolt-head to Rifles No. 1.*—(Spare part bolt-heads, marked " S " on the top, are longer at the front.) Assemble the bolt-head to the bolt, insert it in the body, and test with ·064-inch No. 1 gauge ; should the bolt not close over

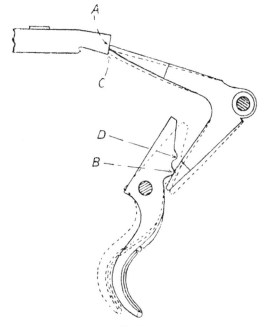

Fig. 1.

the gauge, remove the bolt-head from the bolt, and having placed a piece of emery cloth (No. F) on a flat surface, rub the face of the bolt-head on the emery cloth, maintaining a circular motion in order to preserve a flat surface, until sufficient metal has been removed to enable the assembled bolt to close over the gauge. The bolt should not close over the ·074-inch No. 1 gauge. Care should be taken to keep the face of the bolt-head flat and square.

After fitting and adjusting, the top front edge of the face

of the bolt-head is to be rounded to a radius not exceeding ·02-inch.

Note.—When it is found that the bolts of several rifles turn over the' ·074-inch No. 1 gauge, the bolt-heads should be exchanged among such rifles, as, owing to the varying lengths of bodies and bolts, bolt-heads which are too short in one rifle may be serviceable in another. Bolt-heads that have been replaced in rifles by longer ones, should be kept by the armourer and used whenever possible in rifles requiring the bolt-head replaced, so as to avoid unnecessary use of new spare part bolt-heads. Part-worn bolt-heads held as required by armourers in accordance with the foregoing need not be

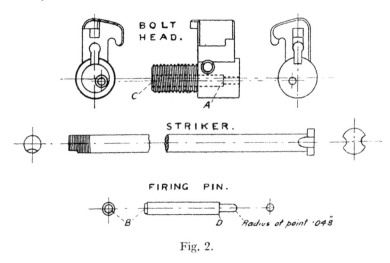

Fig. 2.

accounted for as part of the annual allowance of new spare parts.

8. *Instructions for fitting new No. 2 bolt-heads and firing-pins to rifles No. 2, Mk. IV*.*—(*a*) Assemble the bolt-head to the rifle without the firing-pin, and adjust the front face, where necessary, to enable the bolt to be closed with the bolt-head touching the face of the barrel.

(*b*) Remove the bolt-head from the rifle, insert the firing-pin, and press home to the small shoulder (A) (Fig. 2). If the rear end (B) of the pin is found to project beyond the rear face (C) of the bolt-head, reduce the pin at (B) until it is just below the face (C). This ensures that the bolt-head, and not the small shoulder (D) of the firing-pin, acts as a stop to the forward movement of the striker.

(c) Assemble the bolt complete ; place the cocking-piece in the long cam of the bolt ; test the protrusion of the point of the firing-pin, which should be the same as in the Service rifle (*i.e.*, ·04 inch to ·042 inch), and adjust the point, where necessary, maintaining the radial form at the point, as illustrated.

Note.—The internal shoulder (A) in the bolt-head controls the firing-pin in its most forward position, and when the firing-pin is properly adjusted, prevents it from striking the edge of the chamber when snapping. Therefore, when adjusting the rear-end (B) of the firing-pin, care should be taken to see that the pin is not more than ·003 inch below the rear face (C) of the bolt-head, as whatever distance it is below, so there will exist a similar clearance between the shoulder (D) of the pin and the shoulder (A) of the bolt-head when the pin is gauged for protrusion, and this, added to the amount of protrusion as gauged, gives the amount of protrusion of the striker point in its most forward position.

9. *To re-line the windgauge or cap of the backsight of rifles No.* 1 *and No.* 2.—The tool, sight line, and scriber will be used in the following manner and as shewn in Fig. 3.

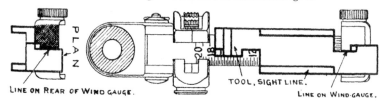

LINE ON REAR OF WIND GAUGE.   TOOL, SIGHT LINE.   LINE ON WIND-GAUGE.

Fig. 3.

First re-brown the windgauge, assemble it to the No. 1 " A " sight leaf, and adjust it to its central position, *i.e.*, with the original top centre line (now browned over, but visible) in correct alignment with the centre line on the leaf, and with the windgauge screw spring engaged in a notch in the screw-head. Next place the sight line tool over the windgauge and leaf, and see if the lines on the windgauge are in correct alignment with the tool ; reverse the tool to verify. Then, with the scriber (which should not be too sharp), trace over to brighten the lines at the front and top of the windgauge, reversing the tool as necessary.

The above instructions, so far as they apply, will be followed when re-lining the fixed cap of the No. 1 " B " leaf.

10. *Fitting washers to take up backlash of the windgauge screw fitted to No. 1 " A " sight leaf.*—In cases where backlash of the windgauge screw exists, owing to the distance between the removable head of the windgauge screw and the right side of the windgauge being too great, one or more washers, ·005-inch thick, will be placed in the recess on the left side of the windgauge under the small slotted head of the windgauge screw. Before fitting the washers, care should be taken to see that the backlash is not due to any defect of the windgauge screw spring, which, if defective, should be exchanged.

11. *Fitting a No. 1 head to the windgauge screw of No. 1 " A " sight leaf.*—When fitting the No. 1 head to the windgauge screw of rifles fitted with slides of earlier manufacture, a radial groove is to be filed in the right rear side of the slide, at " A," Fig. 4, to give clearance to the No. 1 head, which is larger than the earlier pattern. The depth to which the groove is to be

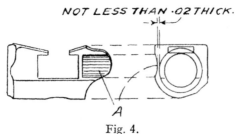

Fig. 4.

filed will be determined by trying the slide on the sight leaf (assembled with windgauge and screw with No. 1 head) until it can be set just below the 200 yards position.

After adjusting the slide to suit the No. 1 head, it will be blacked in accordance with the instructions given for the temporary blacking of sights.

12. *Butts.*—When, owing to shrinkage, the socket end of the butt does not fit the body, the looseness will be remedied by attaching a piece of hard paper to the socket end of the butt. The adhesion and protection of the paper will be effected by applying " hard, white spirit varnish, " with a 1-inch camel-hair brush in the following manner :—

Varnish the wood and paper and allow both to be exposed to the air for about 30 seconds, then apply one to the other. When dry, varnish on the outside and allow to dry and harden. When fitting the butt to the body, lubricate with red mineral jelly.

33

In the event of difficulty in attaching the paper, owing to the presence of oil, the socket end of the butt will be cleaned with " oxalic acid," and water (1 ounce acid to 1 pint water). The acid must be washed off with clean water, and the wood thoroughly dried before applying varnish and paper.

Since the socket end of the butt is tapered, the cutting of the paper will be facilitated by the use of a template made in accordance with Fig. 5.

The varnish, brushes and acid will be specially demanded as required.

Anvils are provided to drive the butts home into the socket of the body. These anvils will also be used with new butts of which the socket end has been compressed in manufacture and left large for a driving fit.

13. *To fit a new fore-end to rifles No. 1* :—

(i) Remove from the unserviceable fore-end :—

> The dial sight complete with fixing screw and washer (when fitted to No. 1 " A " fore-ends).
> The nose cap nut.
> The stock bolt plate.
> The collar.
> The inner band spring washer.
> The protector with screw, nut and washer.

(ii) Select the new fore-end to match reasonably with the butt, and examine it for straightness; assemble the nose-cap with nut and screws, the guard screw collar and stock bolt plate, and examine the location of the barrel hole in the nose cap in relation to the barrel groove in the fore-end.

(iii) Place the front handguard on the fore-end, apply its cap to the recess in the nose-cap, and, if necessary, plane or file the upper surfaces of the fore-end until the cap fits and the handguard lies evenly on the fore-end.

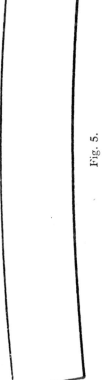

Fig. 5.

(iv) Remove the nose-cap and coat the seating surfaces of barrel and body with lamp black mixed with G.S. oil. Test the seating of the fore-end, and adjust as necessary, taking care to keep the bottom of the groove level with the bottom of the barrel hole in the nose-cap, using a straightedge of sufficient length for the purpose. The fore-end should seat on the base of the body, especially at the front end for $1\frac{1}{2}$ inches at least, on the barrel at the reinforce, and from half an inch in rear of the inner band recess to the nose-cap. The guard screw-collar should bear on the boss of the body, and its outer end should be slightly below the guard seating (about ·01 inch). The fore-end must be clear of the barrel from the front of the reinforce up to a point half an inch from the inner band recess ; it should fit closely between the sear lugs and the face of the butt socket of the body. The inner band recess should be of sufficient depth to ensure that the inner band can be drawn down on to the barrel.

(v) When the seatings and clearances are satisfactory, press the fore-end on the barrel and body, assemble the trigger-guard and screws, and test to see that the barrel is free and that it seats along the bottom of the groove without undue tension. Test the pull-off for double action and, if unsatisfactory, adjust as necessary—*see* paragraph 6. Assemble the nose-cap and screws, test the alignment of the barrel in the fore-end and the barrel hole in the nose-cap, and, if necessary, adjust the sides of the groove to avoid influence on the straightness of the barrel.

(vi) When satisfactory, remove the fore-end, and assemble the remaining components, seeing that the backsight protector is quite clear of the barrel. Lubricate the barrel and body recesses of the fore-end, the groove of the handguards and the barrel and body, with red mineral jelly (at stations abroad, with the mixture referred to in Section 2). Finally, assemble the fore-end to the rifle, seeing that the inner band spring is free to act, that the barrel can be sprung down fully at the muzzle against the tension of the stud and spring, and that the rear handguard does not prevent the backsight slide from seating on the bed at the lower elevations.

(vii) As accuracy of shooting and sighting may be affected by the new fore-end, the rifle should be submitted to the O.C., the Company or Squadron, etc., for accuracy test, the foresight to be adjusted as necessary. (*See* para. 15.)

(viii) Alterations to be made to No. 1 " B " fore-ends when fitting them to rifles with cut-off (*a*) or aperture sight (*b*) :—

    (*a*) The upward extension, on the right side of the stock, which covers the position of the cut-off slot in the body, will be cut away, and an angular recess will be cut to half the depth of the cut-off lug recess, to clear the cut-off joint when the cut-off is opened.

(b) The aperture sight will be replaced by the " washer, spring, bolt locking," but should this component not be available, the pillar of the aperture sight will be filed off at the base and the base disc used as a washer under the spring.

14. *Securing screws.*—Upon re-assembling the following screws they should be secured as described.

(i) *Screw, guard, trigger, front and screw, spring, bolt locking.*—The metal of the components into which the screws assemble will be expanded into the screw-driver slots, after the screws have been carefully tightened, by centre-punching, as illustrated (Fig. 6). Care should be exercised when centre-punching to avoid cutting away the metal of the components.

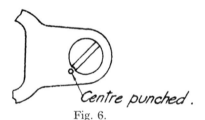

SCREW, GUARD, FRONT.

Centre punched.

Fig. 6.

(ii) *Screw, sear.*—See that the sear screw is screwed tightly home ; make a scriber or pencil mark for the position of the notch on the end of the screw at the bottom edge. Remove the sear screw, and, with a small 3-square file cut a small " V " notch in the end of the screw where marked ; replace the screw and screw home tightly ; then with the centre-punch, indent the metal of the body into the notch (*see* Fig. 7) and re-assemble the rifle.

Note.—This applies to rifles in use in which the bolt-head retaining spring is not held rigidly owing to the sear screw having worked loose ; but it will be carried out also in all rifles undergoing repair and rifles manufactured in future.

(iii) *Swivel screws.*—With the screw head supported conveniently, expand the hollow point of the screws, by means of the centre-punch, sufficiently to prevent them from working loose. The expansion must not be overdone, as this will cause damage to the slot when stripping.

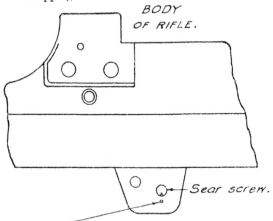

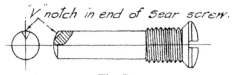

Fig. 7.

15. *To replace and adjust blades foresight.*—Remove the nose-cap screws and nose-cap. Carefully mark the front end of the blade to be replaced, in line with one edge of the block ; drive out the old blade from left to right (taking care not to damage the dovetail of the block) ; mark the new blade to correspond with the mark on the old, drive it in and adjust so that the mark coincides with the edge of the block.

The blades will be adjusted by using the Cramp of " tools, foresight " in the following manner :—

Turn the screws of the cramp back, and place the cramp on the barrel so that the foresight block is between the gap of the cramp. Turn one of the screws up to the side of the foresight it is desired to press, and move the blade to the desired position. Remove the cramp, and replace the nose-cap and screws.

When the correct position of the blade has been determined, the centre-punch will be used to fix it in position.

A quarter turn of the screw of the No. 1, Mk. I Cramp = ·01 inch—*i.e.*, approximately 2 inches on the target for each 100 yards range.

Each division of the scale on the No. 1, Mk. I* and Mk. II Cramps = 4 inches on the target for the same range.

16. *Instructions for correcting the sighting of rifles in R.A.O.C. workshops when barrel with body is exchanged.*— After being fitted with a new barrel and body, the rifle will be tested by being fired on a 100-feet range. Sighting shots will be fired, and the foresight adjusted for lateral deviation, or replaced by another foresight to correct vertical deviation as necessary. The extent of the adjustment of the foresight in the block will be limited by the width of the block, *i.e.*, neither side of the foresight must be within the corresponding side of the block, but may be flush with the block. If this limit of adjustment does not meet the case, the rifle will be examined for alignment of barrel in fore-end and nose-cap, and corrected as necessary. After correction of stocking, the rifle will again be tested.

17. Each rifle must invariably be used with the breech bolt bearing the rifle number, otherwise the lugs may not bear evenly, and the rifle may fire to the right or left ; the distance from the bolt to the end of the chamber may also be affected. When, owing to loss or damage, it becomes necessary to fit another bolt to a rifle, the rifle should be fired for accuracy on the range.

The fore-end and nose-cap are also fitted and numbered to the rifle. Accuracy tests must always be carried out when either or both of these components are exchanged.

18. When spare bolts, sight leaves, fore-ends and nose-caps are fitted to rifles, they will be marked with the body number. When fitting a spare barrel with body, the whole of the components before mentioned will be re-marked with the new body number.

19. *Long-range sights.*—Action to be taken when details become unserviceable.

In consequence of the abolition of long-range sights for Rifles, Nos. 1 and 2, unserviceable components of such sights will not be replaced, and action will be taken as follows :—

    (i) If either the bead, the pointer, the spring, or the pivot screw of the dial sight becomes unserviceable, the whole of these components will be removed and returned to store, the dial plate and fixing screw being left on the rifle for the purpose of covering the hole and recess in the fore-end. The aperture sight will be left on the rifle.

(ii) If either the dial plate or the fixing screw becomes unserviceable, the whole of the dial sight components will be removed and returned to store ; the hole in the fore-end will be plugged with wood, the plug to be glued in.

(iii) If the aperture sight becomes unserviceable, the pillar will be filed off at the base and the base disc used as a washer under the spring. In case of deficiency, the " Washer, spring, bolt, locking, No. 1 " will be employed to replace the aperture sight.

20. *Repair of rifles No. 1 D.P.*—Provision of stocks and handguards is made for the repair and maintenance of No. 1 D.P. rifles. They are supplied, as required, on demand through the usual channels.

These components, marked " D.P.", will not be used for the repair of rifles other than " D.P."

Serviceable stocks and handguards must not be used for the repair and maintenance of " D.P." rifles.

Unserviceable stocks and handguards from service rifles which may be considered as suitable for " D.P." rifles, will be accumulated locally at Command Ordnance Depots and held pending the visit of an examiner from the C.I.S.A., Enfield Lock, who will finally sentence and mark them.

Serviceable components, other than stocks and handguards, may continue to be used for the maintenance of " D.P." rifles provided that the cost is unlikely to exceed the cost of factory repair with " D.P." parts plus cost of transport of the rifles to and from the Royal Small Arms Factory, Enfield Lock.

Rifles No. 3, Mk. I* (T)—fitted with Telescopic Sight.
Rifles No. 3, Mk. I* (F)—fitted with Fine-adjustment Backsight

1. In case of misfires, the mainspring should be weighed from the cocking-piece with the trigger tester, and the protrusion of the striker, from the face of the bolt, and the radius of the point, should be gauged.

The mainspring cannot be weighed with the bolt closed, but only when the latter is drawn to the rear against the bolt stop. The cocking-piece should then be turned into the long camway of the bolt, and the weight of the mainspring tested by applying the trigger tester against the stripping nib of the cocking-piece. To record the weight in the fully cocked position, the cocking-piece should be drawn back until the rear face is approximately ¾ inch in rear of the rear end of the bolt plug.

Misfires are liable to be caused by an accumulation of oil in the spring chamber of the bolt, or at the cocking-piece seating in the bolt plug. These parts of the action should be kept free from heavy oil, mineral jelly, and dirt.

2. *Weights of springs.*—The springs can be tested with the trigger tester and should weigh as follows :—

Pull-off, from 5 lb. to 6 lb.

Pull to move trigger, from 2 lb. to 3 lb.

Pull to move extractor (about) 4 lb.

Pull to lift butt trap by the nib (about) 2½ lb.

Pull to move bolt stop, from 2½ lb. to 4 lb.

Weight of mainspring from cocking-piece with spring eased from 8 lb. to 10 lb.

Weight at full cock from 13 lb. to 15 lb.

3. *Extraction.*—The extracting cam in the body and on the bolt should withdraw the bolt from ·08-inch to ·10-inch.

Failure to extract may be due to a defective cartridge, or to the hook or retaining nib of the extractor being broken.

4. *Ejection.*—In the case of faulty ejection, test the ejector for freedom of movement with the bolt in the position it would be at the moment of ejection. The ejector should be quite free when upward or downward pressure is applied to the bolt lever, and should not friction in the slot in the bolt lug.

If ejection is unsatisfactory, remove the ejector and test its straightness, as a bent ejector will friction in the slot of the bolt. Remove any thick grease, grit, particles of brass, etc., if present in the ejector slot in body and bolt.

5. *Fitting striker.*—In fitting a new striker, care must be taken to adjust it to length ; the " gauge, striker point No. 2 " is provided for this purpose. There is also a similar gauge on the side of the " implement, action No. 2." The striker should also be carefully rounded to the radius in the gauge or implement. A long or badly-rounded striker is likely to cause pierced caps. Before finally assembling the striker in the bolt, the striker should be inserted separately (*i.e.*, without bolt plug, etc.). The protrusion of the point should then be excessive, thus ensuring that, when assembled, the collar of the striker is not bearing at the bottom of the spring chamber.

The forward position of the striker is determined by the cocking-piece seating in the bolt plug ; the nose of the cocking-piece should not bear against the front end of the long cam.

If the protrusion is insufficient, the front face of the cylindrical portion of the cocking-piece should be slightly adjusted by an oilstone until the correct protrusion is obtained.

6. *Fitting sear.*—When fitting a new sear, the height of the stud should be so regulated as to prevent the trigger from functioning correctly until the bolt is fully closed. (A low stud will permit of the sear releasing the cocking-piece with the bolt lever partially raised.)

7. *To correct or adjust " double pull."*—At the top or crown of the trigger, two radial nibs are formed—" A " and " B " (see drawing S.A.I.D. 2059)—the first pull is obtained by the leverage of the front nib " A " against the underside of the body. On continuing to press the trigger rearwards, its movement is checked by the rear of nib " B " coming into contact with the seating at the underside of the body.

Therefore, if the " 1st pull " is too long, the height of the front nib " A " should be reduced with an oilstone, care being taken to maintain the correct shape.

If the " 1st pull " is short, it indicates that the rear nib " B " is too high, and should be reduced.

A short " 2nd pull " or " hair trigger " is a source of danger, and is not permissible.

The bent of the sear, and also of the cocking-piece, should be perfectly square and vertical, and not inclined ; these faces must not receive adjustment during the regulation of the " pull off."

If the weights of the " pull-off " are light, the sear spring should be replaced by a stronger one.

8. *Fitting locking bolt.*—After inserting a new locking bolt, see that the front end does not protrude into the bolt lever way sufficiently to friction against the bolt lever.

9. *Extractor.*—When fitting a new extractor, see that the outside of the leg is not bowed excessively, since, if so, it is liable to friction in the body during withdrawal of the bolt, thereby causing the cartridge-case to be released from the bolt face recess, and resulting in faulty ejection.

10. *Catch, magazine.*—If it is found necessary to adjust the length when fitting a new catch, care should be taken to maintain the bevel at the front end, as this is essential to ensure retention of the bottom plate in case of a jolt or blow.

11. *To fit new stock.*—Remove from the old stock the following components :—Dial sight assembled, fixing screw and washer ; stop band pin ; collars, front and rear ; tie nut and bolt ; screws and bracket, with swivel ; butt plate with screws.

Assemble such of these components as are required to the new stock ; then place the nose-cap on the stock and insert the front end of the handguard ; if necessary, plane or file the upper surfaces of the stock until the handguard fits the nose-cap and lies evenly on the stock.

Place the action in the stock, with the rear handguard retaining ring placed in its correct position ; if necessary, adjust the ring seating in the stock to ensure that the ring is not subjected to excessive stress when the action is screwed down securely, and, if required, plane or file the upper surfaces of the stock until the rear handguard fits in the ring and lies evenly on the surfaces.

The rear face of the transverse rib on the underside of the body should bear definitely against its seating ; in order to ensure this, the stock should be cleared if necessary to prevent the rear end of the body tang from bearing at the end of the tang recess.

The underside and front and rear ends of the body, and the reinforce of the barrel, should bear definitely in the stock. The barrel at the muzzle end should bear lightly against the stock when the body and reinforce bearings have been correctly adjusted.

There should be sufficient clearance in the barrel groove between the reinforce and nose-cap seating to allow a piece of thick brown paper to be passed round and drawn along the barrel.

The length of the guard screw collars should be adjusted so that the trigger guard is tightened against the face of the collar and also the stock.

See that the bolt lever is not prevented by the stock from closing fully down, as this may cause the locking bolt to remain jammed, owing to the recess in the rear face of the bolt lever not being in alignment with the locking bolt. See also that the bolt stop is not prevented, by fullness of the stock, from closing freely.

Before assembling, finally grease the barrel groove of the stock and handguards, and also the barrel and body, with red mineral jelly.

12. *Exchanging bolt.*—When fitting new bolts, the distance of the bolt from the end of the chamber should be tested with the gauges—·064-inch No. 2, and ·074-inch No. 2—to ensure that neither too much, nor too little, space exists between these two points.

The locking lugs must not be oil-stoned, or otherwise adjusted to enable the bolt to close over the ·064-inch gauge ; selection of a bolt that will fit the rifle is the only permissible procedure.

13. *Adjustment of foresight.*—The method of adjusting the foresight laterally is similar to that for rifles No. 1, except that the No. 2 cramp will be used for the purpose.

Sight—Telescopic—Rifles No. 3, Mk. I* (T)

(With leather caps and strap, and case with leather sling and cap, cleaning cloth, wire brush, and eye guard).

General Information, Description and Method of Adjustment

General Information

The telescopic sight is specially adjusted and numbered, before issue, to the rifle to which it is fitted, and forms part of the rifle with which it must always be kept.

Whenever adjustment is necessary beyond that which armourers are allowed to carry out, the rifle complete with telescopic sight and the details mentioned in the heading should be forwarded to the C.I.S.A. in the chest provided.

The sight is not issued separately.

The case, sight, telescopic, with leather sling and cap, cleaning cloth and wire brush, and the eye-guard are issuable separately for maintenance. The cleaning cloth and brush can also be supplied separately for maintenance.

The cloth is provided for cleaning the lenses, and the wire brush for keeping the fittings on the rifle free from dust ; both are carried under the flap inside the cap of the case.

The eye-guard is a conical rubber tube, $3\frac{1}{2}$ inches long, beaded at one end and bevelled at the other. The beaded end fits over the eye-guard body of the telescope.

The two leather caps connected by the strap are provided for protecting the lenses ; care should be taken to prevent oil from getting on to the lenses.

When not in actual use, the telescope should be carried in the case.

Description (Fig. 8)

Telescope.—The telescope consists of a steel body containing a combination of lenses. The two eye lenses are separated by a distance ring and secured by a locking ring. The erector has two lenses—a clamp ring, and a cell-locking ring and stop. It is held by the focussing slide (1) and focussing slide clamping screw (2), on the underside of the body. The object glass is held in a sleeve screwed into the front end of the body and the adaptor (3), with prism in cell (4), is screwed in front of the object glass in the sleeve (5). A ray shade (6) is screwed on a collar (7) fitted on the sleeve. The diaphragm with cross wire and pointer is dovetailed vertically into the sleeve. It is elevated by a screw fitted under the saddle, which is secured by screws passing through the body into the sleeve and stiffening ring. The elevating screw is fitted with a drum head by

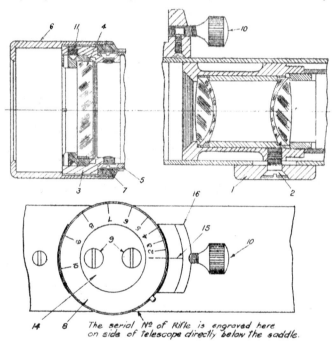

The serial N⁰ of Rifle is engraved here on side of telescope directly below the saddle.

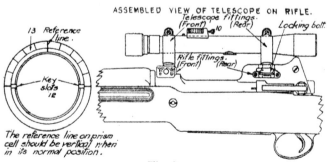

ASSEMBLED VIEW OF TELESCOPE ON RIFLE.

The reference line on prism cell should be vertical when in its normal position.

Fig. 8.

which it is rotated, and an adjustable range scale ring (8) is fitted on the top of the drum head, to which it is fixed by two screws (9) and a washer. A screw with a milled head (10) is fitted in the saddle for fixing the drum of the elevating screw.

Fittings.—The front fitting on the telescope has two legs which hook into the front fitting on the body of the rifle. The rear fitting on the telescope has a single leg, the squared end of which drops into the rear fitting on the left side of the rifle body and is secured by a thumb-locking bolt.

Adjustments

The only adjustments to the telescopic sights of rifles which may be attempted by armourers attached to units are :

The alteration for lateral deflection by means of the prism.

The adjustment of focus, zeroing and setting of the range scale. The interior or other parts of the instrument must not be touched.

Lateral adjustment.—Lateral adjustment is effected by means of a glass wedge or prism (4) mounted in front of the object glass. This prism deflects a ray of light passing through it towards its thicker end. If, therefore, the prism is mounted with its thicker edge on top and horizontal, and the rifle to which the telescope is fitted is laid in rests, so that the bull's-eye of a distant target is found upon the tip of the pointer, then a complete rotation of the prism about the axis of the telescope, in a clockwise direction, as seen from the eye-piece of the telescope, will cause the image of the bull's-eye in the plane of the diaphragm to rotate in a small circle passing, say, from 12 o'clock through 3, 6 and 9 o'clock, back to 12 o'clock. Thus, when the thick end of the prism is horizontal, the image will be positioned either at 12 or 6 o'clock, and the displacement of it, for any small angular displacement of the prism, will be practically horizontal only. This fact is taken advantage of for the purpose of securing adjustment for lateral deflection. The prism is initially mounted as nearly as possible with its thick edge horizontal, so that any required small adjustment for deflection can be effected without materially affecting the adjustment for elevation.

Note.—The prism is in the form of a circular disc, but in this paragraph it is spoken of as though left in its primitive shape of a square.

Method of adjustment.—Remove ray shade (6), slacken the three screws fixing prism cell (11), fit the adjusting key into the slots of the prism cell (12), and rotate to the right or left as necessary. There is a reference line on the ring of the prism cell adaptor (13). If the prism cell is rotated through one of these divisions, it will give approximately five minutes of deflection.

When correct adjustment has been made, tighten up the screws fixing prism cell (11) and replace the ray shade (6).

Adjustment for elevation.—The drum head of the elevating screw is fitted with a movable range scale ring (8) upon which the range scale is engraved. This ring is normally secured by a washer (14) and two fixing screws (9) to the drum head of the elevating screw. If at any time it is found that the elevation indicated by the scale is wrong for any given range, it can be put right by unclamping the range scale ring, adjusting the pointer by shooting at a known range, and then turning the range scale ring to indicate this range before clamping it once more to the drum head of the elevating screw.

Order of adjustment.—It is important to note that whenever an adjustment for lateral deflection by rotation of the prism has been made, the accuracy of the range scale for elevation should be checked, as it may happen that the initial position of the prism was not one in which its thick edge was perfectly horizontal. In adjusting the telescope, therefore, it is important that the adjustment for lateral deflection should be made first ; then, if necessary, the adjustment for elevation should be made. Should the adjustment for elevation be made first, it may happen that the subsequent adjustment for deflection introduces an error in the adjustment for elevation.

To adjust focus.—Remove the telescope from the rifle, release the screw, clamping, focussing slide (2) and adjust the slide (1) to suit the eye, tighten the screw and replace the telescope on the rifle.

To adjust for zero after shooting at 200 *yards.*—Release the screws fixing washer scale ring (9) and turn the range scale ring until the second line corresponds with the zero line (15) on the saddle (16), then re-tighten the screws fixing washer (9).

Clamp the drum with the screw clamping range drum (10) after shooting for zero at 200 yards or adjusting for other ranges.

Packing of telescopic sights during storage.—In order to prevent the formation of verdigris on the brass caps, etc., of the sights during storage, the leather caps will not be placed on the sight, but will be inserted separately in the case.

The steel body tube and brackets of the sight will be cleaned with an oily rag and wiped quite dry ; the telescope will then be wrapped in plain, dry tissue paper before insertion in the case. Care must be taken to see that the tissue paper used is perfectly dry.

The case will be stored in the chest with the rifle.

Tools.—The following tools are provided for the adjustment of telescopic sights :—

Section B. 3

Key, sight, telescopic.

Section F

Screwdrivers, Instrument makers (set of 4)

The above-mentioned tools will form part of the " Box, tool, regimental armourers " in peace, and of the " Bag, armourers, S.A." in war, for units equipped with telescopic-sighted rifles.

Section 5.—Re-browning and Re-blacking

Re-browning

1. For general instructions, assistance to be provided by units, etc., *see* Part I, Chapter III, and Appendix I.

The following components of rifles will be re-browned when required :—

Rifles Nos. 1 and 2.—Barrel with foresight block, inner band and backsight bed ; body ; bolt ; bolt-head ; cocking-piece ; locking bolt and spring ; trigger guard ; magazine ; outer band ; handguard cap ; backsight protector ; nose-cap ; backsight cap (or windgauge) and swivel bracket. Also cut-off of No. 1, Mk. III rifles.

Rifles No. 3, Mk. I* (T) and Mk. I* (F).—Parts of a corresponding nature to those for Nos. 1 and 2 rifles. As these rifles are provided only for sniping purposes, re-browning will seldom be necessary.

The rifles are specially tested and adjusted for accuracy before issue from the factory ; care must therefore be taken to keep the parts separate from those of other rifles ; they should be stripped only when actually necessary for purposes of re-browning, oiling, and minor adjustment or repair.

2. When cleaning off the surplus browning from the frictional surfaces of bolts and bolt-heads and the bolt hole of bodies, care must be taken to avoid the use of sharp abrasives ; it is essential that the size of these parts should be maintained as long as possible.

Oil-blacking

1. Oil-blacking will be limited to foresight blades, swivels, and screws. As foresight blades are hardened and tempered,

the temperature should not be raised above the minimum required for oil-blacking.

2. It should be borne in mind that certain other hardened and tempered parts, *e.g.*, cocking-pieces, locking bolts, cut-offs, etc., which are oil-blacked in factories, are subjected to special treatment and inspection tests which it is not possible for armourers to repeat; when such parts are worn bright, they should be browned.

Temporary Blacking of Sights and other Parts

For the temporary blacking of sights and other parts which are worn bright only at some local point, and which do not require complete treatment by browning, the following process will be found suitable :—

Dissolve 1 oz. of liver shellac in 6 oz. of methylated spirits and add to the mixture as much " carbon black " (lamp black) as will fill six empty ·303-inch cartridge-cases. The carbon black may be obtained by placing a piece of sheet iron over a gas jet, candle, or lamp flame.

Thoroughly free the bright place to be blacked from oil, and coat lightly with the above mixture, using a camel-hair brush.

Care must be taken to keep the mixture securely corked up, otherwise it will evaporate quickly.

Section 6.—Description and Use of Armourers' Gauges and certain Tools

Gauges

Gauges, armourers', ·064-*inch No.* 1 *and* ·074-*inch No.* 1 *for rifles No.* 1.—These gauges are used also for ·303-inch machine-guns, with the exception of the ·074, which is not used for Vickers guns.

The gauges are for testing the distance of the face of the breech bolt from the end of the chamber, or, in other words, the cartridge head space. The diameter of the rim conforms approximately to that of a maximum cartridge. The portion which enters the chamber is merely a guide—not a gauging feature.

When closing the bolt on the gauge, the trigger should be held back to prevent cocking and snapping, which is liable to cause the rim of the gauge to be broken off. Care should also be taken to avoid drawing the gauge back on to, and so damaging, the ejector.

In no circumstances must these gauges be used for No. 3 rifles, as the rim is slightly too large in diameter for the recess in the face of the bolt of those rifles, and, consequently, in addition to giving a false gauging result, will cause damage to the wall of the recess or the projecting horns on the left recoil lug of the bolt.

Gauges, armourers', ·064-inch No. 2 and ·074-inch No. 2 for rifles No. 3.—These gauges are special to No. 3 rifles and must be used only for those rifles. They differ from the No. 1 gauges in that the diameter of the rim is smaller and the portion which enters the chamber is longer, the front end being tapered off.

The instructions given for the use of the No. 1 gauges are applicable also to the No. 2 gauges.

The No. 2 gauges are obtainable on loan from store when required.

Gauges, armourers' plug—·303, ·307, ·308, ·310, *and lead No. 2 with rod, plug Mk. II.*—These gauges are held in R.A.O.C. Ordnance depots and are supplied to circuit armourers at home and abroad when required. The ·303 gauge is supplied to all armourers. At stations abroad, the gauges may also be issued on loan to regimental armourers when the services of a circuit armourer are not available.

The plugs are screwed internally at the rear end to take the rod. The ·307, ·308, ·310 and lead are limit gauges for wear of bore of ·303-inch rifle barrels—*see* Section 3.

The ·308 plug has a line marked round it at $\frac{1}{4}$ inch from the front end, the limit being reached when this line is flush with the muzzle of the barrel.

The ·310 and lead plugs are arranged so that the limit in rifles No. 1 is reached when the rear end of either plug is flush with, or inside, the breech face of the barrel. The distance from the line marked round the ·310 plug to the front end of the plug is the same as the distance from the breech face to the front end of the lead, but as the diameter of the bore and of the front portion of the lead, in new or part worn barrels, is less than ·310 inch, the line will stand out from the breech face of such barrels for a distance which will diminish as wear increases.

In the case of No. 3 rifles, the limit is reached with the ·310 plug when the line on the rod, one inch from the face of the collar, is flush with, or inside, the rear face of the front socket portion of the body ; with the No. 2 lead plug the limit is reached when the line $1\frac{1}{4}$ inch from the face of the collar so enters.

The lines referred to are $\frac{1}{4}$ and $\frac{1}{2}$ inch further from the face of the collar than the M.G. line for machine guns in naval service.

When Mk. I rods, plug, are in possession, and are required for use in gauging No. 3 rifles, they will be altered to Mk. II pattern by armourers by the marking of the two additional lines referred to.

Gauges, armourers', striker point No. 1 for rifles Nos. 1 and 2.—The dimensions for striker protrusion through the face of the bolt-head are ·042 inch high and ·04 inch low, and the radius of the point ·038 inch.

Gauges, armourers', striker point No. 2 for rifles No. 3.—The dimensions for striker protrusion in this gauge are ·055 inch high and ·05 inch low, and the radius of point ·03 inch. This gauge is supplied on loan as required.

Tester, trigger.—This is provided for testing the weight or tension of the various rifle springs and pull-off referred to in Sections 3 and 4, and for pistols, Chapter III. It can be used also for machine-guns when the spring balance provided for use with those guns is not available.

In order to obtain a correct result, it is essential that those working parts of the weapons which are either directly or indirectly linked up with the springs should be thoroughly clean ; when dried oil, mineral jelly or other matter is present, a true reading will not be obtained.

When testing the pull-off of a rifle, the rifle should be, if possible, gripped firmly in a horizontal position in a vice, cut-off side uppermost, the tester then being applied diagonally across the small of the butt in the line taken by the normal finger-pull.

When testing Nos. 1 and 2 rifles, fitted with the No. 1 " B " cocking-piece, for weight of mainspring in both spring-eased and full-cock positions, apply the hook of the tester either in the half-bent or locking bolt recess at the side of the cocking-piece. In order to do this, it is necessary to withdraw the bolt and turn the cocking-piece into the long cam of the bolt, first marking the striker lightly to indicate the full cock position.

Reference gauges and tester, trigger.—A list of these gauges is given in E.R., Pt. I. The gauges are kept at Ordnance depots where armourers' shops are established ; they are to be employed solely for the periodical verification of the working gauges, and must not on any account be used as working gauges.

The working gauges will be tested for comparision with the reference gauges as follows :—

Gauges ·064 No. 1 and ·074 No. 1.—Select No. 1 rifles in which the bolt just closes over the working gauge, then apply the reference gauge.

Gauges, plug.—Select barrels which are worn to the limits according to the working gauges, then apply the reference gauges.

In the case of the ·303-inch plug, select a barrel in which the working gauge runs and is a fit, and then apply the reference gauge, bearing in mind that a very small difference, *e.g.*, ·0001 inch in the gauges, will admit of the smaller entering and the larger being kept out. The ·303 gauge, not being a limit gauge, can be allowed to wear to a greater extent than the limit gauges. ·3025 is a reasonable limit.

Tester, trigger.—Select a rifle in which the first pull and the pull-off are to the minimum weights with the working tester, then apply the reference tester.

When a marked difference from the reference gauges is found, *i.e.*, if the rifles would undoubtedly be sentenced for exchange with the working gauges or testers, but not so with the reference gauges or tester, a report should be made, and the worn working gauges returned to store for exchange.

Similar action should be taken when wear of the ·064 working gauge is such that there is a possibility of rifles, when tested with the gauges, failing to turn over a cartridge with rim of maximum thickness without undue pressure on the bolt handle.

Tools

Implement action No. 1, *Mk. II.*—The various tools and the gauge comprising the implement (*see* Fig. 9) are provided for the following purposes :—

- (*a*) Screwdriver for the following s crews :—inner band, nose-cap (back), trigger guard (front), butt-plate, locking bolt spring and backsight protector nut.
- (*b*) Screwdriver for cut-off, extractor and handguard cap screws.
- (*c*) Screwdriver for the following screws : — outer band, swivels, marking disc, ejector, trigger guard (back), sear, backsight spring and windgauge.
- (*d*) Screwdriver for backsight slide catch screw.
- (*e*) Tool for removing and replacing extractor spring.
- (*f*) Screwdriver for bolt nut of bayonets.
- (*g*) Gauge for projection and radius of striker point (dimensions as for gauge striker point No. 1).

Tools, breeching up.—These tools are now issued only, as ordered, to India and Dominions overseas, but those which may still be available at Command workshops and at Weedon will continue to be used for unbreeching unserviceable barrels from serviceable bodies prior to breaking up the barrels.

Plates, screw and taps S.A.—Particulars of these plates and taps, and the screws, etc., for which they are suitable are given in Appendix VI.

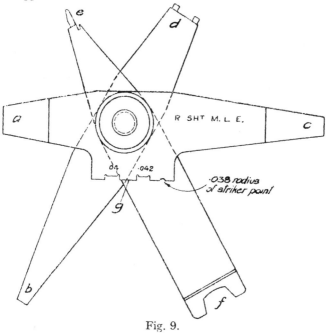

Fig. 9.

CHAPTER II

BAYONETS AND SCABBARDS

Drawing No. S.A.I.D. 2474

Bayonets No. 1, Mk. I

Weight—16 to 18 oz.

Section 1.—Stripping and Assembling

The only parts which are detachable are the bolt with spring and nut and the walnut wood grips with two screws and nuts. As the end of the bolt is riveted over the end of the nut to prevent the nut from working loose, it should be stripped only in the event of a new bolt being required, during re-browning, or when, owing to want of care, it has become rusted in. When it has to be removed and re-assembled, sufficient of the riveted end should be preserved to permit of re-riveting ; when insufficient remains, the nut may be slightly shortened.

The flush end of each bolt is blended off with the pommel during manufacture, consequently, owing to variation in contour, it is necessary to keep each bolt to the bayonet in which it has been fitted.

As some variation occurs also in the contour of the tang of the blade, it is desirable that the grips should be kept to the bayonet to which they are fitted.

Section 2.—Cleaning

When cleaning a polished blade, the nose-cap stud hole in the crosspiece and the sword bar slot in the pommel, care must be taken to avoid the use of abrasives. Worn fine emery cloth only should be employed for removing rust.

When a blade is pitted with rust, no attempt should be made to remove entirely such marks, as the removal of metal involved would tend to weaken the blade.

Section 3.—Examination

1. Examine the blade for straightness, alignment with the tang, and for general condition. When bent, or very rusty, the bayonet will be exchanged—factory repair. See that the crosspiece and pommel remain secure on the tang—they are brazed on in manufacture.

2. At stations provided with a box test, *doubtful* bayonets will be tested as follows :—

Insert the point of the bayonet in the upper end of the block attached to the curve, with the right flat of the blade, marked with an X, on the outer or convex side ; force the blade around the curve—taking care that it is not overstrained beyond the limit of the curve—then immediately release it, and examine for straightness. Blades which take a permanent set after testing must be exchanged (factory repair).

When testing, care must be taken to see that the right flat marked X is always the convex side.

3. Examine the grips for condition and test the security of the nuts on the screws.

4. See that the sword bar slot is clean, that the bolt operates freely, and that the strength of the spring is satisfactory ; then assemble the bayonet to the rifle. If excessively

slack on the rifle, ascertain whether an exchange for a closer-fitting bayonet from another rifle will effect an improvement, and if so, whether the worn bayonet is a better fit on the rifle from which the closer-fitting bayonet was taken. When such an exchange proves satisfactory, re-number the bayonets to the rifles. When a more suitable bayonet cannot be found, the nose-cap of the rifle is probably at fault, and should be brought to the notice of C.I.S.A.'s examiners or the A.I.A. at their next visit. When the sword bar slot and the hole in the crosspiece are badly worn, the bayonet will be exchanged —factory repair. When considerable longitudinal play is found, the fault may be due to a worn bolt in the bayonet, in which case a new bolt should be fitted.

5. Rusty bayonets should be reported to the C.O. for necessary action.

Section 4.—Repairs, Modifications and Adjustments

When fitting new grips, it may be necessary occasionally to modify the contour to conform reasonably with that of the tang and the pommel, but they should be left well prominent to allow for subsequent repair, the edges being rounded off slightly.

When fitting a new bolt, it may be necessary to adjust the locking face slightly to enable the bolt to engage over the sword bar of the rifle nose-cap; the outer end should also be blended with the pommel.

Polishing. — The blades, crosspieces and pommels of bayonets in possession of regular units and regimental depots, during peace, will be kept polished. Bayonets held for mobilization, including those in use in the T.A. and supplementary reserve, have the blades sandblasted, and the crosspieces and pommels browned. When bayonets for peace use of regular units and regimental depots are received unpolished, the polishing will be carried out without removing the grips, screws and nuts, due care being taken to avoid injury to the same.

The removal of grips by troops for cleaning, scraping, or staining with colouring matter, is prohibited ; when met with, armourers should report the matter for disciplinary action.

Re-browning of browned bayonets (including sandblasting) will be carried out at Command workshops as required by the process detailed in Appendix I.

The crosspiece, pommel and tang only will be re-browned, the grips, bolt, nut and spring being first removed.

During boiling, the bayonets should be totally submerged in the boiling water to prevent the blade from rusting.

After browning, and before re-assembly, the underside and ends of the grips should be coated with red mineral jelly.

Sharpening of blades. — The blades of bayonets will be maintained in a sharpened condition, *i.e.*, about ·01 inch wide at the edges. The sharpening, where necessary, will be performed with a smooth file or by grinding ; it should commence at two inches from the crosspiece and finish at the point, the existing angle of the edge being retained.

Bayonets No. 3, Mk. I

Weight—16 to 18 oz.

The instructions contained in Sections 1 to 4 apply generally to this pattern of bayonet.

The blade is identical with that of the No. 1 bayonet, but the crosspiece and pommel and the bolt and grips are special.

The nut and spring and grip screws and nuts are common to the No. 1, Mk. I bayonet.

Scabbard, Bayonet No. 1 (also for Bayonet No. 3)

Section 1.—Stripping and Assembling

It is necessary to remove the locket and chape only when re-blocking the leather, or re-browning the locket and chape.

To remove the locket and chape, cut the wire laces, pull them out and drive the locket and chape off.

To re-assemble these mounts, rub down the ends with glass paper to remove the old glue, then re-glue chape end, press chape on, allow to dry, insert fresh laces (long and short) and clinch them on the mandril.

Assemble the locket by the same method, using a short lace for the purpose. Finally insert several bayonets in the scabbard to see that it is free from obstructions.

Note.—The overall length should not be less than 17⅜ inches.

Section 2.—Cleaning

1. When cleaning, attention should be given to the locket springs, which are liable to become rusty. Rust can be removed from the portions which make contact with the blade by means of a strip of wood, shaped approximately to the bayonet blade, and fine emery ; after cleaning, oil with G.S. oil.

2. When the interior of the scabbard is damp, it should be dried slowly at a temperature not exceeding 80°.

Section 3.—Examination

1. Examine for condition of the leather, fit and condition of the locket and chape.

Insert the bayonet into the scabbard as a test for efficiency of the locket springs, and to ascertain that the scabbard is clear of obstructions. Examine the locket springs for security and signs of rust.

2. See that the locket and chape of scabbards on peace charge of regular units and regimental depots are polished, and that those on scabbards held for mobilization, including the T.A. and the Supplementary Reserve, are browned. Also see that the leather of the scabbards on peace charge is efficiently blacked.

3. When locket springs are defective, the locket will be exchanged—factory repair.

Section 4.—Repairs, Modifications and Adjustments

Re-browning of lockets and chapes.—Re-browning, as required, will be carried out by the process detailed in Appendix 1.

The locket and chape must be removed for the purpose.

After browning, the interior of the locket and chape must be wiped clean and oiled to prevent the formation of rust ; the oil must subsequently be removed before the mounts are re-assembled, to enable the glue to adhere. When re-assembled, allow the glue to become set, and then lightly oil the locket springs.

Black finish.—The leather of brown scabbards on peace charge, and of brown scabbards received from store for peace maintenance (*see* Sect. 3, para. 2), will be blacked as follows under armourers' supervision :—

  (i) Sponge the surface of the leather with boiling water, to which has been added common soda in the proportion of about ½ oz. to the pint.
  (ii) When dry, apply one coat of service black dye.
  (iii) Finish with heel-ball.

Re-blocking of leathers at R.A.O.C. workshops.—Leathers of scabbards marked " W " (paraffin waxed) on the sewn side at about one inch from the locket will be re-blocked as follows :—

  (i) Remove the mounts.
  (ii) Place the mandril in boiling water for three minutes and then insert into the leather.
  (iii) Rub the leather down with a suitable stick, and leave on the mandril until cold.

56

    (iv) Rub down with glass-paper, damp with gum water, applied cold (4 oz. of gum arabic dissolved in one pint of hot water is sufficient for 100 leathers) ; dry naturally, and finally burnish with the stick.

    (v) Re-assemble the mounts.

    (vi) Apply glue to the chape end of the leather, place the chape in position and leave to dry.

    (vii) Fasten the chape by clinching the laces on the mandril.

    (viii) Assemble the locket in a similar manner.

When leathers of scabbards, *not marked " W,"* require repair in R.A.O.C. workshops, they will be treated as follows :—

    (i) Examine stitches of seams for condition, and, if satisfactory,

    (ii) Run shellac varnish down the seam from the inside, and allow the leathers to stand for 2 hours.

    (iii) Place about 20 leathers in the cage of the container in which paraffin wax has been heated to 175° F., and leave them immersed for 4 minutes ; then remove and place each on a mandril, well rub down the surface of the leather with a cloth, and leave for 5 minutes for the leather to set. Remove from the mandril and put in a cool place for 12 hours.

    (iv) Place on mandril, smooth with glass paper, coat with black dye, allow to stand until the surface is almost dry, then burnish with a stick, polish with a cloth, and mark with the letter " W."

    (v) Re-assemble the leathers with the locket and chape.

Note.—The shellac varnish should be prepared by mixing the shellac and methylated spirit to a thick consistency. The shellac takes about 30 hours to dissolve.

Repair of locket tangs of leathers in R.A.O.C. workshops.—When the tangs are broken, they will be replaced by fitting, sewing and glueing new tangs in accordance with the following instructions and the accompanying sketches, using the template (a converted locket), for the purpose.

    Assemble the template (Fig. 1) to the scabbard leather to be repaired, so that the bottom edge of the locket rests on the seam at the back—*see* Fig. 2.

    With a sharp knife cut out the angular piece at " A " (Fig. 2) for the joint of tang.

    Remove the template, insert the scabbard mandril, then glue the tang, previously made, as in Fig. 4, to the scabbard at the joint, and bind in position on the mandril, as in Fig. 3.

Cut away the binding and trim the joint.

With a suitable sewing awl and waxed linen thread, secure the tang to the scabbard on the outside with four stitches, as in Fig. 5.

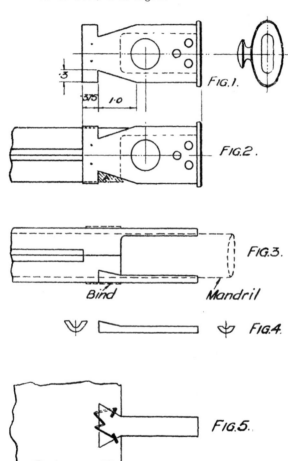

FIG.1.

FIG.2.

Bind   Mandril   FIG.3.

FIG.4.

FIG.5.

CHAPTER III

PISTOLS

Pistols, Revolver, No. 1 (·455-inch Webley), Mks. III, IV,
V and VI (Mks. III, IV and V are obsolescent).

Drawing No. S.A.I.D. 2053

Weight of Mks. III to V (4-inch barrel), approx. 2 lb. $3\frac{1}{2}$ oz.
Weight of Mks. V & VI (6-inch barrel), approx. 2 lb. $6\frac{1}{2}$ oz.

Section 1.—Stripping and Assembling
Stripping

Open the revolver to see that the chambers are empty,
then proceed as follows :—

(i) Unscrew the stock screw, and remove the stock.
(ii) Unscrew the guard screws and remove the guard.
(iii) Lift the mainspring out of the stud hole, press the
arms close together with the pliers and unhook the
claw of the spring from the hammer swivel.
(iv) Take out the mainspring lever.
(v) Unscrew the trigger screw and take out the trigger
with the pawl attached.
(vi) Unscrew the hammer screw and take out the hammer.
(vii) Unscrew the cam lever fixing screw, open the pistol
to the full extent, push the cam lever towards the
cylinder and remove the cylinder from its axis ;
unscrew the cam lever screw and remove the cam
lever.
(viii) Unscrew the joint pin screw, push out the joint pin
and remove the barrel from the body ; the extractor lever can now be removed.
(ix) Unscrew the barrel catch screw and remove the barrel
catch and the spring.
(x) Unscrew the cam screws and remove the cam.
(xi) To strip the cylinder, unscrew the extractor nut and
remove the spring and extractor.

Note.—As the extractor is not interchangeable in cylinders,
care must be taken to keep each extractor to its cylinder. The
cylinder must also be kept to the same pistol. This principle
should be followed throughout in order to avoid adjustment.

Assembling

(i) To assemble the cylinder, replace the extractor and
spring and screw home the extractor nut.

(ii) Replace the cam, replace the cylinder on its axis and see that the cylinder revolves freely.

(iii) Replace the extractor lever in the joint, assemble the barrel to the body, replace the joint pin, taking care that the stud on the pin is opposite the recess in the body, and screw home the joint pin screw.

(iv) Replace the cam lever, cam lever screw and cam lever fixing screw.

(v) Replace the hammer and screw home the axis screw, taking care to ensure that the hammer is free and will drop with its own weight.

(vi) Replace the trigger with the pawl assembled and screw home the axis screw (when replacing the trigger, the trigger nose should be placed between the hammer catch and the full cock bent nose of hammer).

(vii) Replace the mainspring lever.

(viii) Replace the mainspring.

(ix) Replace the guard and screw home the guard screws.

(x) Replace the stock and screw home the stock screw.

(xi) Replace the barrel catch with spring and screw home the barrel catch screw.

(xii) See that the lines on the shield and the body coincide.

Section 2.—Cleaning

1. All parts of the pistol must be kept perfectly clean ; " Oil, lubricating, G.S." only must be used for this purpose ; the use of abrasives, such as emery, sand-paper, etc., is strictly forbidden.

2. *To clean the barrel.*—Remove the cylinder, leave the pistol open, hold the barrel in the vice between the clams and clean with the No. 2 Mk. I brass rod, service flannelette and G.S. oil ; when slight rust is present, a mixture of G.S. and mineral burning oil (paraffin) should be used. If the rust cannot be readily removed by such means, the brass wire, well oiled with the foregoing mixture, may be employed in the eye of the No. 2 Mk. I rod ; 136 strands will, usually, be found sufficient for the purpose without putting excessive stress on the eye end of the rod.

Normally, the barrel should be cleaned from the breech end to obviate any risk of damage to the shield by the end of the cleaning rod.

Finally, wipe out with flannelette and leave lightly oiled.

3. *To clean the cylinder.*—The cylinder should be removed and cleaned similarly to the barrel, except that, when rust or lead deposit is present, the brass wire will be used in the brace

bit, charged with about 90 strands in the rear eye and 76 in the front eye, inserted in the chamber and revolved as necessary with the brace. After use, the brass wire should be preserved on the rod by means of a suitable cap, such as a spent cartridge-case.

4. When revolvers are received from store, and the bore of the barrels and chambers of the cylinder are coated with mineral jelly, the latter must be removed, and the bore and chambers lightly oiled with G.S. oil before the weapons are handed over for use.

Section 3.—Examination

1. Open the revolver to see that the chambers are empty, then examine generally for external condition; see that the numbers on body, barrel and cylinder agree, and that all accessible screws, especially those for the shield, hammer and the trigger guard, are tightened to ensure that the examination of subsequent details is not affected by loose screws.

2. Test the barrel for fit at the joints and for secure engagement of the strap by the barrel catch; the foresight for rigidity and security; also see that it is assembled correctly.

3. Examine the bore of the barrel and the chambers of the cylinder to see if they are free from cuts, rust and lead deposit. Insert the dummy cartridges into the chambers, test the extraction and free return of the extractor and rotate the cylinder to see that it revolves freely both when the revolver is opened and closed.

Examine the ratchet of the extractor for condition.

4. Gauge the distance of the cylinder from the face of the shield by applying the ·052-inch maximum gauge across each chamber when the latter is in the firing position; at the same time see that linear movement of the cylinder is not excessive and that its front end is clear of the barrel. See also that the shield is closely bedded in the body and the face free from burrs. When the gauge enters freely, the revolver must be exchanged.

5. Test the rotary movement of the cylinder by trigger action; see that each chamber is brought into alignment with the bore of the barrel and that no appreciable radial play then exists when the cylinder is held by the pawl and the solid stop of the trigger in the fired position.

During this test see that the trigger stop engages the cylinder when the trigger is released.

6. Test the hammer by hand for free action when the trigger is held back, and for slight overdraw at full cock with the trigger released.

Gauge the hammer projection through the shield—·044 to ·054 inch—and the radius of the nose.

Test for central striking on dummy cartridges ; see that the nose clears the wall of the hole in the body, also the cylinder, when the latter is rotated. When impact is not central, the defect may be due to rotary play of the cylinder referred to in para. 5, or to the hammer. If the latter, the hammer should be exchanged. When in the fired position, see that the shoulders of the hammer seat on the body, that the peak is clear of the barrel strap, and that the rebound arm is clear of the mainspring lever.

7. See that the trigger returns freely and has some initial play, that it does not make contact with the ends of the clearance slot in the guard in its foremost and rearmost positions, and that its nose passes freely on to, and engages securely in, the bent of the hammer. As a test for security of engagement of the nose in the bent, press the peak of the hammer firmly forward, having in mind that when the revolver is loaded and cocked it should not fire if accidentally dropped on the ground.

8. Test the weight of the mainspring. To do this, hold the barrel in the vice, press the trigger firmly in order that the hammer may seat closely on the body, apply a loop of twine attached to the trigger tester over the hammer peak and pull in line with the barrel. The weight registered to move the hammer should be from $3\frac{3}{4}$ to $4\frac{1}{4}$ lb. When outside these limits, and no undue friction is evident, the mainspring must be exchanged and the test repeated.

9. Test pull-off—hammer cocked, 6 to 8 lb.

Test trigger action, 15 to 18 lb.

Test weight to move barrel catch—pistol open, 4 to 6 lb.

When testing the weight of the trigger action, the direction of pull must be in line with the normal finger-pull.

10. See that all accessible screws are screwed tightly home, and that the butt swivel turns freely. After tightening screws, test to see that functioning has not been affected thereby.

Note.—When either the barrel, body or cylinder is unserviceable the revolver will be exchanged (factory repair).

Section 4.—Repairs, Modifications and Adjustments, etc.

Note.—(*a*) For repair work not to be undertaken, *see* E.R., Pt. I.

(*b*) For details, which can be supplied for fitting, *see* Vocabulary of Army Ordnance Stores, Section B.2. For the annual allowance, *see* E.R., Pt. I.

Faulty Extraction :—

(i) Failure of the extractor to rise may be due either to
insufficient freedom of the auxiliary lever in the slot
of the lever, or to the extractor nut not being screwed
home. When failure is due to the former cause,
the slot in the lever should be eased out by filing.

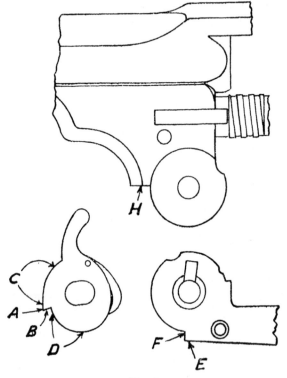

Fig. 1.

(ii) Failure of the extractor to return may be due to a burr
set up either at the inner edge of the circular joint
of the body at " F " on Fig. 1, or on the shoulder of
the extractor lever at " A."

When the obstruction is slight, it can sometimes
be cleared by fully opening the weapon, raising the
extractor by hand to its full extent and then releasing

it sharply ; should this fail, the barrel must be removed to enable the burr to be filed off.

(iii) Short extraction may be due to wear at the shoulder of the extractor lever at " A," at the inner edge of the shoulder of the body at " F," or one of the inner edges of the extractor slot in the barrel.

When worn at " A," the extractor lever should be filed back at " C " and " D " and the shoulder " B " adjusted to ensure contact at the outer edge at " A " with the body shoulder " F." The latter should be set inward at " E " and filed back slightly at " F " to reproduce the full acting corner for engagement with " A."

The shoulder " H " of the barrel should then be adjusted back as necessary to obtain the full throw of the extractor.

Jammed Cylinder.—This may be due to one or more of the following causes :—

(i) *Axis chamber dirty.*—When cleaning, give special attention to the screw thread in front of the cylinder nut.

(ii) *Cylinder frictioning on breech end of barrel.*—This can be remedied by filing the barrel slightly to clear, provided the ·052-inch gauge does not enter between the cylinder and the shield after adjustment.

(iii) *Solid stop of trigger low.*—To remedy, draw the metal up from the sides, and when correct height is obtained, re-test alignment of chambers with the bore of the barrel and set the stop laterally, as necessary.

(iv) *Axis small in diameter.*—In this case, the revolver must be exchanged.

(v) *Trigger stop high.*—*See* remedy for defective trigger stop.

Cylinder not fully turned into position.—When due to the pawl slipping the ratchet, and no defect is found in the ratchet or the pawl, nor excessive space between the cylinder and the shield, the defect may be caused by insufficient pressure of the main spring lever on the pawl. If this is the case, the lever seating on the pawl should be filed back at " A," on Fig. 2, in order that the pressure may be taken at " B."

Radial play of cylinder in fired position.—Slight play is not of serious moment, and a certain amount of wear must be allowed for. An improvement can be effected usually by setting the pawl to make it slightly concave on the right-hand side, so throwing the upper right side edge closer to the teeth of the ratchet of the cylinder ; if this fails and the movement is excessive, a new pawl must be fitted. When fitting a new pawl, see that the trigger is clear of the ends of the slot in the guard, that the solid stop of the trigger engages the shoulder of the cylinder, and that the chambers are concentric with the bore.

Incorrect alignment of the chambers with the bore of the barrel. —When this defect is due to faulty lateral location of the solid stop of the trigger, the revolver should be stripped sufficiently to remove the trigger stop, then, upon re-assembly, the cylinder should be revolved until the stop shoulder makes contact with the solid stop of the trigger. It can then be seen in which direction the solid stop requires setting to produce correct alignment.

When setting the solid stop with a suitable punch, the solid portion of the trigger should be firmly held in the vice near the

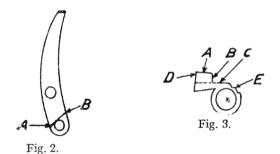

Fig. 2.

Fig. 3.

stop between improvised metal plates, otherwise fracture at the axis hole may occur.

Defective trigger stop.—When high, so causing the cylinder to jam, file down at " A " on Fig 3, maintaining the correct convex form. When low, and not properly engaging the cylinder, reduce at " B " and " C." If the stop does not rise correctly, draw the metal out at " D." If the stop drops on the return of the trigger, file the corner at " E." If it drops on firing, reduce the length of the spring at the acting end. Should the spring be loose on its seating, set it slightly concave.

Excessive overdraw of the hammer. — This will cause the trigger nose to slip under the bent and lock the action. It is due usually to a badly worn hammer or trigger or to wear in both parts. Trial with new parts will indicate which is at fault. New hammers and triggers issued as spare are well up to gauge on the bent and the nose respectively. If adjustment of such is necessary, the surface of the hammer at " A " on Fig. 4 should be filed back until the nose of the trigger engages, and a slight overdraw is obtained.

Adjustment of hammer projection through the shield.—When in excess of high limit—·054—file the hammer nose back, maintaining the radius in accordance with the gauge.

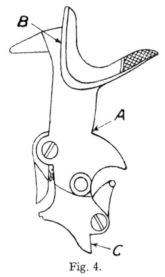

Fig. 4.

When short to low limit—·044—file back the shoulder on each side at " B " on Fig. 4, bearing in mind that it is impossible to obtain extra projection if the rebound shoulder " A " on Fig. 5 of the main spring lever and " C " on Fig. 4 of hammer are not clear when the hammer is in the fired position.

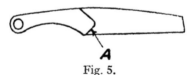

Fig. 5.

Note.—Care must be taken when adjusting the rebound shoulders to ensure that they offer the maximum resistance to an accidental blow on the rear end of the hammer when the hammer is in the rebound position.

Centre-punching of hammer catch screw.—The screw should

be secured by centre-punching the head near the edge. When this has not been done, or whenever the screw has been removed, this operation should be carried out to prevent it working loose. When loose, the catch tends to move forward beyond its normal position, and so fails to clear the nose of the trigger when the latter is pressed during single action, thus preventing the hammer from falling.

Re-browning.—Re-browning, as necessary, will be carried out as for rifles—*see* Section 5, Chapter I.

When re-browning the cylinder, the extractor must be removed, due care being taken to ensure that it is re-assembled to its own cylinder after the latter has been browned.

Pistols, Signal, No. 1, Mk. III*

Drawing No. S.A.I.D. 2530

Diameter of bore of barrel, 1·05 to 1·06 inch.

Weight of pistol, approximately 2 lb. 13 oz.

1. The Mk. III* pattern differs from the Mk. III in that a trumpet-shaped handguard bush is fitted to the muzzle end of the barrel as a protection for the hand when opening the pistol in the event of a hang fire occurring. The Mk. III* pattern only should now be met with.

2. The pistol is of simple construction and calls for no detailed instructions for stripping, assembling and cleaning.

3. When examining the pistol the following points should receive attention :—

    (i) The flange of the handguard bush when distorted should be corrected where practicable.

    (ii) The fit of the barrel joint and the action and condition of the extractor.

    (iii) The condition of the bore and chamber. A fired cartridge case should be tried in the chamber and extracted.

    (iv) The rebound of the hammer and condition of the hammer nose. Protrusion of nose, ·07 to ·075, to be gauged with the gauge for hammer point supplied for the Webley revolver, and adjusted when necessary. When the peak of the hammer does not abut on the barrel catch in the fired position, the pistol must be exchanged (factory repair).

    (v) Weight of pull-off, 8 to 10 lb.

        Weight of trigger spring, 3 to 4 lb.

        Test to ensure that when cocked the bent of the hammer cannot be jarred off the bent of the trigger.

(vi) Functioning of the safety catch. The safety catch must oppose the thumb-piece of the barrel catch when the hammer is cocked, so that the thumb-piece cannot be forced beyond it and the barrel catch disengaged from the barrel. The thumb-piece should be set inward where necessary to ensure this, but friction on the side of the body must be avoided.

(vii) When the barrel or body is unserviceable the pistol must be exchanged (factory repair).

4. Re-browning of exposed surfaces of steel parts is to be carried out as necessary.

Horse-Killer, ·310-in., Mk. I

Diameter of bore of barrel, ·310 inch.
Weight, 1 lb. 7½ oz.

1. The horse-killer is known commercially as " Greener's Humane Horse-Killer." It fires a special cartridge known as " Cartridge, S.A., Ball, ·310-inch, Mk. I, z."

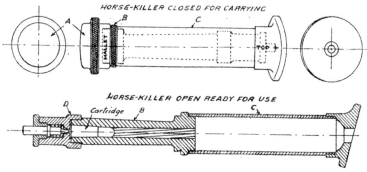

Fig. 6.

2. Fig. 6 shows the weapon in the open position ready for use and in the closed position for carrying. As can be seen, the mallet " A," by means of the plain end of which the firing pin is struck, forms the closing cap. When this is unscrewed the barrel " B " is then unscrewed, reversed and screwed into the tube " C." To load the weapon the firing pin holder " D " is unscrewed, the cartridge inserted in the barrel and the holder " D " screwed home. The base at the end of the tube " C," with prominent end marked " Top " uppermost, is held firmly to the head of the animal.

3. A No. 2 Webley pistol cleaning rod is supplied for cleaning the barrel.

4. When examining the horse-killer attention should be

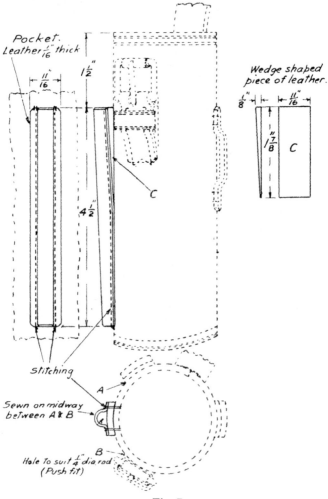

Fig. 7.

given to the condition of the connecting screw threads and of the chamber and the bore of the barrel; the firing pin should be freely retracted by the spring and the radius of the point maintained. The protrusion of the firing pin should be about ·055 inch when pushed home forward. The interior of tube "C" and the base should be cleaned as necessary, having in view the weakening effect of rust pitting on the tube.

5. A leather case is provided for each horse-killer. The Mk. I* pattern differs from the Mk. I in that an external leather pocket is fitted to take the cleaning rod. Mk. I cases can be converted locally to Mk. I* pattern in accordance with Fig. 7. The case also takes a cartridge holder.

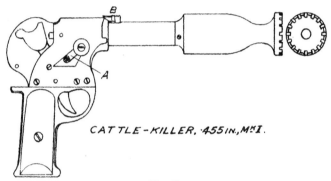

CATTLE-KILLER, ·455 IN., M⁰ I.

Fig. 8.

Cattle-Killer, ·455-in., Mk. I

Diameter of bore of barrel, ·424 inch.
Weight, about 5 lb. 13 oz.

1. The cattle-killer was originally introduced by the R.S.P.C.A. It is a converted trade article, and is not manufactured on an interchangeable basis, so that parts cannot be issued for maintenance. Where not readily repairable locally the pistol will be exchanged (factory repair).

2. The barrel has to be detached for loading purposes. It is assembled to the body on the bayonet joint principle. To remove the barrel, the thumb catch "A," Fig. 8, is pressed downward, the barrel given a quarter turn in a clockwise direction and then drawn forward. The fired cartridge case is removed when the barrel is detached, by pressing the sliding extractor "B" to the rear.

3. The pistol takes the same cartridge as the service Webley revolver. The mechanism is simple and the parts

are accessible for any minor repairs and adjustments which may be found necessary. The barrel can be cleaned with the No. 2 Webley pistol-cleaning rod provided. The enlarged bore of the gun-metal head is liable to accumulate fouling, which can be removed by a cleaning rod and brass wire.

4. When examining the weapon the condition of the chamber and bore of barrel should be observed and attention given to the safe engagement and condition of the bents of hammer and trigger, which must be such as will ensure that the weapon when loaded and cocked will not fire if accidentally dropped on the hard floor of a slaughter-house. The firing pin, which is of floating spring retracted type, must be free, and the barrel securely locked by the thumb catch " A." The castellations in the gun-metal head must be clear for the free escape of the gases, etc., when the head is held in contact with the animal.

The weight of the pull-off should be from 6 to 8 lb.

5. When examining the barrel it should be borne in mind that a weapon of this nature is unlikely to receive the attention in use that is given to military weapons ; moreover, a high finish of bore is not essential. When any doubt exists as to the efficiency of the weapon from a firing standpoint the armourer should have it fired before handing it over for use.

6. A wood case is provided for each cattle-killer. The external dimensions of the case are approximately 11 by 8¾ by 2¾ inches. The lid is hinged and a brass catch and leather handle are fitted. Internally the case has a partitioned-off recess for the barrel and cleaning rod.

CHAPTER IV

SWORDS AND SCABBARDS

Drawing S.A.I.D. 2474 illustrates the various patterns of the swords and scabbards in use, and gives their approximate dimensions and weights. This drawing is provided to facilitate identification.

Section 1.—Stripping and Assembling
Swords and Scabbards

The stripping and assembling, where possible and necessary, is a simple matter. In cases where it is necessary to remove a nut from the pommel of a sword having the tang of the blade riveted over the nut, care must be taken not to reduce the length of the tang more than is necessary having reassembly in mind.

In the case of scabbards with detachable mouthpiece and wood lining, the latter can be removed by holding the scabbard upside down and tapping the loop lightly with a wood mallet.

Section 2.—Examination
Swords

(i) Examine generally for condition, security of the hilt, and, in the case of No. 1 Cavalry Swords, security of the buff piece. See also that buff pieces, where provided for other swords, are present.

If the blade is bent or badly cut on the edge the sword must be exchanged (factory repair). In this connection it must be borne in mind that when a blade has been bent and re-straightened it must be subjected to special heat treatment to overcome the weakness at the point where the bend or set occurred.

If the blade and/or the hilt is rusty, the rust, when not too deeply seated, should be removed. When badly rusted the sword must be exchanged, as excessive removal of material would reduce strength.

(ii) When the box test for blades, supplied for use in the R.A.O.C. quadrennial examinations, is employed, the springing must only be carried out in one direction (x mark on convex side) and once for each sword.

Scabbards

(i) Examine generally for condition, and try the sword in each. Where a detachable mouthpiece is provided remove it and also the lining in order to examine the latter and the internal surface of the scabbard for condition.

(ii) When steel scabbards are too badly dented to be remedied locally, they must be exchanged.

(iii) Rusty scabbards should be dealt with as in the case of swords.

(iv) Where dampness in the scabbard is suspected as a probable cause of rust on the sword blade, the lining, or the scabbard where the lining is non-removable, should be slowly dried and lightly greased with mineral jelly applied to the sword blade.

Detachable wood linings are treated with paraffin wax before issue and should not retain moisture when in normal condition.

Section 3.—Repairs, Modifications and Adjustments

Note.—For details which can be supplied for fitting, *see* Vocabulary of Army Ordnance Stores, Section B.2. For the annual allowance, *see* Equipment Regulations, Part I.

SWORDS.

BEFORE SHARPENING (BLUNT)

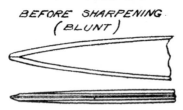

SHARPENED

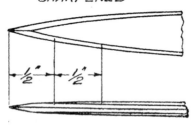

Fig. 1

Swords

Sharpening of No. 1 *Cavalry Sword Blades.*—Upon receipt by the unit of the order to mobilize, the point of the blades will be sharpened as follows :—

Hold the sword, and rest the point in a shallow nick cut in the edge of a hard wood block or bench (or fix in a vice) so that the angle of the edge is horizontal ; then with the 8-inch second cut saw file sharpen in accordance with Fig. 1, commencing at ½ inch from the point and subsequently blending up to 1 inch from the point. Finish off with emery cloth and lightly oil.

To remove dents from guards.—Proceed as for dents in scabbards, except that it will be necessary to extemporize means, such as a hard wood block, for supporting the portion of the hilt affected. When badly damaged, the guard must be exchanged.

To remove dents from steel scabbards.—Insert the mandril, where provided, into the scabbard, with a little wood packing on the side opposite the dent; apply the hammer around the dent to bring the scabbard to its proper shape, then file smooth and polish with emery cloth.

To fit a new tip to steel shoes and new loops.—When the shoe is much worn, file the end flat, bind the new tip on with wire and braze to the shoe. After brazing, file the shoe to proper shape, and finish with emery cloth.

New loops should be similarly bound on, brazed and finished.

To re-secure the mouthpiece of cavalry sword scabbards in which screw holes are badly worn.—Re-tap the screw hole with the No. 5 tap (*see* Appendix VI), and fit a No. 1 " A " or " B " rifle ejector screw after grinding off the point and polishing the head. Tinned copper rivets may also be used for this purpose.

PART III

MACHINE GUNS

CHAPTER I

GUNS, MACHINE, HOTCHKISS, ·303-IN., MKS. I AND I*

Drawing S.A.I.D. 2064.

No. 1.   With butt-stock and leaf backsight.

No. 2.   With Mk. I* pistol grip and tubular backsight ; for Royal Tank Corps.

Note.—(*a*) The Mk. I guns are suitable for strip feed only.

(*b*) The Mk. I* guns are suitable for either strip or belt feed.

Section 1.—General Information

Weight of No. 1 gun, 27 lb.
Weight of No. 2 gun, 26 lb.

1. Mk. I* guns can be identified by the Mark I* on the left side of the receiver and by the marking " strip or belt " on the top of the receiver at the front end.   Mk. I guns are not so marked.

2. Mk. I* D.P. guns have been converted from the Mk. I pattern by deepening the strip grooves in the receiver to take the belt ; such conversion is not practicable for service guns, owing to the weakening of the walls of the grooves.

3. There are two patterns of feed-piece spring—Nos. 1 and 2.   The No. 2, marked with the figure 2, has a deeper pawl tooth to suit the deeper grooves for belt and strip in the receiver of Mk. I* guns, and is suitable for both marks of gun. The No. 1—unmarked—is suitable for Mk. I guns only.

4. The Mk. I* butt-stock for No. 1 guns is strengthened by two enclosed steel plates and has right and left side-grips. The plates and grips are bolted together on the butt by screwed pins and nuts.

5. The barrel and spare will bear the same number as the

gun and will only be used with that gun. When replacement is necessary the procedure described under Section 5 will be followed.

The barrels, encircled with a band of white paint, held in mobilization store will be allocated and numbered to guns only in the event of mobilization and in accordance with the mobilization scheme of the unit. The two spare foresights which form part of the spares issued with each gun should be the same height as the gun and spare barrel foresights respectively.

A foresight protector is provided for every barrel, the early pattern known as the foresight cover, is of pressed sheet metal and of the slide-on type ; the later pattern is the Mark I foresight protector which is clamped to the stool.

6. The Mk. I* pistol grip in Mk. I* No. 2 guns is bored to take the shoulder-piece and the T-headed fixing pin, with leather thong, for securing the shoulder-piece. The fixing pin is inserted from the left.

Mk. I pistol grips are not bored to take the shoulder-piece ; otherwise they are identical with the Mk. I* pattern.

7. A cartridge case deflector and a cradle for the belt, which is attached to the deflector, are used with Mk. I* No. 2 guns. The deflector is clamped to the gun by two bolts each with a nut and spring washer.

8. The tubular backsights, provided specially for the Tank Corps, are of various patterns. The Nos. 1 and 2, Mk. I sights are of steel. The No. 1 has the tube soldered to two studs riveted to the base plate, the tube being additionally secured by a screw assembled from the underside of the base plate and engaging a boss on the tube in which it is soldered.

The No. 2 Mk. I has the tube dovetailed to a rib formed on the base plate, the tube being secured by a dowel pin.

The Mk. II sight is of gunmetal, the tube being integral with the base. This pattern, which supersedes the Mk. I pattern for future manufacture, is the one mainly in use.

9. There are two patterns of A.A. sights—Mks. I and II. The foresights of both are of the usual elliptical formation, the Mk. II being the larger. The Mk. I is hinged to a block which is clamped to the foresight stool of the gun. The Mk. II is fixed to a stem which engages in the T slot in the foresight protector, where it is secured by a plunger on the stem.

The backsight of the Mk. I is of aperture type, the aperture stem being hinged to a small block attached to the backsight leaf of the gun. The backsight of the Mk. II is of rigid pointer type and is attached to the leaf of the gun backsight.

10. Several patterns of tripod mountings have been issued—Mks. I, I*, II, II* and II**. The Mks. II, II* and II** differ from the I and I* in that the leg bracket and the joint portion of the legs are strengthened, the joint being wider.

The Mks. I* and II* differ from the Mks. I and II in that the legs are set outward to improve support for the gun.

The Mk. II** is a modification of the Mk. II* to enable the mounting to be employed in conjunction with the A.A. mounting, so avoiding the provision of the gun holder. It differs from the Mk. II in that the ground spike is reduced in diameter and secured by a plain flush rivet, a strengthening tube is fitted into the adjustable pillar and both tube and pillar are slotted vertically to receive a grub screw inserted in the leg bracket to retain the pillar in the bracket.

The Mks. II* and II** only are now in use, the earlier marks being obsolescent.

Prior to the introduction of the tripod mounting a barrel rest or bipod was provided ; this was attached to the stud on the underside of the foresight block. It is now obsolete.

11. The gun holder provided for use in conjunction with the A.A. tripod mounting prior to the adaptation of the Mk. II** ordinary gun tripod mounting comprises the upper portion of the tripod mounting down to and including the adjustable pillar, the spike of which is removed ; this portion of the mounting is common to all marks of tripod mountings. The holder is now obsolescent.

12. There are two patterns of A.A. tripod mountings— Mks. I and I*. In the Mk. I the tubular post is in one piece, whereas in the Mk. I* the post is in two parts, the upper or shorter of which is detachable for convenience of pack transport.

Either pattern will take the gun holder or the Mk. II** ordinary gun tripod, but the retaining clip, which secures the gun holder in the upper end of the post, is not required when the Mk. II** tripod is mounted thereon.

13. The box for the 50-round metallic belts is of tin-plate with a detachable lid and internal compartments for 6 belts. The box for the 30-round strips is of wood, strengthened by steel strips ; it has a hinged lid, with a leather handle, and five internal compartments each to contain two strips. The Mk. I pattern has a spring catch, and the Mk. II a leather strap fastening.

A leather case is also provided for 30-round strips carried on packsaddlery.

A box converted from the Mk. II, No. 1 pattern for the 30-round strips, and known as Mk. II, No. 2, is provided for the 14-round strips; it is arranged internally to take 20 strips, 10 in the bottom compartments and 10 in an upper detachable tray. This box is identical externally with the Mk. II, No. 1.

A later pattern of box for 14-round strips, identical externally with the box for the 50-round metallic belt but with five internal compartments arranged to take six strips in each compartment, has been made. It is known as the Mk. III.

The 14-round strips and their box are now obsolescent.

Section 2.—Stripping and Assembling
To Strip the Gun

1. See that the gun is unloaded. If the clamp of the cartridge case deflector is attached to the No. 2 gun, remove it. If the breech is not closed, raise the feed-piece stem by pressing up its lower end till a click is heard, indicating that the piston has been disengaged from the lower arm of the feed-piece and has gone forward till it is held by the block of the sear. Press the trigger, having first set the disc of the cocking handle to " A " or " R."

2. Turn the lever of the cocking handle upwards till it will go no farther. It is then slightly to the left of the vertical, and the tenons will correspond with the tenon recesses in the rear opening of the guard.

Draw back the cocking handle till the tenons are clear; turn to the right so that it is at an angle of 45 degrees with the vertical. This brings the open grooves on the stem opposite the nibs of the collar in the guard and the lugs on the stem in line with the recesses in the collar in the piston. The cocking handle can then be withdrawn, care being taken that the disc is kept to the right of the butt in the case of No. 1 guns.

3. Unscrew and remove the guard locking screw, and, pressing the butt or pistol grip forward and then downwards, disengage the projections on the sides of the guard from the recesses in the receiver, and the trunnions from their hooks. Remove the butt (or pistol grip) and guard.

4. Lift the T-headed arm of the trigger till it is clear of the sear arm, then revolve the milled head till the sear axis can be lifted out. Remove the trigger with sear and spring. Separate the sear and trigger by disconnecting the spiral spring.

5. Take out the recoil spring.

6. Insert the cocking handle in the piston, with its handle at an angle of 45 degrees to the right of the vertical, so that the lugs enter the recesses in the collar in the piston. Turn the lever vertical and draw the piston with the breech block

out of the receiver. *No force must be used in removing these parts*. Lift the breech block off the piston. Turn the upper boss of the firing pin out of the recess, and draw the firing pin backwards out of the breech block, raising its rear end while so doing.

Insert the hook of the hand extractor or a small drift or screwdriver between the two rear coils of the extractor spring and compress the spring. When the base of the spring is clear of its recess the extractor and spring can be drawn outwards and removed from the breech block.

7. Push the feed-piece spring slightly forward to disengage it from the under-cut stud on the stem ; then, lifting the finger-piece, draw it backwards till the tongue is clear of the under-cut recess on the front guide. Care must be taken to avoid lifting the spring more than is necessary, as excessive strain may bend or break it.

8. Open the feed-piece cover and raise the backsight to a vertical position. Lift the stem of the feed-piece and revolve it to the rear till the flat is opposite the opening in the upper bearing, then remove the stem.

9. With the ejector key, unscrew the ejector cap and remove the ejector and its spring.

10. Turn the barrel locking nut to the right, by means of the wrench, as far as the stop will permit, until the left edge of the serrated spring coincides with the inscribed mark on the receiver. Draw the barrel out to the front. Unscrew the gas regulator and remove it. Turn the locking nut slightly to the left to disengage its stud from the handguard and remove the latter. Unscrew the locking nut and remove it, and take out the fermeture nut from the receiver.

11. Unscrew the cartridge stop holder and remove the stop and spring.

12. *To remove the backsight.*—Unscrew the fixing screw in the front end of the backsight bed and remove the spring washers ; press the sight backwards and lift off.

13. *To remove the feed spring without stripping the gun.*— Cock the gun and proceed as in paragraph 7.

14. *To remove the extractor without stripping the gun.*— Remove the feed strip from the gun. If the cartridge case deflector is attached to the No. 2 gun, turn the handle of the latch into the vertical position and allow the deflector to fall clear of the ejection opening. Take an empty case and place it in the front end of the ejection opening. Pressing the trigger

and controlling the moving parts by means of the cocking handle, allow them to go forward slowly till they are stopped by the case. The extractor and spring will then be accessible through the ejection opening and can be removed in the ordinary way.

To Assemble the Gun

Replace the parts in the reverse order to that detailed for stripping. Before replacing the piston and breech block the fermeture nut should be rotated by hand to the unlocked position, where its slot corresponds with the ejection opening in the body, and the upper boss of the firing pin must be placed in the recess in the breech block in order to allow it to lead into the receiver. After inserting the piston and pushing it partly forward it will be checked by the shoulder on its right coming against the lower arm of the feed-piece. The stem of the latter must be pushed upwards to allow the piston to pass and go fully forward. *No force must be used in replacing the piston.* When replacing the guard an inch or so of the stem of the cocking handle should be inserted through the hole in the rear face of the guard in such a manner as to secure the rear end of the recoil spring. The cocking handle should lie diagonally downwards on the right of the butt-stock (or pistol grip) and be grasped, together with the butt-stock (or pistol grip), with the right hand.

When replacing the two spring washers under the head of the backsight fixing screw see that their concave faces are in opposition.

Section 3.—Cleaning

1. The guns should be cleaned as soon as possible after firing, special attention being given to the interior of the barrel, gas cylinder and nozzle, gas regulator, cup of piston, face of breech block, point end of firing pin and interior of handguard. This work will normally be carried out by the troops, but the armourer will ensure that it is carried out in guns when passed to him for overhaul, etc. The spare parts which may also have been used should receive similar attention. Boiling water should be used for the preliminary cleaning of parts in contact with the powder gases whenever possible. Daily cleaning may be necessary in a moist atmosphere. The use of emery or other abrasive substance is strictly forbidden. After cleaning, all parts will be lightly coated with G.S. lubricating oil.

For loosening and removing rust " oil, mineral, burning " (paraffin) or a mixture of this oil and G.S. oil may be employed, in which case the parts must subsequently be well cleaned and dried before being finally oiled with G.S. oil. G.S. oil only is to be used for lubricating purposes.

2. *To clean the barrel.*—For ordinary cleaning the No. 1 rifle rod or single pull-through and flannelette can be employed, care being taken to ensure that the breech block is in its rearmost position and that the end of the rod does not strike the face of the breech block.

When rust or metallic fouling is present the barrel will be removed from the gun, and the double pull-through employed as follows :—

Thoroughly oil the gauze wire, drop the weight through from the breech end and see that the gauze fits the bore tightly. Hold the barrel, suitably protected, in a vice, and with the necessary assistance pull the cord to and fro in the usual manner.

Care must be taken to keep the cord clear of the muzzle and breech ends as otherwise friction will cause a groove to be formed which, at the breech end, will tend to produce a burst cartridge, and, at the muzzle end, seriously affect accuracy.

When the gauze becomes free in the barrel it can be packed as described for rifle barrels in Part II, Chapter I, Section 2 ; it should be replaced by a new piece when no longer effective.

Obstructions due to a jammed pull-through or flannelette will be removed as described in Part II, Chapter I, Section 2.

The chamber must be thoroughly cleaned, care being taken to remove any deposit due to oil or dirt from the walls. It can normally be cleaned with the No. 1 rifle rod or other suitable service rod with oiled flannelette inserted in the eye of the rod, but if badly glazed with deposit it will be necessary to employ a piece of gauze wire let into a slit in a wood stick such as is used for the chamber of the rifle barrel.

When using a steel rod care must be taken to ensure that it is well packed with flannelette and that it is free from sharp edges or burrs.

3. *To clean the gas cylinder and regulator.*—After removing the gas regulator, which, if very tight, should be saturated with paraffin for a time before attempts are made to remove it, clean the stem and head with a piece of oily flannelette and wipe out the gas cylinder.

If hard fouling is present in the gas cylinder, remove it carefully by means of the gas cylinder cleaner, and then wipe out again with oily flannelette, seeing that all chippings are removed. The gas nozzle should be cleaned in a similar manner.

Re-assemble the gas regulator to see that all is clear, and again remove it and wipe both regulator and cylinder dry ;

then, with a piece of clean flannelette, very lightly oil both with G.S. oil, and re-assemble the regulator in the position occupied before first removal.

4. *To clean the cup of the piston.*—Remove fouling with a piece of oily flannelette, leaving the cup slightly oiled unless the gun is to be fired immediately.

Note.—Under no circumstances must emery cloth or emery be used for cleaning the gas regulator, gas cylinder and its nozzle, and cup of piston, as loss in size of such parts will lead to loss of gas power, thus tending to put the gun out of action.

5. *To clean the mechanism.*—The moving parts must be removed, but it may not always be necessary to strip the trigger mechanism, extractor, ejector or cartridge stop, provided they function freely and are clean. Dirt must be carefully removed from all stationary parts, particular attention being paid to recesses which are likely to harbour dirt.

A cleaning brush is provided for the interior of the hand-guard.

After the parts have been replaced the external surfaces of all metal portions should be rubbed over with a piece of flannelette lightly oiled with G.S. oil.

6. *To clean the feed strip or belt.*—Rust should be removed and the strip lightly coated with G.S. oil as a preservative. The " Brush, harness, hard," lightly oiled, is convenient for this purpose.

No more oil than is absolutely necessary must be used, as any excess will be carried into the chamber by the cartridges, where it will affect both functioning and accuracy.

7. *After gas attack.*—Guns should be cleaned and re-oiled at once. Oil cleaning will only prevent corrosion for about 12 hours. At the first available opportunity the gun must be stripped and working parts cleaned with boiling water containing a little soda. Spare parts, strips and belts should be carefully examined and cleaned.

8. *Guns and parts returned to store, etc.*—Before packing for issue or stowing away in any place where examination cannot readily be carried out, the unpainted parts should be coated with a mixture of G.S. oil and red mineral jelly in equal proportions. The mixture should be made hot, and a piece of flannelette dipped into it should be applied to the interior of the barrel by means of a pull-through. To ensure that the whole surface is covered the flannelette must not be tight in the bore.

Section 4.—Examination of the Gun, etc.

The following instructions are for general guidance ; circumstances may arise which may necessitate a change in the
sequence of examination as given, *e.g.* a defect due to unfair
usage or other cause which it is desirable should be looked for in
all guns when discovered in the guns first examined, or when a
brief examination only is called for.

(i) *General.*—Examine the gun generally for damage and
see that gun and barrel numbers—including spare
barrel—agree. If they do not agree and the
barrel numbers do not marry with other guns in
possession of the unit, the gun and its barrels
should be reported for accuracy test.

(ii) *Test cartridge head space.*—Remove the barrel and
handguard, breech mechanism, including feed-
piece and spring, but not the fermeture nut, from
the receiver, and the extractor and spring from the
breech block ; re-assemble the barrel, breech
block, piston and firing pin to the receiver, insert
the gauge in the chamber of the barrel ; the
forward end of the piston should then be con-
trolled with one hand whilst the thumb of the
other hand is applied to the rear end of the breech
block to push it forward, thereby ensuring a light
control on the gauge. The breech block should close
over the ·064-inch but not over the ·074-inch gauge ;
in the latter case the fermeture nut should not
turn into its completely locked position ; if it does
either the breech block or the fermeture nut is at
fault and the gun should be exchanged.

(iii) *Pin, firing.*—Examine for fracture, damage or wear.
If worn or damaged at the point, and well within
protrusion limits, adjust.

The protrusion should be tested with the gauge
supplied in accordance with the instructions in
Section 7.

(iv) *Piston.*—See that it bears the gun number, examine
for damage, fracture and wear, especially at the
sear bent, receiver stop, firing pin shoulder and
camways.

The cupped end should be clean ; if corrosion
is present from firing, the end should be dipped
when possible in boiling water and then well
cleaned.

(v) *Block, breech.*—See that it bears the gun number,
examine for damage, fracture and wear, especially

the screw thread, firing pin shoulder and face, including the firing pin hole. Re-assemble the extractor and spring and try a dummy cartridge in the face, where it should be held securely by the extractor.

(vi) *Nut, fermeture.*—See that it bears the gun number, and examine for damage, fracture and wear. Burrs on the leading edge of the screw thread, where present, should be carefully removed without injury to the thread. When fractured at the feed strip clearance it should be dealt with as described in Section 5.

(vii) *Receiver.*—Examine for damage internally and for wear, etc., of the piston stop, barrel seating, feed tongue, trigger guard seatings, feed-piece cover and spring, cartridge stop and spring, ejector cap, ejector and spring, and condition and functioning of the backsight of No. 1 gun or the condition of tubular sight of No. 2 gun.

See that the feed strip and/or belt passes freely through the guides, and that burrs or sharp edges are removed from the feed tongue.

(viii) *Feed-piece.*—Examine for fracture, damage and wear of arms and top stud.

(ix) *Spring, feed-piece.*—See that the No. 2 spring is assembled to Mk. I* guns ; that the platform of the stop pawl on the left, which rests on the belt or strip, is well rounded on the right corner to provide a lead.

(x) *Nut, locking, barrel.*—Examine for damage, condition of the thread, lugs and spring.

(xi) *Guard, trigger, and butt-stock or pistol grip.*—Examine the guard for damage, etc., especially at the locking screw hole ; condition of the bent of the sear, the hook of the trigger and the spring. When the locking screw hole is damaged it should be dealt with as described in Section 5.

Examine butt-stock (or pistol grip) for damage. When the butt-stock is of Mk. I pattern and repairable, report for exchange and conversion to Mk. I* pattern. See that the shoulder-piece for Mk. I*, No. 2 guns assembles correctly to the pistol grip.

(xii) *Spring, recoil.*—When in doubt as to strength, compare with a satisfactory spring, either from another gun or from spare, for overall length.

A reduction in length up to one inch is not usually detrimental.

(xiii) *Handle, cocking.*—Examine for straightness, and the tenons and channels for damage. Remove burrs where present.

(xiv) *Handguard.*—Examine for damage or distortion and for internal rust.

(xv) *Barrel (including spare).*—Examine externally for damage, especially at the interrupted flanges, at the breech face, muzzle end, foresight and trunnions. See that the foresight is tight in the dovetail, and that the Mk. I fixed foresight protector is well secured.

If the foresight is damaged, but repairable, adjust and reblack.

Examine internally for condition and wear. When badly worn in the lead and bore, report for local accuracy test in accordance with Equipment Regulations, Part I. See that the chamber is clean and undamaged and that sound dummy cartridges enter freely. See that gas nozzle, gas cylinder and gas regulator are clean, that the regulator can be rotated freely in the cylinder throughout its complete travel, and that it is efficiently retained by the nib.

(xvi) *Re-assembly details.*—Assemble the fermeture nut, barrel locking nut, barrel and piston, in order to test alignment of the cupped end of the piston with the nozzle of the gas cylinder ; if not in alignment test with the spare barrel assembled ; if still at fault try a new barrel from other gun spares, when available, and if the defect is still present, report the gun for exchange (factory repair).

Re-assemble the gun, seeing that parts assemble correctly, and test by hand for correct functioning of the mechanism, special attention to be given to the following details :—

(a) Security of the sear in the bent of the piston when set at " safe," with the feed-piece raised clear of the stop shoulder of the piston, and the locking screw removed to avoid damage to the rear wall of the screw hole in guard, ground the butt sharply. When unsafe, *i.e.* when the piston jars from the sear and is driven forward, adjust the bent at fault after comparing with similar parts in good condition from another gun.

(*b*) Insert a few dummy cartridges in a belt or strip and test the feed, taking special care to see that the stop pawl of the feed spring engages fully in the openings in the belt or strip. If the stop pawl does not function correctly try the spare springs ; defective springs should be exchanged (factory repair).

Note.—When any doubt exists as to the serviceability of a gun from a functioning standpoint, the armourer should take the necessary steps to have the gun fired.

(xvii) *Spare parts and tools.*—Examine the spare parts when possible during the examination of the gun parts, and see that they function correctly in the gun. See that the tools are in good working order and that they perform their work satisfactorily.

(xviii) *D.P. Guns.*—See that the nose of the firing pin is removed and that the guns are complete and in working order. Every care must be taken to prevent D.P. parts from becoming mixed with service gun parts. Finish is of no importance, but the guns should be kept as free as possible from rust.

(xix) *Shoulder-piece.*—Examine the fork end for damage or distortion, and assemble to the pistol grip of the gun to see that when attached it forms a rigid connection.

(xx) *Strips*, 30, 14 *and* 9 *rounds.*—Examine for straightness, fracture, especially of the clips, and test with dummy cartridges to ensure that the cartridges are held securely and are correctly located by the base stops. When in doubt of their efficiency, test for correctness of feed in the gun. Sound strips should be resized as necessary with the resizing tool supplied with the gun. A convenient method of testing for fracture of the clips is to place the strip on a bench and pass a light metal bar, under reasonable pressure, along the edges of the clips. It is well to have available a strip which is known to function correctly for comparison with those under examination.

(xxi) *Belts, metallic*, 50 *rounds*—Will be examined on similar lines to the strips ; in addition they will be examined at the link joints for alignment and security of the joint pins. Each belt should pass through the receiver of the gun freely, a receiver well up to size in the grooves being selected for the purpose.

(xxii) *Mountings, tripod.*—Examine generally for damage, etc., see that the gun assembles correctly in the yoke and the catches engage the trunnions of the barrel, that the adjustable parts can be moved within their limits and be securely clamped, the legs are each pressed outward by the spring, and that the nut securely retains the spring.

See also that the shackle which secures the legs of the tripod when in the closed position on the gun is in good order.

(xxiii) *Mountings, tripod, A.A.*—See that the post moves freely in the leg brackets and that the legs when opened out do not overrun their normal movement ; if they do, then the upper end should be repaired in accordance with the instructions given in Section 5.

(xxiv) *Deflector, cartridge case, Mk. II, and ammunition belt cradle.*—Examine generally for damage and distortion. Assemble the deflector to the gun, observe that it can be securely fixed by the clamp, that the chute is sufficiently close up to and in line with the ejection opening in the gun receiver, and the bag is secure and its fastenings in good order. Assemble the cradle to the post of the deflector clamp, seeing that it is properly secured by the plunger ; then hinge the pan down and up to test the efficiency of the catch. When the Mk. I catch is unserviceable the cradle should be exchanged.

Section 5.—Repairs, Modifications and Adjustments

Note.—For parts which, when unserviceable, necessitate the sending of the gun to store for exchange, *see* Equipment Regulations, Part I.

The annual allowance of parts for the repair of the guns is laid down in Equipment Regulations, Part I.

When parts are of necessity withdrawn from the gun spares, indents must be put forward immediately for their replacement.

Parts other than those referred to which may be required for replacement purposes will be indented for as necessary.

(i) *Barrels.*—When a gun barrel is replaced by another, other than by the spare belonging to the gun, the following procedure will be carried out.

The fresh barrel will be assembled to the gun and the mechanism tested for correct functioning.

If the fermeture nut is not free to turn, but is free with the other barrel assembled, the face of the barrel should be carefully eased off, but only just sufficient to enable the nut to turn without play. When the nut is not free with either barrel, the face of the nut should be eased. When correct the gun is to be tested on the range, the armourer to be present if possible. When satisfactory accuracy has been obtained and a foresight of different height letter to that marked on the muzzle side of the foresight stool is fitted, the letter on the stool will be erased or cancelled and a letter corresponding with that on the foresight marked thereon. The lateral position of the foresight will be registered by a line to be marked along the upper surface of the foresight base, or platform, which must coincide with the line on the stool.

The barrel will next be numbered to agree with the gun number on the receiver, the number to be stamped on the surface between and above the trunnions, the original number above the gas cylinder being cancelled by chiselled lines.

The standard heights of foresights are " H " = high, " M " = mean, " L " = low, and " LL " = double low.

When a new height of foresight is so fitted, steps should be taken to ensure that the spare foresight for the barrel coincides.

A range of foresights is supplied to authorised stations upon demand, on the following scale, for the guns in their areas—" H," 15% ; " M," 30% ; " L," 50% ; " LL," 60%.

Note.—When supply facilities are not available for the replacement of barrels, the guns will be sent to store for exchange. This will also apply when no range is available for functioning and accuracy tests.

When fitting a Mk. I foresight protector to the barrel it may be necessary to adjust the radius at the base of the foresight stool at " A " to clear the radius " B " in the protector—*see* Fig. 1.

The protector should be as upright as possible in view of the assembly of the Mk. II A.A. foresight in the vertical " T " slot.

(ii) *Butt-stocks.*—Fitting of oil bottle. When assembling the oil bottle it may be found in some instances that the depth of the butt is too great for the brass tube. Where such is the case the butt will

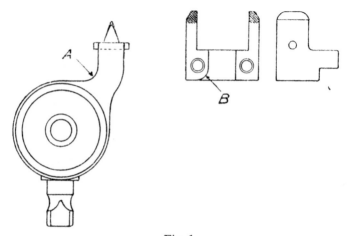

Fig. 1.

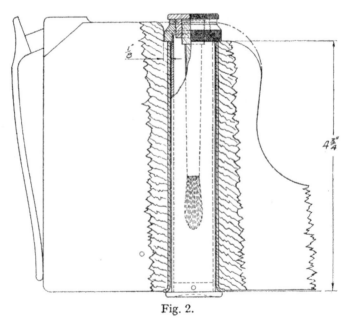

Fig. 2.

be reduced in accordance with Fig. 2. Where butts are found to be insufficiently deep the discrepancy can be catered for by making and inserting leather washers which will engage the oil bottle between the bottom flange and the underside of the butt.

Fitting of leather pocket and strap for the dismounting wrench. Where butt-stocks are not

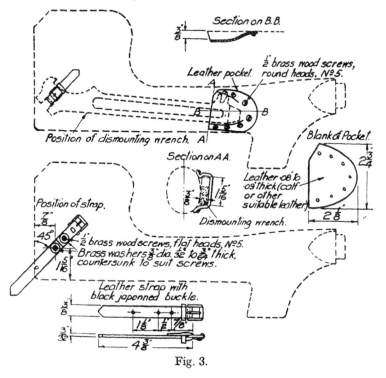

Fig. 3.

already fitted with the pocket and strap they will be fitted with these details in accordance with Fig. 3.

(iii) *Components marked " M " (para. A. 900 L. of C.).—* Fig. 4 illustrates the modifications to the receiver, feed-piece and feed spring referred to in the above-mentioned L. of C. These alterations will normally be carried out to guns when undergoing factory repair, but in special emergency when stoppages in feed occur in guns not fitted with the modified parts, the modifications, other than the setting of the feed spring, can be carried out locally,

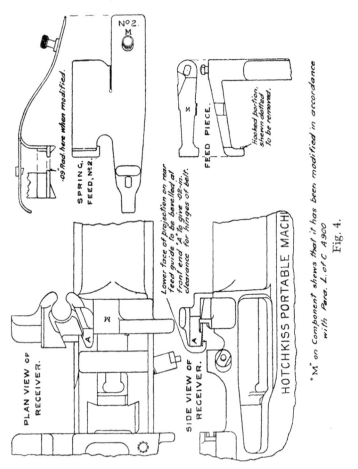

Fig. 4.

provided that the gun is otherwise in good condition and it is certain that the stoppages are not due to other causes, *e.g.* insufficient gas power, defective belts or strips, etc. Feed springs which require setting should always be exchanged—factory repair.

(iv) *Guards, trigger.*—Where the locking screw hole is damaged, repair will be effected, provided the rear wall of the hole is not broken through, by carefully tapping the metal forward from the rear face of the guard to make the hole again cylindrical. It is advisable when doing this repair to insert a piece of wire, slightly smaller than the screw, into the hole. When the hole is broken through, the gun will be exchanged—factory repair. The locking screw should be screwed in as far as possible when the gun is re-assembled after repair.

(v) *Handguards.*—Where badly indented they should, where practicable, be repaired by inserting a suitable mandril or block which will make contact with the damaged part, the block being held in a vice and the dent removed by hammering around the dent. Care must be taken to avoid distortion, as such may affect alignment and re-assembly. Fractures should be repaired by brazing, where possible.

(vi) *Nuts, fermeture.*—When fractured or broken at the point where the construction is weakened by the clearance for the passage of the belt or feed strip, they will be repaired locally in accordance with Fig. 5. The maximum dimension shown on the drawing is to be worked to, in the case of all nuts, but where this is not possible in nuts broken or fractured at a point below this dimension, adjustment may be made down to the minimum dimension shown. If beyond this, the nuts will be unserviceable and the guns will be exchanged.

In order to lessen such damage to fermeture nuts, burrs set up during engagement of the nut with the breech block should be carefully removed by the armourer with a smooth file. The gun barrels should also be kept free from burrs on the breech face and on the interrupted flanges, so as to prevent excessive friction on the nut, which should rotate freely but without longitudinal play when the barrel is assembled.

(vii) *Trigger pull-off.*—Where the pull-off is very harsh it will usually be found due to some slight roughness or burrs on the sear nose or the bent of the piston ; such should be carefully smoothed off in the direction of movement. On no account must attempts

92

Portion of nut shewn dotted to be removed.

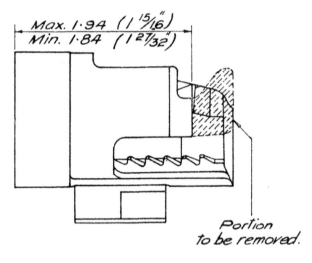

Max. 1·94 (1 $\frac{15}{16}$")
Min. 1·84 (1 $\frac{27}{32}$")

Portion
to be removed.

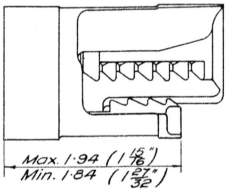

Max. 1·94 (1 $\frac{15}{16}$")
Min. 1·84 (1 $\frac{27}{32}$")

Plan with portion removed.

Fig. 5.

be made to lighten the pull-off by altering the shape
of either part, as such action will make the gun
unsafe.

It should be noted that in this gun the " safe "

position is entirely dependent upon the secure retention of the piston by the sear.

(viii) *Receivers*.—Where indented on the underside owing to excessive downward swing of the trigger guard during its removal from the receiver, thus causing the front end of the guard to lever the metal upward and inward, the indentation, where sufficient to set up friction on the piston, or affect alignment of the piston with the nozzle on the barrel, should be removed on the lines described for the handguard, care being taken that the rivets which secure the bottom plate are not disturbed.

(ix) *Screws, orifice*.—Where not already removed, the head of the chamber orifice screw is to be removed in order to prevent wear and loss of the screw by unnecessary stripping down, the only object of the screw being to plug a hole drilled for manufacturing purposes. In the case of guns in use, the head will be removed locally by sawing or filing off after first ascertaining that the screw is secure and is screwed firmly home in the gas chamber. The end should be finished off flush with the surface of the gas chamber and then painted over.

(x) *Stoppages during firing*.—When stoppages in guns are reported by the unit as of regular occurrence, the armourer should arrange to be present at a demonstration on the range and satisfy himself as to the cause before attempting to remedy the fault (if within his capacity) by repair or adjustment of the gun.

(xi) *Strips, feed*.—When not badly bent in their length, they should be straightened by hand on a bench, care being taken not to overstrain and weaken them. Where it is not found possible to do this, they should be exchanged. The centre clips should be resized where necessary with the resizing tool ; the front and rear clips should be adjusted by pliers, care being taken to compare them with a good strip, which should be held as a guide for form and grip on dummy cartridges. Strips so adjusted should have dummy cartridges inserted and be tested in a serviceable gun.

(xii) *Belts, metallic,* 50 *rounds*.—Resizing of the centre clips with the tool for resizing belts or strips, and of the other clips as described for feed strips, will be carried out only on repair. Where other defects occur, such as distortion at the joints, fracture or breakage of the clip, the belts will be exchanged.

No attempt should be made to replace defective links of one belt with links from another belt, as this involves the setting of the joint pin retaining lip in order to remove the pin, and the links are not interchangeable. When owing to an extreme emergency, repair of this nature is vital owing to temporary shortage, belts of the same make as indicated by the manufacturer's mark on the three link elements should be employed in the exchange of links from one belt to another.

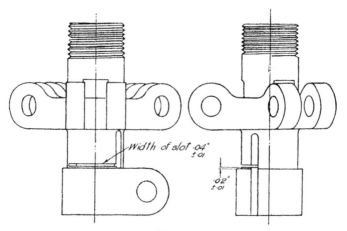

Fig. 6.

(xiii) *Mountings, tripod.*—Legs, when bent, can usually be straightened cold, but when a severe short bend is present they should be heated in order to avoid fracture.

The correct splay when measured from spike to spike is about $9\frac{1}{4}$ inches.

When fitting Mk. II catches to the yoke, steps must be taken to ensure that they do not fit tightly on the gun barrel trunnions, that the latter seat in the yoke, and can be assembled into the yoke without opening the catches by hand. To ensure correct assembly the slope at the upper end of the catches must be central and smooth.

Where the axis pin holes in the yoke have become

enlarged they can be swaged in with a suitable ring punch.

Should it be found impossible to clamp the adjustable pillar tightly with reasonable pressure on the thumb screw of the leg bracket, a slot should be sawn at right angles to the vertical slot in accordance with Fig. 6.

(xiv) *Mountings, tripod, A.A.*—The tubular post when not badly bent, can be straightened in the manner employed for the legs of the M.G. Mk. IV tripod mounting, Chapter IV, Section 4.

Where the legs can be opened to an extent such as will cause the stays to over-run their normal movement, the upper stop at the leg joints should either be swaged or have a piece brazed on to remedy the defect.

When badly bent, the post should be exchanged.

(xv) *Sights, A.A.*—Distortion of the elliptical portion of the foresight, when not severe, can be remedied by setting; where available, an undistorted sight can be utilized as a template.

Section 6.—Re-browning and Re-painting

Re-browning

Re-browning, as required, will be carried out under the same conditions as for Small Arms—*see* Chapter III, Part I.

The following parts of the gun, etc., will be re-browned when necessary :—

Barrel ... } Handguard }	Where not previously sandblasted and painted, or when they have had the browned finish and Commanding Officers prefer to retain that finish.
Guard, trigger	External surfaces.
Handle, cocking ...	Exposed surfaces.
Nut, locking, barrel ...	External surfaces.
Receiver with feed-piece cover	External surfaces. Parts other than the feed-piece cover, but including the feed-piece cover spring, to be removed and replaced after browning.

Regulator, gas ... ... Exposed surfaces.
Bed, backsight.
Catches, slide, backsight.
Slide, backsight.
Sight, tubular, Mk. I (steel).
Sight, fore.
Sights, A.A.

Re-painting

Note.—For materials allowed and surfaces to be painted, etc., *see* Appendix II.

Barrels and handguards which have been sandblasted and painted should be re-painted where necessary. Those which have the browned finish may also be painted, instead of re-browned, at the discretion of Commanding Officers.

The non-working or non-frictional surfaces only of the barrel should be painted ; the handguard should be painted all over externally.

Care must be taken when painting the barrel to see that the registered number, stamped in advance of the annular rings, and the " S.C." marking, where present, on the upper surface between the trunnions, is not obliterated.

Recoil springs of " D.P." guns in possession of units will be painted with a light coat of the M.G. paint, applied with a brush, in order to distinguish them from those used in service guns. The spring must not be dipped in the paint, as that method does not produce a satisfactory result.

Tripod mountings, A.A. tripod mountings and gun holders and ammunition feed strip boxes will also be repainted where necessary in accordance with the instructions given in Appendix II.

Note.—When painting is being carried out the armourer must see that the paint is applied in a manner such as will not affect the functioning of the article. As a general rule frictional surfaces should never be painted.

Section 7.—Description and Use of Tools and Gauges

Machine for filling strips and belts.—The machine consists of four main parts, viz., the bed with its mechanism, hopper, clamp, and handle. The latter three parts are detached when the machine is packed in the box provided.

The action of the machine is as follows :—

The strip slides into the bed at right-angles to the cartridge plunger and is traversed in steps by means of the traversing slide and its pawl. The action slide runs in the bed and is driven by the connecting rod. A cam slot is cut in it which actuates the traversing slide, and the cartridge plunger is attached to it. The strip is kept down by an overhanging bracket while the cartridges are being driven into the clips. The hopper stands up vertically from the bed, and the clamp, which extends vertically downwards, engages in a slot in the underside of the bed. The clamp screw is arranged to take the driving handle of the machine.

To use the machine the hopper is filled with cartridges and the strip is inserted in the bed till the pawl engages behind the first clip of the centre row. The driving handle is then rotated and the supply of cartridges in the hopper replenished till the strip is full. If it is required to draw the strip back in order to fill a space which has been missed, the trigger underneath the bed must be pressed to release the pawl of the traversing slide.

Machines of an earlier pattern were originally supplied for filling strips only. In this machine the channels in the bed plate are not of sufficient depth to take the hinges of the belt. Any machine which is not shown by the name-plate to be suitable for both strips and belts is to be used for filling strips only.

Tool for resizing strips.—The tool is provided to enable the curvature of the centre row of clips on the strip to be restored when, through use or damage, the clips do not properly retain the cartridges. It must not be used for belts.

It consists of a rectangular body of steel, slotted to allow the strip to pass through, two shallow channels being cut in the bottom to clear the strengthening ribs on the back of the strip. A projecting handle is provided at each end. The top of the gap is closed by a plate carrying a roller. The plate is attached to the body of the tool by two screws, and by means of these and of four set screws passing through the body from the underside it can be adjusted for height.

The strip is driven through the body in the reverse way to that in which it passes through the gun, *i.e.* with extension piece leading, the tool meanwhile being held by the handles. The roller makes contact with the upper part of each clip as the strip is driven through, and forces it down, thus restoring its original shape.

Tool for resizing belts and strips.—Is in the nature of a machine, and consists of a malleable cast-iron body, in which a studded feed wheel is mounted on a spindle. Above the wheel is a hardened steel roller mounted on an axis pin in an adjustable bracket fixed to the top of the body. A " T " slot is cut in the underside of the body to take a clamp, with which the tool is secured to any convenient box or bench.

The feed-wheel spindle projects outside the body and takes

the crank handle. (The clamp and crank handle are identical with those in the filling machine.)

To use the tool insert the belt or strip on the left with the clips uppermost and end link first—*i.e.* in the reverse direction to that in which it is inserted in the gun—the first central aperture engaging a stud on the feed wheel ; then turn the crank handle in a clockwise direction and wind through.

The roller bracket can be adjusted up or down on its inclined seating to give the desired result, the latter to be determined in comparison with the grip of the cartridges in a new and satisfactory belt or strip, which should be selected as a standard.

The working parts of the tool should be lubricated periodically.

It may be found necessary occasionally, and more especially in the case of the belt, to adjust the front and rear clips to remedy distortion ; this must be carried out by hand, care being taken to see that the cartridge is gripped satisfactorily after adjustment.

Gauge, Protrusion of Firing Pin.—The gauge consists of a circular cylinder having two flanges, a plunger and spring within the cylinder, and a keeper pin which retains the plunger and limits its travel.

The lower end of the cylinder and the lower end of the plunger are arranged to seat on the face of the breech block and on the point of the firing pin respectively, whilst index surfaces on the upper end of the cylinder and an index shoulder near the upper end of the plunger give visual reading of the protrusion.

The gauge is marked round the upper flange of the cylinder, thus :—

GUN, HOTCHKISS, ·303, PROTRUSION FIRING PIN, ·035 L, ·046 H.

To use the gauge proceed as follows :—

   (i) Remove the barrel locking nut, barrel and handguard from the receiver.

  (ii) See that the piston and breech block are fully home in the forward, or firing, position, and that the face of the breech block and the point of the firing pin are undamaged and clean.

 (iii) Insert the gauge into the front, or barrel, end of receiver and press the cylinder well down on the face of the breech block ; then press the plunger lightly down on the point of the firing pin, and observe the relation of its index shoulder with the index surfaces of the cylinder.

(iv) When correct the shoulder should not descend below the lower or project above the upper surface of the cylinder. When protrusion is excessive, *i.e.* the shoulder projects, the firing pin must be removed from the gun and adjusted ; when protrusion is insufficient the firing pin must be exchanged.

Note.—(*a*) It is essential that the breech mechanism should be completely assembled when the protrusion is gauged, otherwise a false result may be obtained.

(*b*) Brass chippings from cartridges are liable to lodge in the junction thread of the breech block and the fermeture nut, and between the stop shoulder on the piston and the piston stop in the receiver, and so reduce the protrusion ; it is, therefore, desirable, when a low protrusion is obtained, to strip down and examine carefully, then re-assemble and re-gauge.

CHAPTER II

GUNS, MACHINE, LEWIS ·303-INCH, MARK I

Drawing Nos. A.I.D. 1711, S.A.I.D. 2063, 2081

Section 1.—General Information

Weight of Mk. I gun about 26 lb.

1. The Mk. I gun only is in use in the Land Service. Two further patterns of guns—Mks. II and III—are for Air Service, the Mk. III being the one now in use.

The following principal differences in the three patterns are described for identification purposes :—

The Mk. I gun has an aluminium radiator, which fits over and is keyed to the barrel, and a radiator casing in two parts—front and rear—connected together by a clamp ring, in which the foresight is mounted.

A locking piece which forms part of the rear casing is connected to the body of the gun by the barrel and the locking pin.

A butt-stock is fitted.

The Mk. II gun has a single barrel casing only, which leaves the front end of the barrel exposed. It has a locking piece of similar type to that of the Mk. I gun, but forward of that piece the casing is much smaller in diameter. A sleeve interposed between the front portion of the casing and the barrel provides the necessary support at that end.

A spade-handled grip is fitted in lieu of a butt-stock.

The Mk. III gun has an uncovered barrel, which is screwed as usual to the body of the gun and secured by distance pieces, front, centre and rear, the centre piece being rotatable and having projecting lugs for mounting in aircraft.

A gas cylinder protector of pressed steel is attached to the front distance piece and is clamped at its front end to the forward enlarged part of the gas cylinder.

As in the case of the Mk. II gun a spade-handled grip is fitted in lieu of a butt-stock.

The Mk. III guns are usually speeded up (" S.U.") to give a higher rate of fire. Such " S.U." guns have an enlarged gas vent hole in the barrel (Mk. I*), a partially plugged gas regulator (Mk. I*) and a volute spring buffer in the rear end of the piston rod. The S.U. details could be assembled also to the Mks. I and II guns if required. The breech mechanism is common to all marks of guns.

When the spring buffer is employed in No. 1 piston rods in S.U. guns, a " thrust plug " is first inserted in the hole in the rear end of the piston rod—conical end first. The No. 2 piston rod, stamped with the figure 2 in rear of the striker post, is suitably bored and does not require the thrust plug.

2. The magazines in use for Mk. I guns are known as Nos. 5, 6 and 8, Mk. I, and hold 47 rounds.

The No. 5 has a plain No. 1 pan, and the Nos. 6 and 8 have grooves pressed inward at the upper surface of the pan for strengthening purposes.

The strengthened pan of the No. 6 is interchangeable for repair purposes on the No. 5, which then becomes No. 6.

All have the round type of catch, the No. 2 catch having a hole drilled to take a lace for quick disengagement.

Mk. I* magazines—not yet produced—differ from the Mk. I in that a detachable cover plate is fitted to the centre disc to permit of ready access to the catch spring.

" D.P." and Skeleton Mk. I magazines are supplied as authorized. The D.P. is distinguished by bars of white paint, about one inch wide, on the upper surface of the pan, the bars radiating at 90° intervals from the centre of the pan. Skeleton magazines are cut away as described under Section 5.

The magazine in use for Mks. II and III guns is the Mk. II, which holds 97 rounds.

A special form of handle and catch is employed to facilitate handling when in the air.

The pan is strengthened by stays internally.

3. An auxiliary magazine post is required for the gun when the Mk. II magazine is employed ; this post assembles to the magazine post of the body.

The Mk. I magazines can be employed on Mks. II and III guns if required ; so also the Mk. II magazines on Mk. I guns in conjunction with the auxiliary magazine post and a set of Mk. I* magazine feed, left stop pawl, and Mk. I** right stop pawl, but in this case the ordinary gun sights are not then visible for use ; the A.A. sights, being higher, can be used.

4. A cartridge case deflector with bag attached for the empty cases is employed with Mks. II and III guns. It is attached to the sides of the body of the gun near the front end by a clamp which forms part of the deflector.

5. There are certain variations in pattern of component parts of guns, as follows :—

Butt-stock, Mk. I* and Mk. II.—These patterns are fitted with a swivel bracket and oil bottle. The Mk. II pattern, in addition, is arranged to take the Mk. I* butt cap.

The Mks. I and I* patterns are convertible to Mk. II in Ordnance Factory.

Catch, butt, No. 2.—Has a thumb-piece which projects downwards at the rear or butt-cap end. The rear face of the thumb-piece is chequered.

Cap, butt, Mk. I*.—Differs from the Mk. I, in having an additional pair of rearwardly projecting arms which embrace the butt along each side and are connected to each other (through the butt) by two screws. Mk. I butt caps are modified to Mk. I* pattern in Ordnance Factory as required.

Extractor, Mk. II.—Is made up of two pieces, the spring portion being a separate component part from the actual extractor. The extractor is shorter, and is stepped down on its upper surface immediately over the circular stud ; the shoulder thus formed is undercut and forms an abutment for the front end of the spring. The tail end is tapered off to the rear, and the under corner at this end acts as a fulcrum on the surface of the recess in the breech bolt of the gun when the hook end is raised against the pressure of the spring. The corners at the hook end are well rounded off. The spring is similar in shape to the spring portion of the Mk. I extractor and its rear end is formed to fit into the " T " slot in the bolt in the known manner.

Pawls, stop, magazine, Mk. I* (Mk. I modified).—Differ from the Mk. I pawls as follows. The projection of the acting ends is increased by ·05 inch to ·15 inch. The acting end of the right pawl is slightly modified in form, and the acting ends of both pawls are bevelled at the top corner to facilitate assembly of the magazine. Either pattern can be employed, but, where possible, endeavour should be made to arrange that the pawls in the gun are both of the same pattern and that the spares agree.

Pawl, feed arm, Mk. I*.—The projection of the acting end is increased similarly to the stop pawls.

Screw, clamp, ring, No. 2.—Is approximately ¼ inch longer in the stem, and the head of smaller diameter than the No. 1. It is introduced in order to facilitate the removal and re-assembly of the clamp ring and front radiator casing. With this screw the clamp ring can be opened out sufficiently without detaching the screw thread from the threaded portion of the clamp ring.

Guard, trigger, Mk. I* (Mk. I pattern modified).—Has detachable side pieces, secured by means of a screw passing through a steel bush in the right-hand piece and engaging with a screwed bush in the left. It is in use with the Air Service and is approved for future manufacture for Land Service.

Two further patterns of trigger guard, Mks. II and III, have been supplied to the Air Service. These differ from the Mks. I and I* principally in that the bow which guards the trigger is much larger in order to take a thickly gloved hand. In the case of the Mk. II the bow is detachable.

The components for the Mk. III pattern are common to those of the Mk. I* pattern, but the Mk. II, no more of which will be made, has a special sear and spring, and the trigger spring and plunger are omitted, no provision being made for them. Both patterns have been converted from the Mk. I.

6. Some tangent sight leaves are graduated up to 2,000 yds. and others to 1,900 yds. ; there is a slight difference in the graduations ; those sighted up to 1,900 yds. are of later manufacture and, when available, are fitted in lieu of the earlier pattern when guns pass through for factory repair. The difference is insufficient to warrant the withdrawal of the earlier make.

7. Flash eliminators have been prepared for issue when authorized. The eliminator replaces the barrel mouthpiece, and is secured in position by a locking collar with four projections, one requires to be bent after assembly into the spanner grooves in the eliminator, whilst those at the rear engage a groove to be cut in the front of the radiator. Particulars for fitting will be found under Section 5. The flash eliminator is common to the Air Service guns, but is secured in those guns by a nut and spring washer.

Section 2.—Stripping and Assembling

To strip the gun.—The gun is stripped in the following order :—

(i) *Butt.*—With the cocking handle in the forward position, insert the point of a dummy bullet behind the No. 1 catch and press upwards to disengage the catch. With the No. 2 catch press the thumb-piece forward. Rotate the butt one-eighth of a turn in an anti-clockwise direction and withdraw the butt.

(ii) *Trigger guard and pistol grip.*—Press the trigger to withdraw the sear nose and plunger clear of the openings in the bottom of the body, and slide the guard back till it is clear of the body.

(iii) *Bolt and piston rod.*—Draw back the cocking handle to its full extent and withdraw it from the piston rod by pulling outwards. Draw out the bolt and piston rod.

(iv) Unhook the pinion casing.

(v) *Body cover.*—See that the feed arm is over to the right, draw back the body cover till it is clear of the retaining ledges on the body and lift off.

(vi) *Feed arm.*—With the point of a dummy bullet press forward the latch. Turn the feed arm till the key-way in the axis hole clears the key on the magazine post and lift off.

(vii) *Body.*—With the point of a dummy bullet press back the body locking pin, and unscrew the body from the barrel. When the barrel is removed from the body, great care must be taken to avoid damage to the lip on the breech face. The barrel and radiator should never be stood muzzle upwards on any hard surface.

(viii) *Gas Regulator.*—With the point of a dummy bullet lift the key until the stud is clear of the hole in the radiator casing. Remove the key and unscrew the gas regulator.

(ix) *Clamp ring and front radiator casing.*—Unscrew the No. 1 clamp ring screw and remove the clamp ring and front radiator casing. The No. 2 screw should only be unscrewed sufficiently to bring the end flush with the outside of the left wing of the clamp ring ; the lower part of the flange on the front radiator casing should then be sprung out of the recess in the clamp ring by pressing the casing upwards.

(x) *Rear radiator casing.*—Slide the casing off the radiator to the rear.

(xi) *Gas cylinder.*—Insert the piston rod till the rack enters the cylinder at least two inches, and using it as a wrench, unscrew the gas cylinder.

(xii) *Gas chamber.*—Unscrew with the spanner. This part should be removed only when it is necessary to remove the barrel, as frequent removal will tend to loosen it and allow gas to escape.

(xiii) *Barrel mouthpiece.*—Unscrew with the spanner. *This component has a left-hand thread and must be turned clockwise to unscrew.* When the flash eliminator is fitted, the projection on the locking collar must be disengaged before the eliminator can be unscrewed.

> *Note.*—Undue force must not be applied when unscrewing the gas cylinder, gas chamber, barrel mouthpiece or flash eliminator. When set by rust they should be well soaked with paraffin (oil, mineral burning), and left for a time before a further attempt is made to remove them.

(xiv) *Barrel.*—Remove the barrel by means of the screw jack as described in Section 7 and then remove the barrel band from the radiator.

Stripping Various Components

(i) To remove an extractor.—Raise the hook until the stud is clear of the recess of the bolt, and draw the extractor out, care being taken not to strain it by lifting more than is necessary. The Mk. II extractor is removed in a similar manner, the spring being subsequently removed by pressing the point of the mock bullet of the combination spring balance, or the bullet of a dummy cartridge, between the end of the slot in the bolt and the groove in the end of the spring, which can then be withdrawn.

(ii) To remove the magazine stop pawls.—Force the stud on the pawls, spring out of its seating and lift the pawls off their studs. Note that the studs and pawls are marked 1 and 2, to ensure re-assembly in the right order.

(iii) To remove the cartridge guide.—Press the stud down and slide out.

(iv) To remove the ejector.—Raise the rear end of the ejector cover and slide it to the rear.

(v) To remove the return spring complete with casing.—
Press up the arm of the pinion pawl to release the
spring. Unscrew the tension screw and allow the
pinion to drop out of its casing. With the point of
a dummy bullet press on the hub and push the spring
casing out of the pinion.

(vi) To remove sear, trigger, plunger or spring.—Push out
the axis pins.

(vii) To remove the pinion pawl.—Push out the axis pin.

(viii) The foresight can be driven out of its bed with a
punch through the holes in the foresight protector.

(ix) To remove the tangent sight.—Unscrew the fixing
screw and drive off to the rear.

(x) To remove the clamp screw from the clamp ring,
when necessary.—Unscrew and remove the positioning stud by means of the modified barrel
mouthpiece spanner.

To assemble the gun.—Reverse the foregoing operations.
When replacing the barrel and radiator in the rear casing,
care must be taken to avoid damaging the projections on the
rear face of the barrel. Similar care must be exercised in
replacing screwed portions, particularly the gas chamber,
cylinder and barrel mouthpiece. When assembling the clamp
ring with the No. 2 screw, place the clamp ring on the rear
radiator casing ; insert the lower part of the flange on the front
radiator casing into the recess in the clamp ring, then press the
upper part into place, keeping the slot in the casing in line
with the stud under the foresight block. See that the clamp
ring lies evenly around the flanges on the radiator casings,
then tighten the screw.

Before replacing the body cover, it must be seen that the
feed arm is over to the right. When replacing the bolt,
the feed arm should be moved over to the left to allow the feed
arm actuating stud to engage ; also see that the rear end of the
ejector is clear.

Notes.—(a) It may be necessary to move the cocking
handle slightly when raising the pinion casing into
position to enable the rack to engage with the
pinion.

(b) When assembling the barrel band, care must be taken
that the portion marked " F " on the boss is to
the front, in order that the barrel shall assemble
correctly.

(c) See that the return spring is eased.

Section 3.—Cleaning, etc.

The general instructions for cleaning and oiling are contained in Chapter I, Section 3.

Special attention should be given to the barrel, gas cylinder, gas chamber, gas regulator, barrel mouthpiece (or flash eliminator), face and interior of the breech bolt, head and striker post of the piston rod and striker, and interior of the front radiator casing.

Barrel.—The barrel can be cleaned, without stripping the gun down, by means of the cleaning rod and flannelette inserted at the muzzle end.

The double pull-through can be inserted at the breech end after the removal of the butt, body cover, trigger guard, pinion casing, piston rod and bolt. The chamber also can then be cleaned.

Gas cylinder.—Normally this part can be cleaned, without stripping, by means of the cylinder cleaning rod with wire brush or mop attached ; but when hard fouling is present at the front end, the cylinder should be removed and scoured through until clean. The enlarged bore at the extreme end near the screw thread should be scraped out clean.

Care must be taken to avoid distortion of the cylinder when held for cleaning, as, when distorted, especially at the front end, serious loss of power will result owing to escape of gas by the piston head. On no account must emery or other abrasive material be employed for cleaning the cylinder, as such will enlarge the bore and also result in serious loss of power.

Gas chamber and gas regulator.—The interior of the gas chamber can be cleaned whilst in position after removing the gas regulator. When hard fouling is present it should be scraped out, care being taken to avoid injury to the screw thread. Hard fouling can be removed from the gas regulator by means of the gas regulator cleaner ; similar fouling in the vent holes in the regulator should be carefully removed without enlarging the holes.

Magazines.—Care must be taken when cleaning to see that oil is not left on the internal surfaces, as, when so left, it is liable to be carried into the chamber by the cartridges and so affect functioning and accuracy.

Magazines must on no account be cleaned by washing in hot water, as such will reach parts inaccessible for cleaning. Soda also must not be used, as this will attack the aluminium centre block. This applies also to the radiator of the gun.

Section 4.—Examination of the Gun, etc.

The following instructions are for general guidance; it should be borne in mind that special circumstances may arise which may necessitate a change in the sequence of examination as given, *e.g.* a defect due to unfair usage which it is desirable should be looked for in all guns when discovered in the guns first examined, or when a brief examination only is called for.

(i) *General.*—Examine the gun generally for damage. See that the registered number on body cover, rear radiator casing and clamp ring agrees with the number on body. Then strip and examine as follows :—

(ii) *Butt.*—Test for fit and security in body. Mk. I pattern, where fitted, should be noted for exchange for factory conversion to Mk. II.

(iii) *Guard, trigger.*—Test action of trigger and sear and of butt catch. Examine bent of sear and pinion pawl seating for wear and damage.

Note.—The butt catch may be either No. 1 or No. 2 pattern.

(iv) *Casing, pinion.*—See that the casing is modified to facilitate removal from body. For instructions regarding modification, *see* Section 5. Test action of pinion pawl. Examine teeth of pinion. Remove return spring casing and examine spring for fractures and security of studs.

(v) *Bolt.*—Remove and examine the feed arm actuating stud, and see that its number agrees with that of the bolt. Examine the bolt for fracture, condition of cam slot and of recoil and feed arm actuating stud shoulders, and the face for excessive erosion. See that the striker hole is not excessively enlarged (the limit, ·088 inch, can be determined with a piece of wire adjusted to size). Replace and observe the location of the feed arm actuating stud, which should overturn slightly to ensure free entry into the guideways in the body during the rearward movement. Examine extractors for set and for condition of hook, and see that they do not project beyond the surface of bolt. Weight to lift hook—Mk. I, 3 to 6 lb.; Mk. II, 4 to 6 lb.

(vi) *Rod, piston.*—Examine generally for fracture, and for straightness and security of the stem in the rack; there should be sufficient play between the stem and the rack to allow for free alignment of the stem in the gas cylinder. Examine the striker post and sear bent for smoothness of the working surfaces, and see that the piston head is free from hard fouling ; when removing such fouling care must be taken to avoid reducing the size of the head. See that the striker is secure and that the point is undamaged ; also that the teeth of the rack are clean and undamaged. Gauge the striker protrusion in the bolt—·037 to ·043 inch. Re-assemble the piston rod and the bolt—extractors removed—to the body, and test cartridge head space—·064 to ·074 inch. If the bolt turns over the ·074-inch gauge, assemble the longest bolt available ; if this also turns over, assemble the best barrel available, and if this does not give the required cartridge head space, the gun should be shown for exchange (factory repair).

(vii) *Cover, body.*—Examine for fracture and distortion, especially of the cartridge guide tongue, condition and action of the pawls, which may be either Mk. I or Mk. I* pattern, but preferably of one mark throughout. Measure the projection of the pawls from the curved edge—Mk. I pawls about ·10 inch, Mk. I* pawls ·15 inch. Should the projection of the Mk. I* be very excessive, assemble the spare pawls to ascertain whether the fault lies with the gun pawls or with their seatings. Where the edge in rear of the acting end of the No. 2 stop pawl is sharp, it must be smoothly rounded off to prevent it cutting into the under surface of the body cover. Test the tangent sight for security and action.

(viii) *Arm, feed.*—Check fit on magazine post, and engagement and security of latch. Examine for fracture and distortion, condition of feed pawl and spring, cam groove, and lug at rear end.

(ix) *Body.*—Test to ascertain that the body is firmly breeched to the locking piece of rear radiator casing ; when not firmly breeched, and the fitting of a barrel packing washer is necessary, the cartridge head space may be affected and must be retested. See that the ejector cover does not project above the surface and that the ejector is not excessively worn or damaged. Examine recoil shoulders for excessive wear and damage and for fracture ; when fractured, the fracture is usually visible on the outside surface. Examine key, or feather, in magazine post for security, damage and wear—remove burrs where present; cocking handle slot for excessive wear, applying an unworn cocking handle in cases of doubt; pinion casing hinge pin for security and condition; and safety catch plates for action, and condition.

(x) *Key, gas regulator.*—See that engagement in gas regulator and radiator casing is satisfactory; when distorted, adjust by careful setting.

(xi) *Regulator, gas.*—Examine for damage; see that hard fouling, where present, is removed with the cleaner and that the gas holes are clear.

(xii) *Casing, radiator, front.*—Examine for damage and distortion, and see that it is securely held in position by the clamp ring.

(xiii) *Ring, clamp.*—See that it is undamaged and free from distortion, that the positioning stud is secure and its head correctly located, and that the clamp screw is in good condition.

(xiv) *Casing, radiator, rear.*—Examine for damage and distortion; when it is found that distortion is sufficient to affect adversely the alignment of barrel with body, and consequently the sighting of the gun, the complete gun should be exchanged (factory repair). Minor indentations which affect free assembly of the casing to the radiator should be removed in accordance with the instructions given in Section 5. Special attention should be given to the locating recess for the positioning stud in the clamp ring. Apply a good locking pin to test wear or damage of body locking pin hole.

(xv) *Cylinder, gas.*—Examine for damage and fracture, especially at the corners of the flat surface at the rear end, also for circumferential distortion at the front end, which, when present, can be ascertained by applying the head of the piston rod and then sighting through and testing for inequality of " play." Any internal fouling which may be present on the internal surface should be removed, care being taken to avoid enlargement during such removal. Examine screw threads for condition and fit on the gas chamber; the cylinder should not overturn on the gas chamber in excess of a half-turn, but it should be borne in mind that the fit of the thread is of more consequence than overturning.

(xvi) *Chamber, gas, and band, barrel.*—Test fit of gas
chamber in the band, and see that it does not
overturn on its seating in the barrel; if it does overturn the defect may be remedied by slightly setting
the barrel band, but if this is unsuccessful it will be
necessary to replace one of the components by
interchange with components known to be satisfactory. Screw threads should be carefully
examined. See also that gas holes are clear and
that fouling is removed.

(xvii) *Mouthpiece, barrel.*—See that fouling is removed and
that the L.H screw thread is in good condition for
re-assembly to the barrel. Where the flash
eliminator is fitted in place of the mouthpiece, and
it is necessary to remove it from the barrel, the
engaged retaining lip on the locking collar should
be prized up carefully to avoid fracture.

(xviii) *Radiator.*—Examine for distortion and burring of
fins and damage to barrel keyway. Burrs liable to
affect assembly of other parts should be removed
and distortion and damage corrected and repaired
where practicable.

(xix) *Barrel.*—Examine the lip on the breech face, and the
flange key and screw threads at the breech and
the muzzle for damage and wear. Examine
internally for condition and wear ; when badly
worn in the lead and bore, report for local accuracy
test in accordance with Equipment Regulations,
Part I. See that the chamber is clean and
undamaged and that sound dummy cartridges
enter freely. When the lip is excessively short,
thereby increasing the cartridge head space beyond
·074 inch, and the barrel is otherwise serviceable,
the barrel must be exchanged (factory repair).

(xx) *Gun re-assembled.*—Re-test the cartridge head space
during re-assembly. Test mechanically for correct
functioning. Adjust the return spring to 16 lb.,
and see that the cocking handle can be drawn
right back without jamming the spring ; then
re-adjust to the service weight of 12 to 14 lbs.
Pass a dummy cartridge under the cartridge guide
and observe that it is correctly and firmly held by
the spring. Test feed from magazine with dummy
cartridges, also extraction and ejection with dummy
cartridges and fired cases. Try the pull-off and
apply the safety catch in both cocked and fired
positions. Finally look over the gun to see that

it is complete. When not required for immediate use, ease return spring.

(xxi) *Spare parts.*—Should be examined whenever possible at the same time as the gun, and, where their condition is doubtful, tried in the gun for correctness of functioning.

(xxii) *D.P. and skeleton guns.*—D.P. and also skeleton guns will be examined to see that the nose of the striker is removed, that they function mechanically and are otherwise in a condition suitable for instructional purposes. Finish is of no importance, but the guns should be kept as free as possible from rust.

(xxiii) *Magazines.*—Examine for fracture of pan, and test concentricity of the pan with the gauge ; test separating pegs for security and alignment, and cartridge retaining plates for security ; also freedom and engagement of the catch and action of the spring when the magazine is mounted on the gun. Apply a straight-edge to the surface of the centre block to see that the edge of the pan does not project beyond that surface. Load with 25 dummy cartridges, and turn the pan on the loading handle slightly in each direction, to see that the cartridges are free and that they are retained in the retaining plates when the magazine is held in the loading position. The pan should then be turned to carry the cartridges home to their innermost position to ensure that they travel freely.

(xxiv) *Mounts, field Mk. III.—Mountings, tripod, AA, and Holders, gun.—Accessories and tools.*—Examine generally for serviceability, special attention being given to the efficiency of the stops for the forward location of the legs of the field mount when open.

Note.—Should the armourer be doubtful as to the condition of a gun from a firing standpoint, he should report it for firing trial, and be present at such trial whenever possible.

Section 5.—Repairs, Modifications and Adjustments, etc.

Notes.—(a) For the list of parts which, when unserviceable, necessitate the sending of the gun to store for exchange or factory repair, *see* E.R., Pt. I.

(b) The annual allowance of parts for the repair of the guns is as laid down in Equipment Regulations, Part I.

(*c*) When parts are of necessity withdrawn from the gun
spares, indents must be put forward immediately
for their replacement.

Other parts required for the repair and upkeep
of the guns will be indented for as required.

(i) *Arm, feed.*—In the replacement of an unserviceable
latch, care must be taken when driving out the
axis stud to support the feed arm around the stud.
A metal block having a hole of suitable size should
be employed. The new stud must be inserted from
the underside and securely riveted over the upper
surface of the latch, sufficient freedom for the
rotary movement of the latch being allowed for.

After riveting, the stud must be flushed off with
the surfaces of the feed arm and the latch respectively, and any slight distortion which may have
occurred should be corrected by setting.

When play on the magazine post is such as to
affect the security of the latch, the metal round
the post hole can be drawn inward by carefully
hammering upon a metal block.

After adjustment the arm may require some
setting to remedy distortion.

(ii) *Body.*—*Bevelling of the key of the magazine post to
facilitate assembly of the magazine.*—Where this
has not been carried out, the upper corner of the
front and rear edges will be bevelled by filing to a
depth of $\frac{7}{64}$ inch and inwards towards the centre
line so as to leave the width at the top $\frac{1}{16}$ inch ;
the edges to be slightly rounded off. Should the
key be loose in its recess it must be removed,
expanded at the seating face and made a tight fit ;
after expansion the acting width must not exceed
·193 inch.

(iii) *Bolt.*—Burrs or roughness in the camway, on the
recoil studs or on the actuating stud, when too hard
to file off, should be removed with the carborundum
stick provided and then smoothed off with fine
emery cloth.

(iv) *Butt.*—(*a*) *To fit marking disc.*—The disc and screw
are the same pattern as those in the butt-stock of
the service rifle. Where not already fitted, proceed
to fit as follows :—

1. Mark the disc with the corps marks and consecutive
numbers, employing the $\frac{5}{64}$-inch stamps for the
purpose.

2. Remove the butt from the gun.

    3. Mark off, on the right side of the butt, a centre point at a distance of one inch forward of the oil bottle on the centre line of the butt.

    4. With a suitable centre bit in the Mk. III brace, cut a recess $\frac{1}{8}$ inch deep to take the disc; assemble the disc and re-assemble the butt to the gun.

    (b) *To fit a fresh Mk. I* butt cap.*—In order to bring the holes in the tangs and side arms in alignment with the screw holes in the butt it may be necessary in some cases to adjust the cap seating of the butt or to set the side arms slightly to ensure a close and rigid attachment. When setting the arms, care must be taken to support them at the base and so avoid loosening the rivets.

  (v) *Cover, body.*—As this part is not strictly interchangeable, it may be necessary, in the event of replacement, to adjust the flanges or the side grooves at the front end to suit the body. When doing this the bearings should be smoked in order to ascertain the tight points. Care must be taken to ensure that the cover is kept in correct alignment and that its rear end flushes with the body.

    In order to ensure that each body cover is kept to the gun to which it has been fitted, it will be numbered to agree with the gun number on the body. The majority of covers already bear the body number with a cancellation mark through it; this cancellation mark will be ignored. Where the number disagrees with that on the body, and the cover fits satisfactorily, it will be cancelled with a chisel mark and the body number stamped on in rear of it. Where unnumbered, the number will be stamped on the upper surface in front of the sight bed. The $\frac{5}{64}$-inch stamps will be employed.

  (vi) *Casing, pinion.—Modification to facilitate detachment from body.*—In the event of this modification not having been carried out, it will be made in accordance with Fig. 1.

  (vii) *Casing, radiator, rear.*—

    (a) *Removal of minor dents which affect free assembly to the radiator.*—To enable this to be done a strong bar of iron or steel, such as a crowbar, can be utilized to form the basic portion of a mandril; to this a block of hard wood, shaped suitably to cover more than the area of the dent, should be clamped. The bar should then be gripped in the vice, the wood block projecting sufficiently to enable the casing to be passed over it up to the required position. The dent can now be removed by lightly hammering the metal at the part of the casing surrounding the dent.

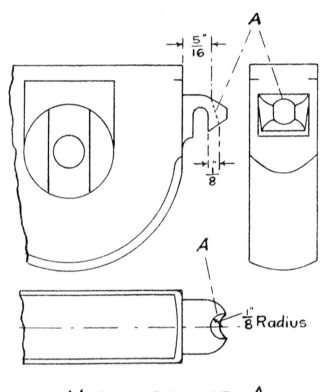

MODIFICATION AT A.

Fig. 1.

(b) *Distortion of the body breeching face of the locking piece*.—When this face has been forced outward due to force having been used during assembly of the casing to the barrel and radiator, it should be carefully set back until the face is truly flat when tested by a straight-edge. It should be borne in mind that any error in this face is multiplied in the length of the casing and will affect foresight alignment and accuracy of shooting accordingly.

(c) *Damage to the locating recess for the clamp ring.*—When damaged and enlarged sufficiently to affect rigidity of the clamp ring location, the metal can be drawn by careful hammering, the portion of the casing affected being supported on a suitable metal block.

(d) *Wear in locking pin hole.*—The limit of wear is governed by its effect upon the relationship of the upper surface of the locking piece and the body, the lateral deflection of the foresight and the freedom of the piston. When such are liable to be affected seriously the gun must be exchanged (factory repair).

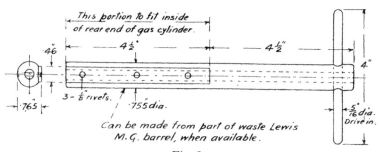

This portion to fit inside of rear end of gas cylinder.

·46

4½"

4½"

4"

3 - ⅛" rivets.

·765

·755 dia.

·755 dia.

⁵⁄₁₆ dia. Drive in.

Can be made from part of waste Lewis M.G. barrel, when available.

Fig. 2.

(viii) *Cylinder, gas.*—

(a) When fractured at the corner or corners of the flat surface formed on the rear part, repair can be effected by brazing ; if badly fractured and distorted, the cylinder should be exchanged. Fracture is due usually to attempts made to unscrew the cylinder when very tightly held by fouling and also to insufficient engagement of the piston rod in the cylinder when unscrewing. A tool made to Fig. 2 will be found more suitable for armourers' use than the piston rod.

(b) When fitting a new cylinder and the screw threads happen to fit the gas chamber very tightly, first see that all fouling is removed by means of paraffin from the thread of the gas chamber, then, if still very tight, ease on by the use of a little oil-stone dust and oil. It is not essential that the face of the cylinder should abut on to the gas chamber ; fit of the screw thread is of much more importance in sealing the chamber.

(ix) *Eliminator flash.*—In order to fit this to the gun it is necessary to cut a groove in the front of the radiator to take the projections of the locking collar. This will be done, upon the receipt of eliminators, in accordance with Instructional Print A.I.D. 1711, which includes also the setting down of one of the two front projections into one of the spanner grooves of the eliminator, the second projection being kept in reserve for use if the other breaks during subsequent stripping and reassembly.

(x) *Guide, cartridge.*—The function of this component is to ensure that the base of the cartridge is held well down for the positive drive forward by the face of the uppermost extractor on the bolt, and also that the point of the bullet is directed correctly to the

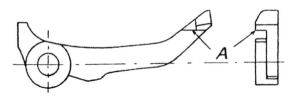

Fig. 3.

chamber. The strength, angle and lead of the spring therefore are of great importance and should be carefully observed during examinations, or when malfunction is reported by the unit, and compared with a new spare spring or one which is known to function correctly. If nothing amiss is found, the cartridge guide should be tried by actual firing in another gun, as slight variation in the guides of the body may exist and so accentuate the effect of small differences.

The weight of the spring when tested by a push rod applied to the spring balance at the point of cartridge contact should be about 2 lb.

(xi) *Pawl, stop, magazine, right, No. 2.*—When the rear edge at " A " on Fig. 3 is sharp, it should be rounded off with an oilstone to prevent cutting into the body cover.

(xii) *Plates, safety catch—Modification to Mk. I*.*—Where not already modified, Mk. I plates will be altered to Mk. I* by filing a gap near the front end to engage the cocking handle in accordance with the location and dimensions given in Fig. 4. This additional gap enables the safety catch to be applied in the home position. After modification the plates are to be marked as shown.

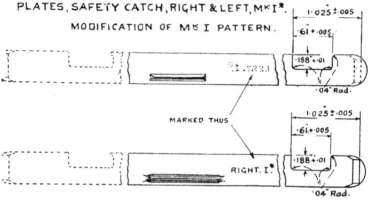

Fig. 4.

(xiii) *Ring, clamp—Numbering to body.*—Where not numbered, or the number disagrees with that on the body and does not agree with the number on any other gun in possession, the body number will be lightly stamped with the $\frac{5}{64}$-inch stamps on the front of the stool at the wider part. The clamp ring should be assembled and clamped to the casings by the screw when the marking is carried out.

(xiv) *To assemble a return spring from retaining collar to casing.*—Return springs are normally issued with casing and hub in tin box, but in the event of springs in collars being met with and having to be fitted, the spring should be inserted into the casing whilst in the collar, the latter being gradually withdrawn as the spring is pressed home into the casing. It may be found necessary in some instances to ease out the slots in the casing slightly to enable the spring to enter without causing distortion of the casing, which may prevent assembly to the pinion.

(xv) *To fit washers, packing barrel.*—The washers are ·005 inch thick, and are provided in order that play between the rear face of the locking piece of the rear radiator casing and the front face of the body, where present owing to wear, may be taken up and rigid breeching again restored. The washer, or washers where it is possible to fit more without causing excessive cartridge head space, is assembled from the breech end of the barrel up to the flange, and is secured by the locking piece of the radiator casing. It is essential that the cartridge head space be re-tested whenever a washer is fitted, as it has the effect of drawing the barrel forward in its relation to the body by taking up wear in the breech screw thread.

(xvi) *Handle, carrying.*—The handle assembles to the rear radiator casing of the gun between the two rear collars, and can be assembled from the front of the gun. It should be free to rotate when the band is clamped by the detachable screw and wing nut, which are secured by a 3-inch length of M.G. brass chain and two M.G. " S " hooks. The prongs of the fork of the stirrup-shaped handle are covered with asbestos cord or sheet, which in turn has a covering of leather.

The parts detailed in the Vocabulary of Army Ordnance Stores are obtainable for local maintenance. In an emergency No. 6 S.W.G. soft steel wire (Section C.2 of V. of A.O.S.) can be utilized in lieu of the rivet for the wood grip by reducing it slightly as necessary.

(xvii) *Magazines.*—

(a) *To remedy distortion of pans and separating pegs.*— The pans can be trued up by means of the tool provided, which enables the rim and the pegs to be levered in the desired direction. Concentricity should be checked by the gauge supplied, the pans subsequently being examined to see that they are not fractured, and the magazines, filled with sufficient dummy cartridges, tested both off and on the gun.

(b) *To fit a new catch spring.*—The fitting of a new spring in replacement of a broken or weak spring is a lengthy operation and will not normally be undertaken locally, but in the event of armourers being called upon to undertake the work at R.A.O.C. Workshops the following instructions will be followed :—

1. Detach the centre disc by shearing off the rivets with a sharp chisel and punching out the rivets. In this operation care must be taken to avoid damage to the centre block, which is very thin between the inside face and the bottom of the rivet holes.

2. Remove the unserviceable spring, insert the new coil spring, re-assemble the centre block and centre disc and re-rivet with six new centre disc rivets, taking care not to compress them unduly in view of possible damage to the centre block by doing so.

3. Retest magazine.

Note.—In the event of magazines being converted to Mk. I* pattern with cover plate for the spring, it will then only be necessary when replacing the spring to detach the two fixing screws and nuts which secure the cover plate, remove the latter, replace the spring and re-assemble. The two screws and nuts take the place of two of the six centre disc rivets.

(c) *Skeletonizing of magazines.*—Magazines required as " skeletons " will be converted from worn magazines in accordance with the following instructions and Fig. 5 :—

1. Mark off the portion of the centre disc which covers the engaging end of the magazine catch, as shown on Fig. 5 at " A." Place the aluminium centre block on a flat metal surface and with a keen-edged chisel, ground at a sharp angle, cut out portion marked off, care being taken not to cut into or damage the magazine catch. The cut part can be removed by inserting the chisel under the outer edge of the disc and tapping it upward. The sharp edges are to be smoothed off after removal of the cut portion.

2. Mark off the magazine pan inside to agree with

external view shown on Fig. 5. Place a round piece of metal, corresponding in diameter to a corrugation in the magazine, under the pan, and with the chisel cut through each corrugation separately, in the direction of the arrow. Place the pan on a flat metal surface,

MAGAZINE, LEWIS ·303-ɪɴ. M.G.
SKELETON.

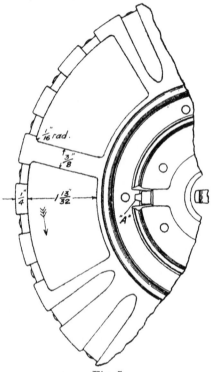

Fig. 5.

cut through remaining portions and remove. Smooth off the sharp edges and remedy any slight distortion which may have occurred by setting.

Note.—Care must be taken not to damage the raised portions of the magazine pan or the centre disc, as such damage may prevent the magazine from functioning when on the gun.

(xviii) *Mounts, field, Mk. III.*—

    (a) *Repair of leg joints.*—The parts most subject to wear are the upper joints of the legs and the leg joints of the saddle, more especially at the stop surfaces which limit the angular thrust of the legs, and the hinge screws and screw holes. When the stop surfaces are so worn as to render the legs insufficiently secure to support the weight of the gun, and the hinge screws are not unduly worn, the stop surface of each joint of the legs or the corresponding surfaces of the saddle, whichever are most worn, should be repaired by fitting and brazing on a strip of sufficient thickness to withstand the thrust. Care must be taken when fitting strips to the saddle to avoid weakening the latter unduly.

    (b) *Modification of shoes.*—In the event of shoes being met with which have not been modified by curving the lower end upward to enable it to automatically swing outward when the spike is pressed into soft ground, modification will be carried out in accordance with Fig. 6.

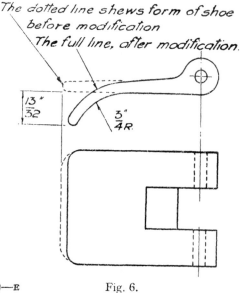

Fig. 6.

(xix) *Sights, A.A. fore and back, Mk. II.*—The foresight when in use is clamped to the rear radiator casing just behind the foresight or further back to shorten the sight radius according to the speed of the target. On account of its size the elliptical plate is liable to become distorted during use and may require re-setting. An undistorted sight can be used as a template for the correct form.

The sight should be upright on the gun when the pointer is central with the ordinary gun foresight. The base of the backsight is clamped between the tangent sight slide and the upper end of the slot in the tangent sight leaf, and is secured by a clamping plate, spring washer and screw. The sight is assembled from the graduated side of the leaf and the clamping plate, etc., on the opposite side. If the aperture of any backsight is found to be fitted with cross-wires the latter should be removed by cutting them off close to the edge of the aperture and blending off with a smooth file. The face of the sight should be smoothed and re-blacked with the temporary blacking referred to in Part II, Chapter I, Section 5.

(xx) *Mounting, tripod, A.A.*—For particulars, repairs, etc., *see* Chapter I, Section 5.

(xxi) *Box, carrier, magazine—Conversion to Mk. I*.*—In order that the contents of the boxes may be protected as much as possible from the entrance of sand, etc., Mk. I boxes will be converted to Mk. I* when undergoing repair in R.A.O.C. Workshops, by cementing strips of "fearnought" (Section H2 of V. of A.O.S.) $\frac{5}{8}$-inch wide, around the inside of the lid to form a seating on the rim of the body of the box. The strips are to be butted at the corners of the lid. A strip 4 feet long is sufficient for one box. Chatterton's compound (Section W2 of V. of A.O.S.) is a suitable cement.

(xxii) *Adapters, holder, A.A. Mk. I.*—The adapter provided for use with the No. 1, Mk. II, rifle aiming rest, enables the gun to be mounted thereon for elementary instruction in A.A. Training.

In order to ensure that the gun-holder may be fixed rigidly to the adapter, the top of the upper joint of the adapter is left full for adjustment to enable it to be made to seat closely on the inner surface of the vacant leg joint slot of the gun-holder when the leg hinge screw is assembled.

An additional leg hinge screw, with split pin, is required for assembly.

The lower end of the adapter assembles into the aiming rest socket in place of the rifle carrying arm and is secured by the arm axis screw.

(xxiii) *Box, battalion spares.*—In the case of units supplied with holdalls, etc., for spare parts and tools, the obsolete chests for belt-filling machines, with the internal fittings removed, are utilized for the carriage of certain spare parts left in the care of the armourer. The boxes will be re-stencilled in white paint on the front in 1¼-inch block type :—

" BATTN. SPARES, LEWIS ·303 M.G.

The work will be carried out in R.A.O.C. Work-shops.

(xxiv) *Carriers, magazine.*—These vary somewhat in material and colour. A ring of cane is sewn round the carrier at about 5 inches from the base, and another similar ring or a disc of plywood or fibre inserted in the base for stiffening purposes and for protecting the magazines. Materials for repair can be obtained upon demand. When fitting new turnbuckles and eyelets the internal pad of leather or canvas must be maintained.

(xxv) *Pouches, magazine, web—Modification.*—Pouches of later manufacture have the straps attached at a higher position on the back. Pouches of earlier pattern will be converted as follows :—

Remove the 2-inch and 1-inch straps by cutting the stitches, care being taken not to damage the webbing. Remove the 2-inch buckle and re-sew it on about the centre of the 2-inch strap. Re-sew the 2-inch strap so that one end crosses the top of the pouch, and re-sew the 1-inch strap so that the bottom edge of the strap comes about the centre of the back of the pouch. Sample pouches to guide alteration and the following material will be supplied as necessary :—

Thread, drab, No. 18, 3 oz. for every 100 pouches.

Where it is found that the webbing has broken on the top of the pouch a strip of 2-inch or 2¼-inch thin webbing should be sewn over the broken part. The necessary webbing and thread should be demanded as required.

124

(xxvi) *Chests, Vickers or Lewis M.G., Mk. III—*
    (a) *Modification to Mk. IIIB.*—In the case of units
        supplied with the holdall instead of the bag for
        spare parts and tools, one chest for every four
        guns will be modified in accordance with Fig. 7 to

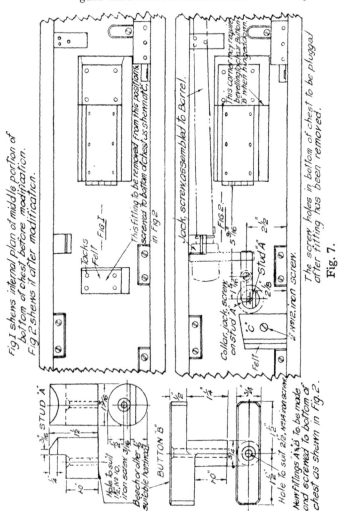

Fig. 7.

take, in addition to the gun, a barrel with the jack screwed to it and the collar of the jack. A piston rod, a gas cylinder and a No. 1 filled wallet also will be carried in this chest, the two former in the right bottom corner at the front in the existing fittings, and the wallet at the bottom of the chest. The parts carried in this chest are separately demanded and accounted for. Chests so modified will be stencilled :—

" GUN, LEWIS, ·303, MK. I & S."

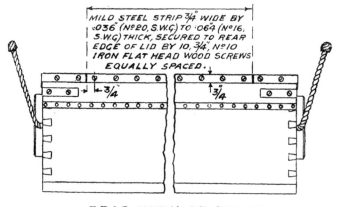

REAR VIEW OF CHEST
AFTER CONVERSION

Fig. 8.

(b) *Conversion of Mk. II chests to Mark III.*—The conversion consists of the fitting of a mild steel strip to the rear edge of the lid. The strip also replaces the basil leather strip for securing the top edge of the canvas backing. Conversion will be carried out in R.A.O.C. Workshops in accordance with Fig. 8.

The following material will be required per chest : one mild steel strip, $\frac{3}{4}$ inch by $37\frac{1}{2}$ inches approx., ten screws, wood, flat head, $\frac{3}{4}$ inch, No. 10.

(xxvii) *Other equipment.*—The various other accessories, *e.g.* aim correctors, gun covers, etc., should be repaired as necessary to maintain them in a serviceable condition.

Section 6.—Re-browning and Re-painting
Re-browning

Re-browning, as required, will be carried out under the same conditions as for small arms (*see* Part II, Chapter I, Section 5).

The following parts will be re-browned when necessary :—

Arm, feed.
Band, radiator casing, front.
Bed, tangent sight.
Body.
Blade, foresight ... ... As an alternative this may be oil-blacked, care to be taken not to overheat and so affect the temper.

Bottle, oil, butt.
Bracket, swivel, butt.
Cap, butt.
Casing, pinion.
Casings, radiator front and rear
Catch, butt.
Cover, body.
Cylinder, gas ... ... Exterior only. To be cleaned with the wire brush and oiled internally after browning.
Eliminator, flash ... ... Or barrel mouthpiece, whichever is in use.

Guards, trigger, Mk. I*
Handle, cocking.
Leaf, tangent sight ... Including graduated surface.
Plate, safety catch.
Plate, butt.
Regulator, gas.
Ring, clamp.
Slide, tangent sight.

Notes.— (i) Mk. I trigger guards which have fixed wood side-pieces will be painted.
(ii) Swivels and exposed screws and pins will be oil-blacked.

Re-painting

For materials allowed and surfaces to be painted, *see* Appendix II.

When the paint is dry, the working parts in close proximity to the painted surfaces should be tested for free action.

Section 7.—Description and Use of Tools and Gauges

*Jack (with collar) for assembling and removing the barrel.—
To remove the barrel from the radiator.*—Place the collar on
the breech end, screw the jack home to the collar, and strike
the projecting arm a smart blow with the rawhide mallet to
start the barrel out of the radiator. The jack must not be
driven further than is necessary to loosen the barrel, otherwise
damage to the keyway in the radiator will result.

To replace the barrel.—Screw the jack (without the collar)
well home to the breech face of the barrel, pass the barrel into
the radiator, seeing that the key is central in the key slot, then

MODIFICATION TO TAKE CLAMP RING POSITIONING STUD

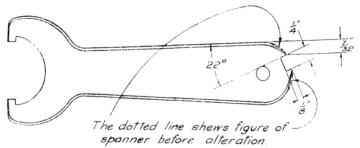

*The dotted line shews figure of
spanner before alteration.*

*All sharp edges of gap to be removed.
The end of the spanner may require to be softened
sufficiently to enable the gap to be filed.*

Fig. 9.

drive the barrel home by striking the end of the jack with the
mallet.

Note.—A jack for the removal only of the barrel was
originally issued. This being bored throughout cannot be
used for assembling purposes.

Spanner.—This is provided for the barrel mouthpiece but
can be used also for the gas chamber, and, when modified in
accordance with Fig. 9, for the positioning stud of the clamp
ring.

Where not carried out, the modification will be made
locally by armourers.

The spanner is issued with the gun spares.

Plug, clearing.—Like the clearing plug issued with the
Vickers ·303-inch gun, this is supplied with the gun spares for
removing the front portion of a separated case from the

chamber ; also the end of the handle is formed as a jaw for use as a hand extractor for removing a live round or an empty cartridge case from the chamber. To remove a portion of a separated case, press the centre pin well back, insert the tapered split screwed stem into the chamber, ease the gun bolt forward, and, pressing firmly on the cocking handle to ensure that the pin expands the screw threads into the metal of the case, rock the plug handle to left and right to enable the screw to cut into the metal; then pull back the cocking handle, raise the safety catch, lever back the plug handle, withdraw the plug, knock back the centre pin and remove the portion of the case from the plug.

In the case of a number of clearing plugs of earlier supply, the end of the handle was not formed as a jaw. If met with they will be modified by armourers in accordance with Fig. 10.

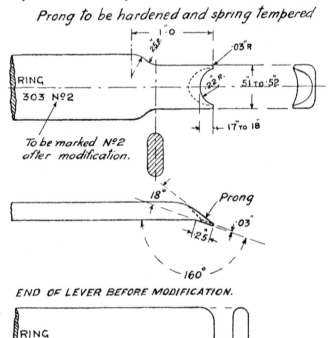

Fig. 10.

Cleaner, gas regulator.—This is in the form of a cutter with a wooden handle and is supplied with the gun spares for removing fouling, chiefly metallic. It may require occasional sharpening with an oilstone.

Gauge, striker point.—This gauge, the dimensions of which are high ·042, low ·037 inch, is applied to the face of the bolt when the striker post of the piston rod is home to the inner stop face at the front of the cam slot in the bolt. When the protrusion of the striker is greater than the high limit the point will be adjusted, the radius at the point being maintained. When less than the low limit, the striker will be replaced. The piston rod and bolt must be removed from the gun to enable the gauge to be applied.

Gauge, concentricity of magazine, and tool for setting.—The gauge is for use when testing the true spinning of the pan from the centre of the magazine, and also the uprightness and even distance of the cartridge separating pegs from the same centre. The gauging wing is intentionally made to clear the rim of the pan, as otherwise it would not be possible to detect eccentricity, where present. For the same reason the space between the studs is also left larger than the diameter of the pegs.

The tool for adjusting the magazine is made of round bar steel and is double-ended, one end being bored to engage a separating peg and the other slotted to engage the rim of the pan over a cartridge retaining plate. The tool should not be used on the outer corrugations of the pan, as if so used it is liable to cause local distortion and fracture.

Gauges for testing cartridge head space.—The gauges for the rifle—·064 and ·074-inch, No. 1—will be used in accordance with the instructions given in Section 4.

CHAPTER III

GUNS, MACHINE, VICKERS, ·303-IN., MK. I

Drawing No. S.A.I.D. 2062

Section 1.—General Information

1. In addition to the Mk. I water-cooled gun which is employed in Land and Naval Services and for ground use in the Air Service, there are three air-cooled patterns special to the Air Service, the Mk. I*, Mk. II and Mk. III. The Mk. I*,

not now in use, is a conversion from the Mk. I and can be identified by louvres formed near the rear end of the tubular portion of the barrel casing, and by the opening out of the front end of the end cap of the barrel casing. The Mks. II and III have a perforated barrel casing much smaller in diameter than the casing of the Mks. I and I*, the end cap and trunnion block being correspondingly smaller to blend with the barrel casing.

The barrel and the main portions of the mechanism are identical, but divergencies from the Mk. I exist in certain details, such as the contour of the crank handle, " S.U." (speeding up) cylinder and buffer spring in the muzzle attachment of Mks. I and II, and the handle arms, firing lever and safety catch, etc., are omitted from the rear crosspiece ; also the sliding shutter is omitted from the underside of the breech casing and the front and rear covers are " special."

The Mk. III gun has several new features, *e.g.* new alternative types of muzzle attachments, with and without a flash eliminator, a laterally operated rear cover catch and a rearcrosspiece to suit it and an adjustable loading handle which forms a permanent fitment of the gun.

Two further patterns of water-cooled guns, converted from the Mk. I, which will be known as Mks. IVA and IVB, have been introduced for use in armoured fighting vehicles. Particulars and instructions with regard to the care and repair of these patterns and the mountings for them will be published separately.

The Air Service guns cannot be mounted on the Land Service tripod and cone mountings owing to the gap between the elevating joint lugs being filled in by a distance-piece ; a special inner elevating screw is employed in the Air Service when it is desired to fire a Mk. I* or Mk. II gun on a Mk IV tripod mounting.

The following paras. have reference to the Mk. I pattern.

2. Weight of gun—from $28\frac{1}{2}$ lb. to 32 lb.

3. The tubular portion of the barrel casing may be either corrugated or plain ; the plain casings are made of thicker material to compensate for loss of strength due to the omission of corrugations.

Barrel casings of early manufacture were pressed inward on the underside, adjacent to the end cap, to form an assembly guide or " lead " to the front bearing for the muzzle end of the barrel, but as with this pattern the internal protecting coat of tin became damaged and the casing rusted through, a short separate tinned brass guide riveted to the casing was introduced in lieu ; subsequently a tinned brass trough extending from the front barrel bearing to the trunnion block was introduced and this pattern is fitted to most of the guns in the Service.

4. The trunnion block, *i.e.* that part which connects with the breech casing and the tubular portion of the barrel casing, in guns of early manufacture was lightened by recesses in the rear face. The recesses were subsequently omitted in order to obtain greater resistance to distortion in the event of the gun receiving a blow or strain such as would tend to throw the barrel and breech casing out of alignment. For this reason it is now the practice to employ guns with lightened blocks for "D.P." only.

5. A number of lightening operations on the gun were omitted during the Great War to facilitate production; differences therefore exist in various detail, but they do not affect interchange and may be ignored; such operations will not be carried out in future manufacture.

6. There are two patterns of front cone for the muzzle attachment. The Mk. I is flat-fronted, with an annular recess, whilst the Mk. II is coned and made bullet-proof. Both patterns are interchangeable in the outer casing of the muzzle attachment and take the removable disc which protects the inner coned face.

For the automatic firing of blank ammunition a special front cone with adjusting screw and nut and a special muzzle cup replace the corresponding parts of the ball attachment.

7. Feed block bodies may be either of gunmetal or steel. Future manufacture will be of gunmetal and fitted with a belt guide rib of steel on the bottom surface of the opening. The strip is already fitted to many existing gun-metal feed blocks; it was introduced primarily to withstand wear from the steel belt links employed in the Air Service. A left-hand feed block in addition to the normal right-hand block is employed in the Air Service and the Royal Tank Corps. In this block the slide with top pawls is common to the right block, the front pawl then being at the rear and the rear pawl at the front *; special top levers are provided for the operation of the slide, the bottom lever only being common to the R.H. feed block.

The belt-retaining pawls are pivoted to the upper portion of the left side of the block, the tie piece for hand release being located at an angle of about 40° upward from the horizontal in order that both the retaining and feed pawls may be operated as required by the thumb of the left hand.

* A special pattern of single top pawl is fitted to Mk. III Air Service guns.

8. Check lever brackets are of two patterns, Mk. I and Mk. II.

The Mk. I is suitable only for the lightened pattern of outside plate of breech casing and is grooved horizontally on its seating face to engage the centre rib in the plate.

The Mk. II is suitable only for plates of unlightened pattern ; it has two studs which engage holes bored through the plate. Both patterns of bracket are secured by two upper and two lower rivets.

Mk. II brackets of early manufacture had one stud only, but this was found insufficient, so a large rivet, representing a second stud, was employed for such brackets.

Mk. I brackets of early manufacture were formed with a stud to receive the thrust of a piston in the check lever. As the piston—with spring—is obsolete, the stud is now omitted from brackets when manufactured.

9. The Mk. II barrel differs from the Mk. I in that it is screw threaded at the muzzle end, whereas the Mk. I—since converted to Mk. II—had an annular groove only, to take the transverse screw of the obsolete Mk. I muzzle cup.

Barrels marked " S.C." on the breech face have the small cone enlarged in diameter by ·002 inch to provide additional clearance for the cartridge. Such barrels, where available, are selected for use on mobilization, but when not available barrels not so marked may be employed.

Barrels marked " T " on the breech face are tubed. They are not to be used on mobilization, and as they are experimental any exceptional points affecting serviceability which may be noticed should be reported to the A.I.A.

" D.P.B." barrels used for automatic firing of service blank ammunition are fitted with a bush choke at the front end of the chamber to ensure more regular pressure from the charge, and the breaking up of the wads. Such barrels will not take ball ammunition. They are converted from service barrels worn out internally.

10. Gibs in extractors of locks are of three patterns, Nos. 1, 2 and 3. Nos. 2 and 3 are practically identical, the former being a conversion from No. 1 and the latter for future manufacture. Nos. 2 and 3 differ from No. 1 in that the upper " lead " portion of the acting surface is bevelled instead of rounded, whilst the lower inclined portion of that surface has a lesser projection and the edges bevelled. The No. 1 is in general process of conversion to No. 2 pattern (*see* Section 5 of this chapter).

11. Check levers Nos. 1 and 2 differ in that the No. 1 was originally fitted with a piston and spring ; whereas in the

No. 2 no provision is made for these details, and it is made larger and heavier at its upper end. Either pattern may be used.

12. Two patterns of lock springs are in use—Nos. 1 and 2 ; they differ only in form at the bend—*see* Drawing S.A.I.D. 2062. The No. 2 pattern is of later manufacture. No more of No. 1 pattern will be made.

13. There are two patterns of firing pin—Nos. 1 and 2. The No. 2 is shorter than the No. 1 in rear of the tumbler bent and the rear end is cut at an angle—*see* Drawing S.A.I.D. 2062. Either pattern may be employed in Mk. I guns. The No. 2 was specially produced for Air Service guns in order to reduce weight and so speed up the firing action of the lock. The No. 2 is the universal pattern for future manufacture.

14. Extractors and extractor levers of No. 1 pattern are modified, when passing through the R.S.A.F., to the No. 2 pattern—see Drawing S.A.I.D. 2062. The object of the modification is to prevent the lower portion of the acting end of the levers from falling over the stop ledges at the sides of the extractor and checking the descent of the extractor. The removal of the lower portion of the acting end of the levers and a portion of each side of the extractor above the side plate spring recesses enables the levers to clear.

15. There have been several progressions in the patterns of tangent sight. The latest pattern now in use is the Mk. III**, which consists of the Mk. II stem having a battle sight, sighted for 400 yards range, in addition to the normal graduated plate for ranges up to 2,900 yards, and the Mk. II** tangent sight slide, which is of the split type and fitted with aperture pillar, friction spring and washer and clamping nut with thumb-piece. An improved pattern of slide has been approved, but has not yet been manufactured. Particulars of this pattern will be published at a future date. The advent of this slide will further advance the mark of the sight.

The Mk. III* differs from the Mk. III** only in that the friction spring and washer and thumb-piece are not fitted to the slide, which is Mk. II*. The Mk. III is fitted with a Mk. II slide, with plain " U " sighting, otherwise it is identical with the Mk. III* and is convertible to that pattern and to the Mk. III**.

The Mk. II had the Mk. II stem and the Mk. I slide, which was of Maxim gun type with ratchet and pawl. This slide could only be moved along the stem by rotating the milled head.

The Mk. I had a Mk. I stem without battle-sight, and the Mk. I slide.

Section 2.—Stripping and Assembling

Note.—These instructions are for general guidance. It will rarely be necessary completely to strip the whole gun, but only the parts necessary for cleaning, examination, and replacement purposes.

To Strip the Gun

See that the gun is unloaded. For preference mount on a Mk. IV tripod mounting, drain out the water from the barrel casing, and proceed to remove the parts in the following order :—

(i) *Lock.*—Raise the rear cover, pull back the crank handle, lift out the lock from the guides on the side plates, rotate it 60° on the connecting rod and lift off. Press back the trigger to ease the lock spring and turn the crank handle forward.

(ii) *Feed block.*—Turn up the front cover catch, raise the front cover and lift out.

(iii) *Fusee spring box with spring, etc.*—Press the box forward to clear the front and rear studs, draw outward and detach the hook of the spring from the fusee chain. Turn the fusee rearward and pull out from the crank.

(iv) *Muzzle attachment.*—Unscrew the front cone, pull out the split keeper pin, turn the outer casing 60° and draw it off from the gland. Unscrew and remove the muzzle cup and the gland and withdraw the asbestos packing. Should the details special to blank firing be assembled, and it is desired to remove the adjusting screw from the front cone, the lock nut may be unscrewed before removing the cone ; the adjusting screw can be unscrewed from the inside end of the cone when the latter is removed and held in a vice.

When owing to the presence of fouling any of the parts have become set they should be saturated with paraffin and, if possible, left for a time before again attempting to remove them.

(v) *" T " fixing pin.*—Raise the rear cover, unscrew and remove the " T " pin and hinge down the rear crosspiece.

(vi) *Slides, left and right.*—Withdraw them from the outside plates of the breech casing.

(vii) *Recoiling portions.*—Grasp the crank handle axis, draw out the recoiling portions sufficiently to enable firstly the left side plate and secondly the right side plate, with the crank, etc., to be disconnected from the barrel ; then remove the barrel.

Note.—The foregoing operations, apart from the removal of the fusee, front cone and gland of muzzle attachment, are necessary in order to remove the barrel.

(viii) *Tangent sight.*—Unscrew and remove the axis pin, and remove the sight, piston and spring.

(ix) *Rear cover lock.*—Unscrew and remove the axis pin, and remove the cover lock and spring.

(x) *Trigger bar.*—Remove the spring and withdraw the bar.

(xi) *Front and rear covers.*—Drive out the keeper pin (plain pin riveted over), or remove the split keeper pin, unscrew the check nut and press out the joint pin. Connect the nut, joint pin and keeper pin to prevent mixing with similar parts of other guns.

Note.—These parts should be removed only when replacement is necessary, and must be kept to the same gun.

(xii) *Front cover catch.*—Press the plug, in the end of the catch arm, inward with a screwdriver, give a quarter turn and slowly release, when the plug will be forced out by the spring ; turn the plunger to clear the lugs in the arm and remove.

Remove the split keeper pin and catch from the cover.

Note.—The catch can be removed as a single unit without removing the other details if desired.

(xiii) *Rear crosspiece.*—Remove the split keeper pin, unscrew the check nut and press out the joint pin.

Note.—The note to (xi) applies here also.

(xiv) *Foresight.*—Carefully mark location of the sight in the dovetail and then drive out the sight through the right hand protecting wing of the bracket with a No. 3 punch.

(xv) *Steam tube.*—Remove the keeper screw and partly unscrew the tube, then remove the gun from the mounting, up-end the gun (rear end of the casing on protecting material on the ground) ; unscrew the tube and lift it out.

Note.—It is unnecessary to remove the tube when the sliding valve is free ; this can be ascertained by lifting the front and rear ends of the gun alternately, when the movement of the valve can be heard.

(xvi) *Sliding shutter.*—Place the gun casing underside up on a bench, press the catch inward, and push the shutter forward to the stop ; maintain pressure on the catch, press in the plunger with the No. 3 punch, and push out the shutter to the front.

(xvii) *Check lever.*—With the gun casing in position as for (xvi), drive out the keeper pin and remove the lever.

    Note.—This component must not be removed except for replacement purposes. It is sometimes necessary to drill the pin out owing to seizure, whilst in other cases the pin is liable to damage during removal. A little oil on the pin is helpful against seizure.

To Re-assemble the Gun

Reverse the foregoing sequence of operations.

When assembling the steam tube see that the slide valve is free, and the screwed head secure ; also that the acorn end is inserted into its socket on the inside face of the trunnion block ; the adjacent corrugation in the case of corrugated barrel casings forms a useful guide for locating the socket. The tube should screw home freely when correctly located.

After assembly, the slide valve should again be tested for freedom of operation—*see* note to (xv).

When assembling the barrel and side plates into the casings care must be taken to see that the bullet lead on the barrel face is above the chamber, also that the side plates are home on the barrel trunnions, as otherwise the parts will not enter the casings freely and damage may ensue.

The gland of the muzzle attachment must be screwed tightly home to the barrel casing, the packing being adjusted as necessary to enable this to be done. The split pin should be inserted in the lowest hole in the outer casing and gland ; when inserted in the top hole the connecting chain is liable to enter one of the gas vents in the outer casing and foul the muzzle cup.

The sliding shutter must be open when the lock is assembled.

To Strip and Re-assemble Details of Component Parts

To strip the feed block.—Force out the split pin fixing the top and bottom levers ; separate the levers by driving out the hexagonal stem of the bottom lever from the top lever, and remove the slide ; draw out the bottom pawls axis pin and remove the spring and pawls.

Remove the top pawls from the fore and aft ends of the axis pin in the slide and press out the spring from the lug on the slide. The axis pin should not be removed unless unserviceable.

To re-assemble the feed block.—Reverse the foregoing sequence of operations, taking care to ensure that the top and bottom levers are assembled in correct co-relation and with the gap for the bottom lever in the extension of the left side plate of the gun, also that the split pin is assembled to the top and bottom levers from the top side of the block.

Note.—Care must be taken to avoid damage to the hexagonal portion of the stem of the bottom lever during assembly to the top lever, which should be substantially supported on the face around the stem hole when driving the stem home.

To strip the lock.—Cock, by pressing up the free end of the side levers. With a No. 5 punch or cupped end of a " T " fixing pin force out the split keeper pin and axis bush of the side levers ; remove the side levers and left and right extractors levers, and extractor ; ease the lock spring, by pressing the sear and trigger out of engagement, to release the firing pin ; push out the tumbler and trigger axis pins and remove the tumbler, trigger, lock spring, firing pin and sear with spring.

To strip the extractor.—Press or tap out the gib spring cover from the dovetailed groove, and remove the gib spring and gib.

To re-assemble the lock.—Reverse the foregoing sequence of operations, except in the case of the lock spring, which should be assembled last of all, when the lock is in the fired position, by forcing it downwards, the long arm to the front.

Note.—The firing pin should never be released in the completely assembled lock unless the extractor is up against the stop on the lock casing, as otherwise it may be damaged by contact with the inside face of the extractor.

To strip the rear crosspiece.—Unscrew the firing lever and safety catch axis pins and remove the firing lever with pawl and safety catch and piston with spring ; lift out the trigger bar lever.

To re-assemble the rear crosspiece.—Reverse the above order, taking care to ensure that the pawl on the firing lever engages the trigger bar lever.

To strip the roller.—Take out the split pin No. 2 (brass) or drive out the No. 1 pin (steel) from the collar and remove the collar and roller.

To re-assemble the roller.—Reverse the above order.

To strip the tangent sight, Mk. III**, and slide, Mk. II**.— Unscrew the upper graduated plate screw from the stem and remove the slide, care being taken to prevent loss of the friction spring. If necessary, for replacement purposes, the graduated plate can be removed by removing the lower screw.

Take out the split pin from the slide screw, unscrew the clamping nut and remove the right-hand portion of the slide, washer and pinion.

Note.—The slide should be stripped only when it is necessary to do so for thorough cleaning or replacement purposes. Care should then be taken to prevent the parts from becoming mixed with parts of other slides in order to avoid adjustment, etc., on re-assembly.

To re-assemble the tangent sight.—Reverse the foregoing order, and do not omit the friction spring.

To strip the sliding shutter.—Hold the shutter in a vice, drive out the catch pin with the No. 5 drift, withdraw the drift and at the same time support the catch to prevent it from flying out ; then remove the catch with spring and plunger.

To re-assemble the sliding shutter.—Hold in vice, insert the plunger and spring, introduce the catch and insert drift ; before re-assembling the pin remove burrs and straighten if necessary or fit a fresh pin ; then press in the catch to overcome spring pressure and insert and drive in the pin, which should follow up as the drift is withdrawn ; test to see that the catch and plunger work freely, rivet the pin over slightly to secure it, lubricate and again test catch and plunger.

To remove the crank handle and the crank from right side plate.—Unscrew crank handle fixing pin, support inside the face of the crank handle, close to the axis, on two suitable steel plates across the jaws of a vice, place a small flat piece of brass on the end of the crank, and, with a stout drift, drive out the crank handle and remove the side plate.

The crank pin can be removed from the crank after driving out the fixing pin.

Note.—The crank handle should be removed only for re-browning or when replacement is necessary.

To re-assemble the crank handle.—Place the right side plate on the crank, hold the crank vertically, resting the fusee end suitably protected on a block, drive on the crank handle, protecting the outer face as necessary, and screw in a fixing pin.

Section 3.—Cleaning, etc.

The instructions of a general nature for cleaning and oiling contained in Chapter I, Section 3, apply to the Vickers ·303-inch machine guns also. Therefore the following instructions have reference only to the parts of this gun which require special mention.

Barrel.—In addition to the cleaning of the bore and chamber, the external surfaces should be kept clean and oiled and free from rust, more especially at the front and rear bearings, to ensure free sliding in the bearings of the barrel casing.

The bearings must not be filed or otherwise reduced in diameter, as such reduction is liable to affect accuracy of shooting. When it is necessary to remove any roughness which may have developed, a piece of worn fine emery cloth only should be employed for the purpose. When the gun is standing by for a time the water in the barrel casing should be drawn off and the external surfaces of the barrel lightly coated with mineral jelly ; the screwed and cork plugs should be removed in order to avoid condensation of moisture in the casing ; also the front and rear packing should be removed and thoroughly dried and oiled before being again used.

The " D.P.B." barrel employed for firing blank ammunition is to be cleaned similarly, special attention to be given to the cleaning of the mouth of the choke bush at the front end of the chamber, which is liable to become corroded. No attempt should be made to clean the ·303-inch bore in advance of the bush, as this may lead to the bush, which is slightly tapered and driven home from the breech to a shoulder, being loosened.

Lock.—Particular care must be taken with those parts which come into direct contact with the propellant gases, *e.g.* the face of the extractor, the gib and the firing pin. The gib spring, firing pin channel in the extractor and lock casing, and the other internal parts of the lock are also liable to become affected by the gases. Boiling water as used for barrels should be employed whenever possible for washing such parts, which should be dealt with in detail after stripping the lock. It is essential that the lock be kept thoroughly clean and well oiled with G.S. oil. Mineral jelly, with which the locks are preserved when issued from store, must be entirely removed before the locks are put into use, as its presence will make the action sluggish and may cause stoppages in firing.

Feed block.—Steel blocks and the steel parts of gunmetal blocks must be kept free from rust and all working parts clean and oiled.

Other working parts.—All other working surfaces such as the lock guides of the side plates and rear cover, the trigger bar, crank axis, crank pin, ramps of rear cover, axes of parts jointed to the rear crosspiece, axis of check lever, rear cover lock and front cover catch, roller and left and right slides should be kept clean and oiled.

Muzzle-attachment.—Fouling, which is principally metallic, similar to that found in the bore of barrels, must be removed ; it usually adheres very firmly to the muzzle cup and disc on the front cone, and has to be chipped off. When carrying out this operation, care must be taken not to damage or cut the parts, as when so cut, fouling will subsequently occur more rapidly ; for this reason the surfaces should be left as smooth as possible. When the thin metal disc which is provided to protect the inside face of the front cone is badly fouled, it should be removed and replaced. As it is liable to become set in its position, it will usually be necesssary either to drive it off or split it with a chisel to relieve the outer wall, in which case care must be taken to avoid damage to the thread of the front cone.

The parts should be washed in boiling water whenever possible, then dried and very lightly oiled.

The muzzle cup, adjusting screw and front cone for blank firing are also to be kept clean and lightly oiled ; the fouling in these parts is a carbon deposit and therefore more easily removed.

External surfaces of guns.—Should be wiped clean and unpainted surfaces with an oily rag.

Spare parts and accessories.—These should be cleaned and oiled when the guns are dealt with, and put back into their receptacles in proper order.

Care of the gun in frosty weather.—Guns will not usually be filled with water when handed to the armourer, but when owing to exceptional circumstances they are so handed over, the water should be emptied out. If glycerine or glycerine residue has been added to the water (this should be ascertained) the mixture should be preserved and the casing refilled with it before re-issue.

Section 4.—Examination of the Gun, etc.

These instructions are for general guidance. Circumstances may arise which may necessitate a change in the sequence of examination.

(i) *General.*—See that the gun is unloaded, and remove the lock. Record the gun number (on top of trunnion block). Examine the gun generally for external damage and for fracture, especially observing—the junction of the trunnion block and breech casing, check lever and its bracket, and the front lower corner of side plate guide gap in the rear end of the right outside plate of the breech casing ; condition and fit of screwed and cork plugs and their connections, condenser boss thread and protector, or adapter, whichever is fitted. Where there is any suspicion or indication of leakage of steam or water from the barrel casing, ascertain whether any such leakage has been observed and act accordingly (*see* Section 5). The spare parts supplied with each gun should be examined and applied where necessary during examination in detail to ensure that they are fit for use.

(ii) *Mounting joints.*—Select the largest joint pins available on a Mk. IV tripod mounting (maximum sizes ·56 and ·44 inch) and insert them in the joint pin holes to see that the holes are not excessively worn. Limit gauges are provided for the use of Assistant Inspectors of Armourers and C.I.S.A.'s Examiners, who will give sentence in such cases.

(iii) *Covers, front and rear.*—Examine for fit at the joints, for security and freedom from movement at locked ends, for excessive wear of extractor stop of front cover, and fracture on either side of that stop. Examine also the condition of the ramps of rear cover, and of the trigger bar and spring and the rear cover lock and spring.

Note.—Where the cover joint is very slack, due to wear of the holes in the outside plates, the gun should be reported for exchange—factory repair.

(iv) *Sights.*—Examine the foresight for condition, and test for security in the dovetail of the bracket ; the tangent sight for condition and fit at joint, the slide for free movement and firm clamping, and when of Mk. II** pattern that it is complete with friction spring and washer. See that the axis screw is home and that it does not rotate with the stem, also that the stem is firmly held in both horizontal and vertical positions by the piston and spring.

(v) *Shutter, sliding.*—Test for free sliding and for security in the closed and open positions, also that the catch and plunger operate freely, and that the parts are clean. If the shutter does not slide freely, examine the bottom plate of the gun, which may have been indented by the end of the connecting rod after removal of the lock.

(vi) *Muzzle attachment.*—Test the fixing pin for security, and the outer casing for fit on the gland during removal ; unscrew the muzzle cup and examine the screw threads in the cup end on the barrel ; see that the cup is free from fouling. If the disc on the front cone is badly fouled, re-assemble the outer casing and fixing pin to the gland, unscrew the front cone, replace the disc with a new one, and re-assemble. The details special for blank firing should be similarly examined. For the adjustment necessary when assembling these details, *see* Section 5.

(vii) *Block, feed.*—Test the action of the levers by operating the recoiling portions ; insert a few dummy cartridges in the belt, see that the top or feed pawls carry the first cartridge up to the stop when the recoiling portions are home, also that the bottom pawls act on the adjacent cartridge and prevent the belt from falling out when the top pawls are disengaged.

Remove from the gun, examine the pawls and springs for wear and action, and the cartridge guides, belt surfaces and stops for excessive wear or damage. Test the tension of the top pawls spring by applying the " tester trigger " to the end of each thumbpiece—$1\frac{1}{2}$ to $2\frac{1}{2}$ lb. to start. Test the bottom pawls spring by applying the tester to the extremity of the tie piece—$1\frac{1}{2}$ to $2\frac{1}{2}$ lb. to start.

(viii) *Box, fusee spring.*—Remove with the spring ; examine lugs of the box for distortion, the spring for security on the nut and hook, and for condition ; see that the adjusting screw and vice pin are in good order, and that the studs and mounting stop on the left side of the casing are firmly secured.

(ix) *Recoiling portions.*—Remove from the gun, and detach and examine the parts, giving special attention to the lock guides and springs on side plates, ends of recess in extension of left side plate, the condition and fit of connecting rod on the crank pin, the crank handle on the crank and the fusee in the crank.

Remove burrs where present.

(x) *Tube, steam.*—Test for free sliding of valve by inclining muzzle end of gun upwards and downwards, when the movement should be heard as the valve makes contact with the end fitting of the tube. When not free, the tube must be removed and cleaned, and, if bent, straightened with the rawhide mallet, care being taken to avoid damage and distortion.

(xi) *Barrel.*—Examine externally, special attention being given to see that the bearings are smooth and the screw thread for the muzzle cup undamaged, the trunnion block free from damage and burrs, that it is bevelled at the upper and lower edges of the breech face to clear the extractor levers, and that the bullet lead to mouth of chamber is cut in the breech face (*see* Section 5).

Examine internally for condition and wear. When badly worn in lead and bore, report for accuracy test in accordance with Equipment Regulations, Part I. See that the chamber is clean and undamaged, and that sound dummy cartridges enter freely.

" D.P.B." barrels should be similarly examined externally. Internally the chamber and bush only are of consequence. In order to check the location of the bush, obtain a blank cartridge case which has been fired in a barrel little used and ease the outside down until it enters the chamber freely; if this case enters up to its rim the location of the bush is correct; if it does not, the bush has probably been driven backward by a cleaning rod, in which case the barrel must be exchanged.

When erratic firing has been reported with a barrel, it should be set aside for gauging by the A.I.A. or C.I.S.A.'s Examiners—the limit is reached when a ·167-inch gauge passes through the bush.

If the barrel is satisfactory, grease internally, repack the cannelure if necessary and re-assemble; if necesssary repack the gland and then work the parts backwards and forwards to seat the bearings and ensure retention of water in the barrel casing. With cord of spring balance applied to the boss of crank handle test the weight to move— 4 lb. for ball ammunition, 2 lb. for blank ammunition. When fresh packing is being inserted it is usually necessary to pack a little tighter to allow for working down, *e.g.* 6 lb. for ball ammunition and $2\frac{1}{2}$ lb. for blank. For fuller details of packing, *see* Section 5.

Re-assemble the muzzle attachment, apply mirror reflector to the chamber and see that the bullet exit is in alignment with the bore of barrel.

Should barrels be found unnumbered on the trunnion block, application will be made to the A.I.A. for numbers, which, on receipt, will be stamped on the upper surface of the trunnion block with the $\frac{5}{64}$-inch stamps.

Note.—Worn out Service and D.P.B. barrels which are in good condition externally will be returned to R.A.O.C. store.

(xii) *Lock.*—Examine internally, especially for damage at the upper right side of the cartridge guide of the extractor and fracture at the extractor stop on the casing. Test the action by cocking the lock by hand, seeing that the point of the firing pin is withdrawn—if broken, the point will remain forward—and that it does not friction in the extractor ; also that the trigger engages the tumbler before the bent of the sear engages the firing pin. Then slowly hinge down the side levers to press the sear out of engagement with the firing pin, carefully observing at the same time that the bents of the side levers lift the extractor right up to the stop of the casing when the sear disengages ; on releasing the trigger, the firing pin should be propelled forward freely by the lock spring.

When extractor and extractor levers of No. 1 pattern are fitted, see that the arms of the side levers confine the extractor levers sufficiently to prevent them from riding down over the lower ledges on the sides of extractor ; if they do ride over, the lock must be exchanged, as friction so set up may cause a cartridge to be exploded in the feed block if a first position stoppage occurs.

Apply the rim of the ·064-inch gauge right through the cartridge grooves in the extractor, and see that it depresses the gib and is held firmly in the recess in the gib. A dummy cartridge with rim of minimum thickness—·058 inch—should also be similarly held. Test the weight of the gib spring—4 to 6 lb.—by depressing the gib with a rod applied to a trigger tester.

Test the weight of pull to move the side levers when in the cocked position—12 to 14 lb.—with the cord of the spring balance applied at the connecting rod end of the levers.

If the lock is satisfactory in the above respects, place it in position in the gun, leave the covers raised, and test the cocking action by pulling the crank handle back very slowly when the trigger and subsequently the sear are about to engage, in order to detect their respective engagements. Slowly reverse the crank movement and observe the lift of the extractor and release of the sear.

Lower the rear cover, carry out the firing action, raise the rear cover and see that the tail of the tumbler is not bearing hard on the side levers.

The spare lock should be similarly examined and tested. For examination in detail strip each lock and proceed as follows, giving special attention to any points found to be defective in the foregoing examination and tests.

Casing, lock.—Examine for fracture at the extractor stop and for distortion ; axis bush hole and pin holes for excessive wear and sear axis pin for security. When the casing is unserviceable the complete lock must be exchanged.

Note.—Excessive wear in the axis bush hole and pin holes may affect the lift of the extractor to the stop and the time of engagement of the bents.

Should any locks be found unnumbered, application should be made to the A.I.A. for numbers, which, on receipt, should be stamped on the underside of the lock casings with the $\frac{5}{64}$-inch stamps.

Extractor.—Place on the casing, insert the firing pin, and check protrusion by comparison with a new spare firing pin if available ; the thickness of rim of the ·064-inch gauge may also be taken as an approximate guide. When protrusion is obviously excessive, either the shoulders of the firing pin or the seating in the lock casing is worn ; when short, look for an obstruction. The point of the firing pin must not be adjusted, as interchange of pins would thereby be affected. Exchange of the defective part is the remedy.

See that the size of the firing pin hole is not excessive—a piece of wire ·088-inch diameter should not pass through—and that burrs on the lower side ledges of the No. 1 extractors are removed.

Levers, side, and extractor.—Examine for fracture, and see that burrs are removed. In cases where the extractor was not held well up to the stop in the assembled lock, the spare extractor levers should be assembled for comparison. When the side levers are at fault the complete lock must be exchanged.

Tumbler.—Examine for fracture and for wear and damage at the bent, firing pin head, and tail.

Sear and trigger.—Examine for fracture, wear and damage at the bent, and set and tension of the sear spring.

Gib and spring.—Examine for fracture and condition.

Bush, axis, side levers and pins, various.—Examine for general condition. Wear can usually be detected readily, but when in doubt compare with corresponding spare parts in the major part of the lock.

Finally, re-assemble the lock, insert into the gun and test cartridge head space—·064 inch—with the longest lock (gun or spare) and adjust as necessary (*see* Section 5).

(xiii) Complete the re-assembly of the gun, carrying out the following examination and tests whilst so doing.

Test the bearing of the crank on the crank stops of side plates by inserting a piece of cigarette paper, or the like, between crank and stops, where it should be held firmly; at the same time lightly rock the check lever to see that it is not then in contact with the crank handle. The object of this test is to ensure that the blow is taken by the stops and not by the check lever. Ascertain also that wear and lateral movement of the check lever are not such as to cause the lever to jam on the side of the bracket.

See that the screw thread on the " T " fixing pin has a secure hold in the thread of the rear crosspiece, and that the roller on the right slide is clear of the tail of the crank handle when the recoiling parts are home. This clearance may vary somewhat owing to varying combinations of manufacturing limits; the minimum clearance can be determined by a No. 2 washer (·005-inch).

Finally ascertain that all fixing pins are secure and that the gun is complete and in working order.

(xiv) *D.P. and skeleton guns.*—D.P., and also skeleton guns where on authorized charge, will be examined to see that the projecting point of the firing pin is removed, and that they function mechanically and are otherwise in a condition suitable for instructional purposes. Finish is of no importance, but the guns should be kept as free as possible from rust. D.P. locks are coppered for ready identification.

(xv) *Accessories.*—Examine generally for serviceability.

Belts, ammunition.—Carefully overhaul for soundness of fabric, security of strips and alignment of long strips; the pockets should be tested for size with dummy cartridges.

To clean a dirty or greasy belt, soak it for two hours in a solution containing 1 part soda, 3 parts soft soap, and 10 parts water. The belt should then be scrubbed and hung up to dry. When dry the pockets should be plugged.

Boxes, belt, ammunition, Nos. 7, 8 and 9.—See that the sides are not distorted to an extent such as will prevent the belt from moving freely, and that the lid joints, fastenings, lid linings and straps are in good order. When the tab provided for holding the left half lid open is unserviceable, it will not be replaced (*see* Section 5).

Boxes, cases and wallets for spare parts and tools. —See that they are in good order and have their complete contents.

Foresight, bar, deflection.—Assemble to the gun, and see that it is securely held and that the bar is at right angles to the tangent sight when the latter is up. It is desirable, in view of the occasional necessity for setting the foresight protecting wings of the gun to obtain horizontal alignment of the bar, to keep each sight to its own gun where possible.

Condenser, steam.—Assemble the joint on the flexible metallic tube to the gun and see that the cone seats closely in the cone of the steam escape hole of the gun; this can be ascertained by blacking the cone and observing the bearing marks. Closely examine the tube at its junction with the joint for fracture, also the remainder of the tube for damage and fracture.

Examine the condenser bag where supplied and fill it overnight about half full with water. It is difficult to maintain these bags watertight, therefore, provided the leakage is not found to have been unduly excessive by the next morning—say more than one-third of the contents—the bag may be considered serviceable.

Petrol cans, where supplied, should be tested for leakage, and their fitments, *i.e.* wire clip-on handle, brass filler with connecting chain, etc., and shackle securing the cap of the can, examined for condition and security. When distorted, the nozzle of the filler should be applied in the filling hole of the gun to ensure that it is fit for use. To avoid damage, the tubing must not be left on the gun during transit.

Sights, night.—See that the spring arms of the foresight and spring clip of the backsight are not fractured or distorted and that they are securely fixed by the screws. Apply the foresight to the foresight bracket of the gun, and also to the sliding sight of the deflection bar foresight, to see that it is securely held in position. Also apply the backsight to the tangent sight slide of the gun as a like test.

Section 5.—Repairs, Modifications and Adjustments.

Note.—For parts which, when unserviceable, necessitate the sending of the gun to store for exchange or factory repair, *see* E.R., Pt. I.

The annual allowance of parts for repair of guns is as laid down in Equipment Regulations.

The spare parts belonging to the gun are not to be drawn upon to replace gun parts until the annual allowance of parts has been used up. When it is necessary to draw upon the spares, indents must at once be put forward for replacement.

Parts, other than those referred to, which may be required for replacement purposes will be indented for as necessary.

(i) *To test and adjust cartridge head space.*—Remove the fusee spring box with spring, raise the rear cover, turn back the crank handle to cock the lock, insert from the underside of the gun the ·064-inch gauge in the extractor over the firing pin hole, hold it there, and at the same time push the extractor right up, see that the barrel is home and then turn the crank handle gently forward and guide the gauge into the chamber. If no check is felt on the crank handle with the gun lock before the crank is home on the side plates, repeat the test with the spare lock; if still no check, add washers as required on the outer face of the adjusting nut of the connecting rod until a slight check is felt with the longest of the two locks, and then assemble the required washers between the nut and shoulder of the connecting rod, seeing that the nut is screwed tightly home with the combination tool.

Re-test to ensure that adjustment is correct. The resistance offered during the release of the sear must be borne in mind when carrying out this test.

As the maximum thickness of the service cartridge rim is also ·064 inch, the check felt on the gauge must not be excessive.

(ii) *To weigh and adjust fusee spring.*—Remove the lock, place the loop of the spring balance over the knob of the crank handle, and, resting the arm on the rear cover, pull the balance vertically upward. Note the weight, which should be between 7 and 9 lb. for ball ammunition and 4½ lb. for blank, when the crank handle just moves from rest.

Adjust as necessary by turning the vice pin of the adjusting screw clockwise (looking from rear of gun), to reduce weight, and vice versa to increase weight. Six clicks—three revolutions—make a difference of approximately 1 lb.

(iii) *To repack cannelure of barrel and gland.*—If the cannelure is rusty, clean with paraffin and lightly oil with G.S. oil ; wind an oiled length of about 16 inches of the asbestos packing, supplied as spare with each gun, evenly around the cannelure, pressing it close with a thin piece of hard wood or other convenient means as winding proceeds, until the space is filled, then oil and smooth down until it is nearly flush with the outer periphery of the barrel.

Assemble the barrel and recoiling portions to the gun, seeing that the packing is not rucked and that it is a good fit in the bearing.

To repack the gland after the muzzle-attachment gland has been unscrewed and the old packing removed, oil a length of about 30 inches of the packing and wind it loosely but evenly around the barrel, pressing it into the seating, as winding proceeds, by any convenient means. Screw the gland in by hand to compress the packing, when correctly packed the gland should not screw right home, a little draw being left for final tightening up with the combination tool after the packing has been well seated by the following operation.

Turn the crank handle upward and, holding it with the right hand and the fusee with the left, work the recoiling portions backward and forward to settle the packing, until the weight to move when tested by spring balance looped on to the axis boss of the crank handle is about 6 lb. for ball ammunition and 2½ lb. for blank ; this allows for subsequent running in, down to the regulation weights of 4 lb. and 2 lb. respectively.

It is essential that the gland be screwed home tightly up to the end cap of the barrel casing. Removed packing which is in a serviceable condition should be preserved for use again by hanging it up to dry; several short lengths can be used for packing either the cannelure or gland.

(iv) *To fit a spare disc to muzzle-attachment.*—Unscrew the front cone; with a sharp chisel cut the periphery of the unserviceable disc in line with the axis, prize up the metal, where cut, to provide a hold for the pliers, and withdraw.

When fitting the fresh disc it may be found necessary to tap it on.

Care should be taken when screwing in the front cone to see that the edge of the disc does not foul the thread in the outer casing of the attachment.

(v) *To adjust foresight.*—This is usually carried out by a qualified machine gunner on the range, but if the armourer is called upon to carry it out he should first mark the existing location of the foresight before altering its position, and take care to support the bracket when tapping the blade over.

Moving the blade to the right will throw the shots to the left, and vice versa.

·01 inch represents about one inch on the target per each 100 yards range.

Only one height of foresight is provided; if the elevation is found to be greatly in error at short ranges—200 to 400 yards—alignment of the barrel and breech casings may have been disturbed, in which case the attention of the A.I.A. or C.I.S.A.'s Examiners should be specially called to the gun when they visit the unit.

(vi) *To remedy distortion of outer casing of muzzle-attachment.*—Such distortion, which may be caused by a blow, occurs at the bayonet joint end and is liable to affect concentricity of the bullet exit with the bore of the barrel. The mirror reflector when inserted in the barrel chamber will shew up any serious eccentricity, but it is desirable that armourers should provide for their use a plug of sufficient length which will fit the bore of the barrel and pass through the bullet exit hole in the front cone. Provided the plug is smoothly finished it need not be hardened, but should be tested periodically for straightness. The outer casing can be corrected by gripping the prominent portion in a vice or setting it by means of hard wood blocks shaped to conform to the curvature.

(vii) *To remove a barrel bulged in front of gland.*—Remove the outer casing and muzzle cup of muzzle-attachment and file off the enlarged portion. Remove the unserviceable barrel, replace it with a serviceable barrel, and re-assemble the muzzle cup and outer casing.

Note.—When the bulge is covered by the gland extension it will be necessary to cut the extension off in order to obtain access to the bulge.

(viii) *To repair a barrel casing perforated by bullets, etc.*— In the event of the barrel casing being pierced by bullets, etc., the gun being thus put out of action, repairs will be carried out in accordance with the following methods to enable the gun again to take its place in the firing line with the least possible delay :—

(a) Temporary " first aid " repairs.
(b) Semi-permanent repair.

(a) A pad of luting, preferably wrapped in a piece of flannelette or cloth to prevent it from being squeezed through the hole or holes, is pressed over the latter and covered with an oiled pad of flannelette. The whole is then bound round with flannelette folded in two to increase its strength, the flannelette being tied to make it fast. This, whilst not preventing leakage entirely, should do so sufficiently to enable the gun to be kept in action.

(b) The jagged edges of each hole should be hammered level with the casing and the casing cleaned around the hole. A piece of sheet tin, DXX (·02 inch thick), sufficient to overlap the hole considerably, should then be shaped, by means of a hammer and a piece of hard wood, to conform to the shape of the barrel casing, and to fit evenly over the hole. It should then be soldered in position. This, when done properly, makes a thoroughly sound repair.

When the front of the end cap is pierced it may be found possible to plug it temporarily with a piece of wood. For a more permanent repair a piece of the sheet tin can be soldered on.

Materials allowed are detailed in E.R., Pt. I.

(ix) *Barrels, Mk. II—Modifications.*—Barrels which have unlightened trunnion blocks, *i.e.* not recessed at the upper and lower surfaces, and which are not already bevelled as shown at B, B in Fig. 1, will be so bevelled in order to ensure clearance for the front end of the extractor levers. The portions A, A, shown in dotted lines, will be removed by filing, the barrel being held in a vice.

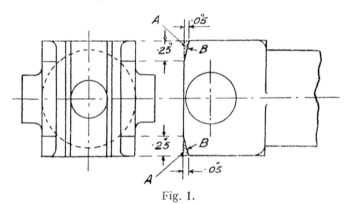

Fig. 1.

Where the bullet lead in the breech face, to prevent the possibility of the bullet of a cartridge becoming lodged or checked on the breech face during feed into chamber, has not already been cut, it should be made by filing, in accordance with Fig. 2. Care must be taken not to damage the chamber or to cut the lead deeper than shown ; excessive depth will cause the cartridge to bulge or burst owing to the removal of chamber wall support. The lead should be finished smoothly with fine emery cloth. Damage to the opposite wall of the chamber can be avoided by protecting it with a fired cartridge case suitably sectioned. The portion of the breech face opposite to that marked with the letters " S.C."—which denote enlarged small cone of chamber—only is to be so modified, and after modification this becomes the top side for assembly into the gun.

(x) *Block, feed—Repair, etc.*—When the acting end of the top pawls is worn, the serrations can be touched up by filing, provided the pawls are not shortened to an extent which will affect functioning (*see* Section 4). The slight rounding off of the bottom edge must be maintained ; if left sharp it is liable to catch the brass strip, and also to tear the fabric of the belt. It will rarely be found necessary to touch the acting end of the bottom pawls, but if

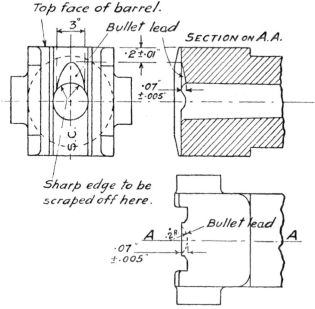

Fig. 2.

there is a tendency for the belt to slip back, the end of each pawl and the height of projection into the opening should receive attention.

The bottom pawls are issued in pairs as one unit with tie-piece or finger plate, and will be dealt with as such.

When the top pawls fail to carry the cartridge well into the feed position the fault may be due either to wear or play in the top and bottom levers, wear of the rear end of the recess of the extension of the left-hand side plate, short top pawls or to a combined effect of two or more of these features.

Where the defect cannot be traced by exchange and trial of parts from correct feed blocks, the defective feed block will be exchanged (factory repair).

Feed blocks marked with a star in the upper recess above the rear cartridge guide have a clearance of ·01 inch on the stop to allow a slight

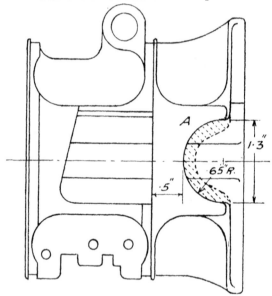

Portion of top part of feed block A
shewn by cross dotted lines,

to be removed.

Fig. 3.

overdraft of the cartridge and so relieve pressure on the right guide of the extractor. This clearance is cut only during factory repair.

Omission of this clearance does not necessitate exchange.

Modifications—Enlargement of thumb clearance.— Where not already enlarged this is to be carried out in accordance with Fig. 3 to facilitate access to the top pawls.

Bevelling of left side of slide.—Where not already done it is to be carried out in accordance with Fig. 4 to provide a lead when the slide passes under the left bridge of the block. The right upper edge of the top lever should also be slightly bevelled to prevent it from fouling the edge of the right bridge of the block under which it passes.

(xi) *Casings, barrel and breech.*

(a) *Bracket, check lever—Instructions for fitting.*— The Mk. I bracket for breech casing plates of lightened pattern requires only to be securely riveted on by means of the two upper and two

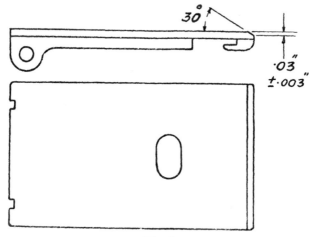

Fig. 4.

lower rivets provided. The bracket must seat closely on the rib of the plate to ensure that the rib takes the stress when the crank handle strikes the check lever; the stress must not be on the rivets. The Mk. II bracket for breech casing plates of unlightened pattern has two studs, which engage in holes in the plate and take the stress referred to. These studs should be a good fit in the holes. The rivets are identical with those for the Mk. I bracket.

A certain number of guns with unlightened breech casing plates were fitted with a bracket of Mk. II type, but with only one stud on the seating face ; these brackets are liable to work loose, and when they are met with during repair, they will be replaced by the Mk. II bracket with two studs. To enable this to be fitted locally the following tools will be supplied on loan, upon demand, for the boring of the second stud hole required :—

Drill   1
Jig   1   with two $\frac{1}{8}$-inch bolts, each with nut.
Rimer 1
Drill, stock, breast 1

The jig will be positioned by the existing stud hole in the breech casing of the gun, and by the two $\frac{1}{8}$-inch bolts, which will be assembled in two of the existing rivet holes. Care must be taken to see that the drill is correctly ground in order that it shall not drill too large for the rimer.

After the Mk. I or Mk. II bracket has been securely fitted, the bearing of the crank on the crank stops of the side plates must be tested in accordance with para. xiii, Section 4, and the check lever adjusted if necessary (*see* para. xiv).

(b) *Bracket, foresight.*—When loose, the gun must be exchanged (factory repair). When the protecting wings are damaged—bent—they should be carefully reset, care being taken to support the bracket to prevent it from becoming loose.

In the event of the deflection bar foresight not seating correctly when assembled to the wings, the latter should be set sufficiently to bring the bar level.

(c) *Cams.*—These may be either solid with or riveted to the outside plates ; where riveted, and they become loose and cannot be tightened, the gun should be exchanged (factory repair). Where the stops for the horns of the extractor are damaged or liable to cause the horns to slip they should be carefully adjusted by means of a short portion of a smooth pillar file.

(d) *Indentation of bottom plate.*—Where such affects the travel of the sliding shutter, the plate must be suitably supported on the inside and the dent carefully hammered out.

(e) *Mounting stop.*—When slightly loose the stop can usually be tightened by punching up the rivets, but when very loose it will be necessary to remove the rivets and fit fresh rivets, which should be obtained locally. A round nail of suitable size will make an efficient rivet.

(f) *Rear cover seating ledges on breech casing.*—Any burrs or other damage to these ledges should be carefully removed ; in addition to forming a seating for the cover, and so controlling the height of the tangent sight axis, they are employed as a base for the M.G. clinometer.

The ledges referred to are those below the upper edges of the casing.

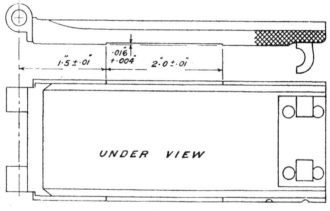

Fig. 5.

(g) *Studs, fusee spring box.*—In most guns access is given to the riveted end of both studs for tightening or replacement, on the inside face of the left outside plate, but in some guns access to the end of the front stud is not provided. In such cases the stud must be soldered in, care being taken to use an anti-rust flux and apply heat within as small an area as possible.

(xii) *Cover, front—Modification to clear top lever of feed block.*—In order to ensure clearance for the travel of this lever when vertical " play " of top and bottom levers is present, clearance will be filed in the under edges in accordance with Fig. 5.

(xiii) *Cover, rear.*—When fitting a new stud for rear cover lock spring, it must be ascertained, before riveting the end over the upper surface of the cover, that the space for the prongs of the spring is right and that the acting end of the spring is correctly located on the cover lock. A snap head should be produced, when riveting the stud, to ensure security.

When smoothing ramps, care must be taken to avoid excessive removal of metal, as such removal will increase the space between the rear end of the cams in the breech casing and the extractor horn contact point on the ramps, and tend to produce explosion of a round in the feed block when a late first position stoppage occurs.

A slack joint, due to lateral wear, can be tightened by assembling a rifle inner band spring washer under the head of the joint pin.

(xiv) *Lever, check.*—When the crank handle bears hard on this lever instead of the crank on the crank stops of the side plates, and there is no evidence of distortion of the crank handle, the check lever must be eased off by filing the bearing until it has the requisite freedom. The crank handle must not be filed ; if distorted it must be exchanged (factory repair).

If the check lever has excessive lateral movement on the stud of the bracket, demand and fit a No. 2 " S " check lever which is supplied with a keeper pin.

The axis hole in this lever is ·002-inch smaller than in the normal check lever. When fitting the No. 2 " S " lever, it may be necessary to adjust the stud on the bracket with a smooth file and emery cloth to remedy irregularity due to wear.

No. 2 and No. 2 " S " levers, when unserviceable owing to wear in the axis hole, are to be returned to Store for factory repair.

(xv) *Lock—Repair, etc.*—Other than the replacement of defective parts, there is little, beyond the removal of burrs, which is within the armourer's province. On no account must adjustment be made which would be liable to affect interchange of the parts, which are carefully gauged in detail before issue. The normal sequence of stripping and assembly should be followed when replacing parts. In the case of a lock spring where the broken parts fall, or can be shaken out, another spring can be assembled without stripping the lock.

In the event of a breakage occurring which prevents the withdrawal of the lock in the gun, *e.g.* the spring lug of the firing pin partly broken and jammed under the ledge of the spring seating in the lock casing, so preventing withdrawal of the firing pin by the tumbler, it will be necessary to remove the recoiling portions in order to obtain access to the lock.

When the upper end of the cartridge guide of the extractor—usually the right side—is found damaged and burred, it should be carefully smoothed where possible without further reducing its strength. Such damage is generally due to bad faults in feed caused by badly filled belts and excessively heavy blows on the crank handle during attempts to clear such stoppages. When such damage is found, armourers should endeavour to ascertain the cause with a view to calling attention to the matter.

Many extractors have been damaged beyond repair during setting up of such stoppages for practice purposes. When the horns of the extractor become damaged and burred, and smoothing is necessary, care must be taken to maintain their form in order that they may rest securely on the stops of the cams in the breech casing, move up or down in front of those cams without undue friction, and act smoothly on the ramps of the rear cover.

Modification of No. 1 gibs to No. 2 pattern.—The modification consists of a reduction and alteration in profile of the front face, and is made in order to reduce friction on the cartridge, and to prolong the life of the gib and gib spring. An Instructional Print, A.I.D. 1914B and the gauge illustrated on the print are supplied upon demand, as required, to enable the modification to be carried out.

The modification is carried out in Home Service in R.S.A.F. and R.A.O.C. Command Workshops.

When too hard to file, the gibs must not be annealed and rehardened locally, but must be exchanged for modification in R.S.A.F. The modification does not affect interchange in locks.

(xvi) *Plates, side, left and right—Fitting of new springs.*—
Before finally riveting on new springs, it should be

ascertained by trial that the set is such as will ensure correct functioning on the stop ledges of the extractor without causing undue friction. The effect can best be ascertained by assembling the recoiling portions together and placing them on a flat surface. If any adjustment in set is required, it should be made preferably at the base after removal from the side plate, care being taken to avoid fracture when setting. The object of the springs is to retain the extractor in its uppermost location, when the gun is not loaded, until such time as the horns reach the cams in the breech casing.

(xvii) *Rear crosspiece.—Adjustment to ensure correct action of the trigger bar on the trigger of the lock.* When excessive lift of the safety catch unduly restricts the forward movement of the firing lever, and in so doing reduces the movement of the trigger bar lever, the rear crosspiece will be adjusted in accordance with Fig. 6. A set of ·03-inch is usually the maximum required and should not be exceeded, as there is then a risk of fracture. A suitable punch for the purpose will be made locally by the armourer.

Before making the adjustment it should be ascertained that the trigger bar lever, firing lever pawl, and trigger bar are in good order.

In the event of further adjustment being necessary, the upper end of the firing lever may be set outwards by placing the thumb-piece lever uppermost, on the open jaws of a vice and setting it down at the centre. To avoid damage some suitable material should be laid over the vice jaws.

Adjustment of rear cover lock catch hook ledges.— When the ledges are worn and the rear cover is not held closely down on to its seating ledges on the breech casing, the hook ledges should be adjusted by expanding—drawing down—the metal from above ; when doing this the inside face of the rear crosspiece must be solidly supported. The ledges will require final adjustment with a smooth file to ensure a good bearing. If possible some "draw" should be left on the catch to allow for subsequent wear.

(xviii) *Sight, tangent.—*

*Fitting of new pinion.—*The teeth of the new pinion may require slight adjustment at the edges to enable it to run freely along the rack; the edges should be left quite smooth after adjustment.

Securing upper fixing screw of graduated plate.— As this screw has a tendency to jar loose when it is not a tight fit in the stem, it can be tightened by

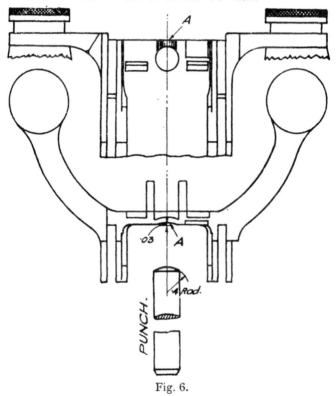

To be set at A.A. with punch, the set not to exceed ·03 inch.

Fig. 6.

expanding the end; to do this, place the screw head downwards on a metal block and lightly tap the small end with a hammer.

Nut, clamping slide, No. 2.—In cases where the outer edge of the thumb-piece is found to foul the crank handle when the sight is hinged down and the slide is in its most unfavourable position on the stem, the edge is to be filed back to clear the crank handle. The maximum amount of reduction necessary should not exceed ·05 inch.

When the nut fails to clamp the slide firmly, an additional washer may be inserted on the inside face of the slide. When the outward travel of the nut is excessive, so permitting the slide to become detached from the stem, one washer or more, as required, may be inserted between the nut and its keeper pin.

(xix) *Adjustment of muzzle-attachment details for blank ammunition.*—The special details for blank ammunition, which are assembled to the muzzle-attach-

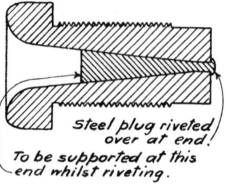

Steel plug riveted over at end.

To be supported at this end whilst riveting.

Fig. 7.

ment for ball ammunition, consist of the front cone, adjusting screw and nut and muzzle cup, the front cone and muzzle cup for ball ammunition being removed. The adjusting screw is assembled to the front cone from the inside end, and the nut on the outside. When assembled complete, the adjusting screw should first be screwed inward up to the muzzle cup until it is seen that the recoiling parts of the gun begin to move ; it should then be unscrewed $2\frac{1}{2}$ turns and locked in position by the nut. Under no circumstances should the screw be less than one turn back from the cup, as otherwise the attachment is liable to be forced off and damaged by the barrel when the latter expands lineally by heat.

Adjustment should be made in $\frac{1}{4}$ turns as required. When the Mk. I*, No. 1 or 2 adjusting screw is fitted it should rarely be necessary to adjust the screw closer than $2\frac{1}{2}$ turns from the cup.

Note.—The weight to move the recoiling portions of the gun should be reduced to 2 lb., and the weight of the fusee spring to $4\frac{1}{2}$ lb. when firing blank.

When the gun is fitted with the blank attachment details it cannot be placed in its chest unless the outer casing with its fitments is first removed.

On completion of blank firing the gun must be restored to its normal condition for ball firing.

(xx) *To convert a Mk. I adjusting screw for blank ammunition to Mk. I*, No. 2 pattern.*—The Mk. I, which has a through hole, is converted to Mk. I*, No. 2, by assembling a plug, supplied on demand from store, into the front portion of the hole from the rear end of the screw, and riveting over the projecting end at the front, as illustrated in Fig. 7. All Mk. I screws are to be so converted.

(xxi) *To fit adapter for steam condenser tube, pattern " B ", to gun.*—Referring to Fig. 8 : screw the adapter A as far as possible up to the shoulder of the condenser boss B of the gun by means of the combination tool supplied with the gun spares.

Test the position of the adapter by inserting the plug of test plug C (obtainable on loan from store) in the conical mouth of the steam outlet *d* of the gun, passing the two projections *e* of the cap through the open interruptions *f* in the adapter, and turning the cap until the projections engage the inner inclined interruptions *g*.

On pressing the conical end *h* of the test plug home in the outlet *d* and drawing the cap well back on the inclined interruptions *g*, the outside face *j* of the cap should be flush with the shoulder *k* of the test plug. If not flush, remove the adapter and file off sufficient from the small end to produce the required result. When satisfactory fix the adapter to the condenser boss by centre punching the smaller diameter of the adapter. When the condenser tube is available it should be tried on to see that assembly is satisfactory. When correctly assembled the full tension of the spring in the cap should be on the elbow joint, pressing the conical joint home into the mouth of the steam outlet of the gun, and the elbow joint should be free to turn in the gunmetal cap under spring tension, so that the tube can be inclined at any convenient angle in the plane of movement.

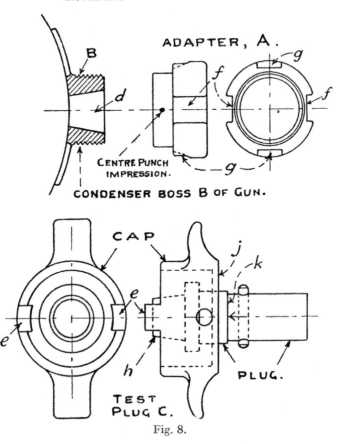

Fig. 8.

The spring in the cap should be greased occasionally with mineral jelly.

In order to maintain an efficient steam joint the conical end of the elbow joint must be free from burrs and distortion. The adapter will remain a permanent fixture on the gun, the condenser boss

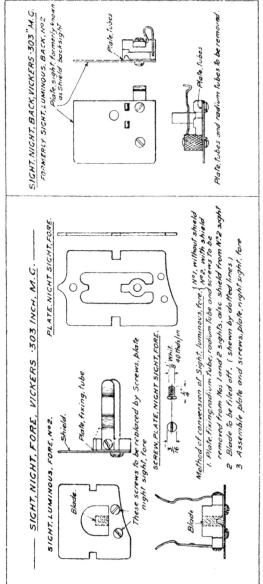

Fig. 9.

protector with chain and swivel being returned to store for disposal.

Accessories.—

(xxii) *Conversion of luminous sights to night sights.*—The conversion of luminous sights Nos. 1 and 2 to night sights, where not already done, will be carried out in accordance with Fig. 9.

The following parts of luminous sights not required in the conversion will be returned to store :—

Foresight.—Plate, fixing tubes and two screws ; shield (from No. 2 foresight) and radium tube.

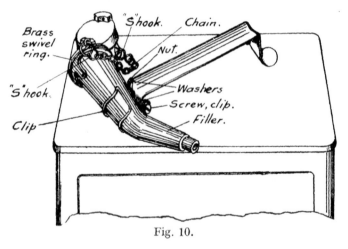

Fig. 10.

Backsight.—Plate, tubes and two radium tubes. The box—Mk. I or Mk. II—for the luminous sights will also be returned to store.

The new parts for use in conversion will be demanded as required. In the case of conversion from No. 1 luminous backsight (without shield) the plate, sight, will also be required.

(xxiii) *Attachment of filler and connection of cap to condenser can (two-gallon petrol can).*—(i) The filler when in use is screwed to the ordinary outlet of the can in place of the screwed cap. When not in use it is kept on the can and held in position by the wire clip as shown in Fig. 10. The clip is secured to the handle of the can by a screw with nut and two washers. The filler is connected to the fixed eye on the outlet of the can by a brass swivel ring with a 4-inch length of M.G. chain, a M.G. " S " hook and a special " S " hook for the eye.

The filler and details are supplied ready for assembly. The " S " hooks should be closed in after assembly, and the spout of the filler kept free from burrs and distortion to ensure free entry into the filling hole of the gun.

(ii) The cap is connected to the can by means of the shackle shown in Fig. 11, which is to be made by armourers as required in accordance with the

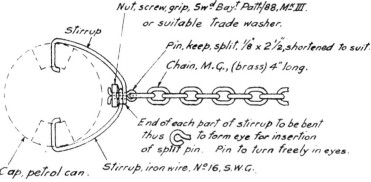

SHACKLE, CONDENSER, STEAM, Mᵏ I.

Nut, screw, grip, Swᵈ Bayᵗ Pattⁿ/88, Mᵏ III.
or suitable Trade washer.

Stirrup

Pin, keep, split, ⅛ x 2½, shortened to suit.

Chain, M.G., (brass) 4" long.

End of each part of stirrup to be bent thus to form eye for insertion of split pin. Pin to turn freely in eyes.

Cap, petrol can.   Stirrup, iron wire, Nº 16, S.W.G.

Fig. 11.

particulars given. The split keep pin is common to that supplied with the gun spares for the Mk. IV tripod mounting. The stirrup is to be secured by setting the ends over after they have been passed through the existing holes in the lugs of the cap.

(xxiv) *Repair of ammunition belts (strip type)*.—(i) The fitting of new strips and eyelets provided for use in replacement of those found damaged and unserviceable is a simple matter when using the belt-repairing tool supplied with the gun spares or the eyeletting tools supplied to R.A.O.C. Workshops. The eyeletting tools consist of a rectangular steel block having a number of holes, with recesses for eyelets, bored vertically through it, a guide pin and a punch.

The tools are used as follows :—

(a) place the eyelet in a recess over a hole in the block ;

(b) insert the small end of the guide pin through the eyelet into the hole in the block ;

(c) place the belt with the new strips in position over the guide pin and eyelet, and press down on to the block ; and

(d) remove the guide pin, place the punch in position over the eyelet, and with a few light hammer blows turn over the edge of the eyelet until firmly fixed on the belt.

The projecting or dished end of each pair of long strips should be connected by a short eyelet before the strips are placed in position on the webbing. The large eyelets are for use in the turned over portion of the belt, and the short eyelets for the other portion.

It is essential that the eyelets be pressed as far as possible through the strips before turning the edge over, and, when using the belt-repairing tool, to give it a rotary movement.

(ii) To repair a torn belt, cut out the torn portion and replace it with webbing, already prepared, and with the eyelet holes punched ready for the strips, as supplied from store. The ends of the new portion of webbing should be well secured by the strips and eyelets and then trimmed off. The ends of the upper piece should not coincide with the ends of the lower piece, and all ends should be secured by not less than two pairs of strips and eyelets.

When repair has been effected, the pockets should be tested for size with dummy cartridges; if too tight they must be expanded with the belt plug supplied with the gun spares.

(xxv) *Repair of belt boxes.*—(i) When adjusting the metal boxes to remedy distortion, see that the sides are set parallel so that the filled belt is free. The belts should not have excessive side play, as such tends to cause the cartridges to work out of position during transport.

(ii) Lids should be repaired by re-soldering at the joints where necessary, the non-rusting flux being employed. If the body is perforated, and repair cannot readily be carried out, the box should be exchanged.

(iii) Leather fittings, when insecurely attached or perished, should be re-riveted or replaced. The tab, provided for holding the left half lid open, will not be repaired or replaced. When no longer efficient, the free portion is to be cut off; the riveted portion should be left in position in order to avoid the plugging of the rivet hole. Neither the tab, nor the stud for it on the right half lid, will be fitted to boxes manufactured in future. When the handles are unserviceable the box should be exchanged.

(xxvi) *Re-blocking of Cases spare parts and tools.*—When these cases are in a greasy and limp condition, they will be re-blocked in R.A.O.C. Workshops.

Process

(a) Immerse in warm soda water solution—temperature about 110° F.—for 8 to 10 minutes.

(b) Scrub thoroughly inside and out.

(c) Wipe down and insert blocks. The ends of side flaps of lid to be tacked to sides of cases to prevent distortion.

(d) After 4 hours remove blocks and allow to dry.

(e) Examine stitching, particularly ends of hems, and repair as necessary.

(f) Treat straps with dubbin.

Material required :

1 lb. soda crystals (Sec. H.1) to 2 gallons water.
Wood block in 3 wedge-shaped pieces :—
Overall size of block :

Height	..	$7\frac{3}{4}''$
Width	..	$5''$
Depth	..	$3\frac{3}{4}''$

Section 6.—Re-browning and Re-painting

Re-browning

This will be carried out under the same conditions as for Small Arms. (*See* Part I, Chapter III, and Appendix I.)

The following parts will be subject to treatment.

In order to avoid unnecessary work in adjustment after browning, it is advisable to keep the parts as far as possible with the gun from which they were taken; the more important in this respect are specially mentioned in the following list:—

Barrel	When cleaning off before browning, care must be taken to avoid reducing in diameter the front and rear bearings, and the trunnions.
Block, feed (steel)	External surfaces only of the block. Slide; top pawls; bottom pawls, and axis pin.
Box, fusee spring ..	Externally only.
Casings, barrel and breech	Externally only. As the barrel casing is painted it will only be necessary to re-brown it when both paint and browning have been worn off. If the painting is properly attended to, the browning should remain in good condition.
Catch, front cover	The plug plunger and spring to be removed.
Catch, safety.	
Cover, front.. .. .. Cover, rear	Remove detachable parts. The covers and joint pin with nut to be returned after browning to the same gun.
Fusee, with chain.	
Handle, crank	Remove from the crank, and return, after browning, to the same crank.
Lever, check.	
Lever, firing (with pawl) ..	The pawl axis pin to be well oiled after browning.
Lock, cover, rear.	
Muzzle-attachment ..	Remove the disc before browning the front cone.
Rear crosspiece	Remove details; see that the firing lever is returned after browning to the same rear crosspiece, and the latter to the same gun.
Shutter, sliding and catch..	Remove the catch and details and return after browning to the same shutter.
Sight, fore.	

Sight, tangent	Remove details. The two parts of the slide body to be kept together.
Foresight, bar, deflection ..	Remove details.
Sights, night, fore and back	Remove details.

(*Note.*—D.P. guns and parts are not browned.)

Re-painting

For surfaces to be painted, *see* Appendix II.

When painting, see that the gun number on the trunnion block of the gun is not obliterated, and that the free operation of the parts is not affected by the paint when dry.

After re-painting belt boxes see that the stencilling and any other authorized marks are renewed.

CHAPTER IV

MOUNTINGS FOR VICKERS ·303-INCH M.G's

Mounting, tripod, ·303-inch M.G., Mk. IV

Drawings S.A.I.D. 2081 ; D.D. (E) 871 ; D.D. (E) 1000

Section 1.—General Information

1. This mounting was originally introduced for use with the Maxim machine gun, for which there had been three earlier patterns.

2. A packing block was provided for the Maxim ·303-inch converted Mks. I and II guns ; this block was fitted to the crossweb of the crosshead, between the joint lugs, to position the gun when inserting the joint pin. The two rivet holes for the block are still bored in the crossweb to enable the block to be fitted for Maxim guns where the latter may be still in use overseas, *e.g.* India.

3. Centring blocks are attached to the crosshead joint, one to the inside face of each jaw, by two screws each ; these blocks were originally provided for Maxim ·303-inch guns, but they serve also for the adapter for Lewis ·303-inch machine

guns and for the Overbank mounting for Vickers ·303-inch machine guns ; they do not function with the Vickers gun, which has a ledge on the right side of the crosshead joint arranged to rest on the upper surface of the crosshead above the joint pin hole. The right block is secured by the two direction dial pointer screws, which are longer than the screws which fix the left block.

4. The inscription plate and the strap for the legs when closed for packing are obsolescent and have been removed from the majority of mountings.

5. Two patterns of direction dials—Mks. I and II—are in use. The Mk. I, which is obsolescent, is in one piece and is not adjustable. The Mk. II is fitted with a rotatable graduated ring, attached to the flange of the body of the dial by means of a plain ring and screws which connect the two rings. The rings can be fixed at any desired setting by means of a set screw fitted to a stud in the body of the dial. The two rings with screws are supplied as a single unit when required for maintenance purposes.

6. Two patterns of direction dial pointers are in use ; both assemble in the same way to the right side of the crosshead by means of the two screws which secure the right centring block. The Mk. I has an index pointer which forms part of the casting, whereas the Mk. II has a vertical index plunger, with spring and split keep pin, fitted to the body of the pointer. The Mk. I pointer may be employed with either pattern of dial, but the Mk. II is suitable only for the Mk. II dial.

7. The elevating dial is obsolescent in view of the graduation of the elevating wheel. It will become obsolete when all elevating wheels have been graduated to " B " pattern.

8. The elevating dial pointer, now known as the elevating pointer, remains unaltered apart from a modification changing its location from the centre of the clamping lugs of the tumbler to the outside face of the left lug.

Section 2.—Stripping and Assembling

Stripping

The following instructions cover complete stripping, which is usually necessary only during repair or replacement of certain parts.

It is essential when more than one mounting is being

stripped that the parts of each be kept separate. The elevating screws and nut must be kept together as one unit ; the elevating screws, which have double threads and can therefore be started in either one of the two positions, should be re-assembled in the most favourable position for fit.

Gear, elevating.

(i) Remove the split pin from the " T " head of the inner screw to disconnect the chain.

(ii) Unscrew the tumbler nut. In the absence of a calliper tool with studs, which can be made by armourers, the nut can be tapped around anti-clockwise by means of a suitable punch.

Now lift out the inner and outer screws with elevating nut, and preserve any packing washers which may have been under the tumbler nut.

(iii) Unscrew the elevating wheel nut. This nut may be jammed up tightly and require to be driven round anti-clockwise by means of a suitable punch.

(iv) Remove the elevating wheel. When tight on the bush it can be driven off by light blows applied as closely as possible to the centre boss ; a block of hard wood should be interposed between the hammer and the wheel, the dial, if assembled, being first detached.

(v) Remove the feather from the elevating wheel bush.

(vi) Unscrew and remove the jamming bolt with nut and pointer, or, to relieve tension on the tumbler, slacken the bolt only.

(vii) Remove the elevating wheel bush by pressing it upward, seeing that the featherways in the collar coincide with the feathers in the tumbler.

(viii) If not already marked, lightly mark the tumbler pins and sides of crosshead arms as a guide for subsequent replacement, and remove the fixing pins, tumbler pins and tumbler.

Crosshead.

(ix) Slacken the traverse check clamp screw to the full extent and lift out the crosshead from the socket.

Dial, direction.

(x) Slacken the three set screws and lift off the dial from the socket.

Legs.

(xi) *Front.*—Remove the keep pin, unscrew the stop nut and jamming handle and remove the spring disc and leg from the stud.

(xii) *Rear*.—Drive out the keep pin from the jamming nut, unscrew the nut, drive out the joint pin and remove the leg.

Note.—The shoes of all legs are brazed and riveted, and the upper joint of the front legs riveted to the tubular portion. The upper joint of the rear leg is built up and riveted to the tubular portion. Each leg forms a complete unit, and armourers are not required to strip them down for repair, which will normally be carried out only in R.S.A.F. Clutch plates on socket are not interchangeable and are not to be detached.

Assembling

To assemble the mounting, reverse the foregoing order and give special attention to the following details :—

(i) *Handles and nut jamming legs*.—That they are screwed on in the position which ensures that the handles of the front legs are upward and about 25 degrees beyond the vertical when fully tightened, the handle for the left leg being rearward and the handle for the right leg forward when the legs are at position marked " 20 " in relation to the zero mark on the clutch plates ; the handle of the right front leg must not foul the elevating gear during traversing ; the vice pin of the jamming nut for the rear leg should be approximately in alignment with the leg, the rear end being slightly downward in relation thereto when fully tightened.

(ii) *Dials and Pointers*.—That they are correctly positioned and well secured ; see also that the direction dial does not prevent the crosshead from seating on the top of the socket.

(iii) *Screws, elevating*.—That the inner screw has the same projection above the outer screw as the latter has above the top of the tumbler nut.

(iv) *Nut, elevating*.—That all vertical play is taken up when the packing washers and tumbler nut are replaced.

(v) *Pins, joint*.—That they are well secured by the chains.

Section 3.—Examination

(i) See that the number on the crosshead and socket agree and look over generally for damage and wear.

(ii) Assemble to the mounting a serviceable gun, which is known to be not unduly worn in the joint pin holes, tightly clamp the crosshead and legs, which should be well spread out, apply the M.G. clinometer to the rear cover seating ledges of the gun, and, lightly holding the front end cap of the barrel casing, apply sufficient pressure vertically up, and then down, to take up all play in the mounting joints, elevating gear, etc. The extent of such play should not exceed 10 minutes of angle as indicated by the clinometer.

When wear is such as to cause the limit of 10 minutes to be exceeded, and cannot be readily located and remedied, proceed as follows :—

(iii) Select the largest joint pins available and check the joint pin holes in the crosshead and elevating gear, which should not be excessively large to such pins. Limit gauges are supplied to A.I.A.'s and C.I.S.A.'s Examiners for the holes and the pins.

(iv) Test the elevating gear for vertical play of the inner screw in the outer screw, the elevating nut in the tumbler, the trunnions of the tumbler in the bearings of the crosshead arms and on the tumbler pins. For wear which can be taken up by adjustment, *see* Section 4.

(v) Test the fit of the crosshead pivot in the socket. For action when slack, *see* Section 4.

(vi) Examine the legs for fit at the joints and for secure and rigid engagement in the clutch plates; also see that the clutch plates are securely fixed to the socket.

When it is found after all adjustment possible has been made that the total vertical play still exceeds the permissible limit, and that a new set of elevating screws with nut is unlikely to overcome the defect, the mounting must be exchanged (factory repair).

When satisfactory continue as follows :—

(vii) See that the jamming handles of the front legs and the handle of the jamming nut of the rear leg are in their correct position when fully tightened, and the former also when slackened (*see* Section 4).

(viii) Assemble the gun to the mounting at the crosshead joint only, apply the joint pin and test for fit of the gun in the jaws by lightly pressing the rear end of the gun laterally to and fro. When side play is noticeable, adjust the joint as necessary (*see* Section 4).

(ix) Remove the gun and crosshead and examine the

traverse check clamp screw and jamming block in the socket.

The vice pin and block must be secure and the acting face of the block and the screw in good order. The screw must not project beyond the face of the block.

(x) Examine the direction and elevating dials * and pointers for condition and security ; see that the Mk. II direction dial rotates freely, that the zero screw is secure, and the set screw in good order ; also that the dial does not prevent the crosshead from seating on the socket, and that it is not located too low in relation to the pointer ; also that the Mk. II direction dial pointer, where fitted, does not rotate in its socket and so cause errors of indication.

See that the elevating dial pointer is of modified pattern and of correct set (*see* Section 4).

(xi) Finally look over the mounting when completely assembled and see that it is in good working order, chains secure, and the paint in fair condition.

For list of polished parts and surfaces of mountings held by regular units for peace use, *see* Appendix III. When any unauthorized polishing has been carried out, it should be reported for disciplinary action.

Notes.

(a) Dents in the legs are unobjectionable, provided the legs are straight and strength is not appreciably affected.

(b) The shoes on the legs of the Indian Pattern have conical ground spikes in place of the rib on the Home Pattern ; they are also drilled for nailing down purposes. The I.P. will not be used in Home Service mountings, and vice versa.

(c) Instances have occurred where, owing to unauthorized washing of the mountings in tanks containing a caustic soda solution, the legs have become very badly eroded, the tubular portion being eaten through from the inside ; indication of the commencement of erosion due to this cause is usually given by a whitish deposit around the vent holes or at the junction of the tubular portion with the shoes or joints. Where mountings in this condition are met with they should be reported

---

* The elevating dial will become obsolete when all elevating wheels have been graduated.

for exchange (factory repair). On no account should mountings be immersed for cleaning or any other purpose.

Section 4.—Repairs, Modifications and Adjustments

(i) *General.*—As accurate shooting with the gun depends largely upon the mounting, it is most essential that the mountings should be kept in good condition. The quarterly examination should be thoroughly carried out, and wear and play taken up wherever possible. It should be borne in mind that, in view of overhead fire, the limit of 10 minutes allowed for vertical play is the maximum permissible, therefore every endeavour must be made to keep the mountings well within that limit and so prolong their life to the utmost before factory repair becomes necessary. Cleaning and oiling must invariably be attended to.

(ii) Ordinary repair is to be carried out in accordance with Instructional Print D.D. (E) 871 and with the tools illustrated thereon.

Bushing and re-bushing of crosshead joint pin holes will be carried out only at the undermentioned stations at home and abroad in accordance with Instructional Print D.D. (E) 869 and with the tools illustrated thereon. When such is necessary in the case of mountings with other units, depots or stations, the mountings will be exchanged— factory repair. The bushes will be left and right hand respectively ; they will be made of harder material than hitherto and will be supplied, when required, upon demand.

The I.P. D.D. (E) 869 will be supplied only to the undermentioned stations—

Home Stations :—
Small Arms School, Netheravon.
Armourers' Training Centre, Hilsea.
R.A.O.C. Depot, Weedon.
Aldershot Cd., Aldershot.
Northern Cd., York.
Scottish Cd., Stirling.
Southern Cd., Hilsea.
Western Cd., Burscough.

Overseas Stations :—
Ceylon ; Egypt ; Gibraltar ; Hong Kong ; Jamaica ; Malta ; Singapore ; Tientsin.

(iii) *Crosshead.*—(a) Fitting of gun stop to the rear cross-web where necessary. In cases where it is found that the stop on the gun does not seat on the web, a stop will be made and fitted in accordance with Fig. 1. The object of the stop is to prevent damage to the fusee spring box by contact with the crosshead. If gunmetal is not available, steel may be used.

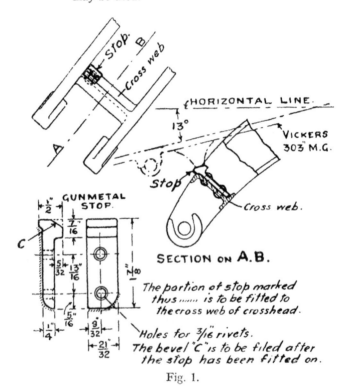

The portion of stop marked thus ...... is to be fitted to the cross web of crosshead.

Holes for 3/16 rivets.
The bevel "C" is to be filed after the stop has been fitted on.

Fig. 1.

(b) *Fitting of dovetail piece for centring of gun.*— See Fig. 2. Where the distance between the upper edge of the joint pin hole and the top at A of X is less than ·45 inch, so permitting the Vickers ·303-inch M.G. to enter too far into the joint to allow of free centring of the joint pin, a strip of gunmetal, filed to the dimensions shown at Z will be fitted and soldered into a dovetail of corresponding size, filed in the crosshead in the location shown and dimensioned at X. After so fitting, cut off the surplus portion of the strip, file the ends of the fitted piece flush with the sides, round off the inner end to blend with the boss, as at Y, drill hole for the keep pin in the position shown at X and Y and fit pin. If the pin is a tight fit drive it in, if not, solder it in. Finally file off the upper

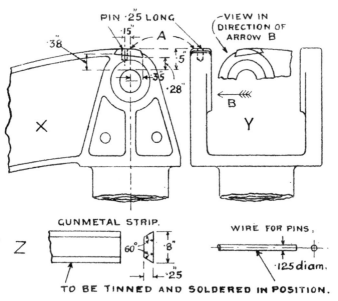

Fig. 2.

surface as required to the ·50 dimension shown and see that the gun will mount correctly.

(c) *Numbering of crosshead to socket.*—Where the numbers on the crosshead and socket are omitted they will be marked with a serial number, which is to be obtained upon application to the D.A.D.O.S. of the area. Where the numbers do not agree, and it has been ascertained that the crossheads and sockets of mountings on charge have not been intermixed, and fit is satisfactory, the crosshead will be re-numbered to the socket, the incorrect number being cancelled. The numbering should be on the top of the right side of the crosshead and on the right side of the rear web of the socket.

(iv) *Dials, direction, Mks. I and II—Fitting to socket.—* When fitting a fresh dial care must be taken to ensure that the dial is concentric with the pivot hole in the socket, parallel to the crosshead bearing, slightly below the bearing, and clear of the crosshead.

Where the existing conical centres in the socket for the set screws are not in a correct position to give the required result, and it is impracticable to adjust them, they should be drilled out, and tightly plugged with suitable screwed plugs to enable fresh centres to be made.

Where the existing set screws are of insufficient length to ensure the rigid attachment of the dial, and the length cannot well be increased without unduly weakening the head, screws $\frac{1}{8}$ inch longer should be demanded.

(v) *Legs.*—When not too badly bent they should be heated in the forge to a red heat and straightened, care being taken to ensure that the tubes are not unduly distorted nor the brazing affected during the process.

The work of straightening will be facilitated by the employment of hard wood blocks, grooved to suit the tube. When badly bent or dented the legs must be exchanged.

The teeth at the joints which engage the clutch plates on the socket must be kept free from burrs, which are to be filed off smoothly.

When the teeth of the front leg joints do not marry correctly and evenly all round with the clutch plates, the studs which are screwed and riveted to the socket have probably been bent, in which case they must be unriveted from the socket, unscrewed and straightened as required, after heating in the forge, to give the desired result, which should be obtained before re-riveting the stud in position.

When straightening, care must be taken to avoid damage to the screw threads.

When the joint of the rear leg, which is usually secured to the tubular portion by two rivets, is not rigid, the rivets should be tightened ; if appreciable play still exists, the leg should be exchanged (factory repair).

Drilling of vent holes.—In order to provide an outlet for any liquid which may have got into the legs by unauthorized immersion of the mountings in a tank for cleaning purposes, each leg must have two vent holes, each about $\frac{3}{16}$ inch in diameter, drilled through the underside of the tubular portion, one near each end, at about $2\frac{3}{4}$ inches from the point of abutment of the tube on the shoulder of the leg joint and shoe respectively. The larger of the six drills supplied with the hand drill stock will serve the purpose.

If upon drilling these holes in the legs, liquid is found to exude, the mounting will be exchanged (factory repair).

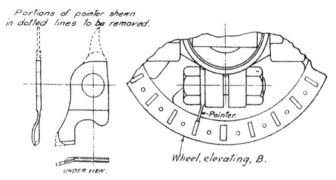

Portions of pointer shewn in dotted lines to be removed.

UNDER VIEW.

Wheel, elevating, B.

Fig. 3.

(vi) *Plates, clutch.*—Where badly worn, the mounting must be exchanged—factory repair. Burrs must be smoothly filed off, and when slack on the socket owing to loose rivets the latter must be tightened, due care being taken to avoid injury to the teeth.

(vii) *Pointers, elevating—Modification.*—Where the modification consequent upon the change in location from the centre of the clamping lugs on the tumbler to the outside face of the left lug has not been carried out, it will be made in accordance with Fig. 3. The index end must be heated to avoid fracture when setting it to the required form.

(viii) *Wheels, elevating, B.*—Instructions for graduating
"A" pattern wheels are given in Instructional
Print D.D. (E) 1000. The template, with nut
and washer, and the special regular cut file with
depth gauge at end will be supplied, on loan, upon
application.

(ix) *Adjustment of clamping handles of front legs.*—When
the tightened handles are not in the required
location (*see* "Assembling," para. (i), Section 2)
adjustment can be made in several ways.

(a) Change the starting position on the screw threads
of the stud.

(b) Exchange handles and/or spring discs with those
from other mountings when adjustment of such
mountings also is necessary.

(c) Reduce handle contact face or leg contact edge
of spring disc.

(d) Increase or decrease the doming of the spring
disc. To increase the doming, place the convex
side of the disc over a suitable hollow block
(an unserviceable muzzle-attachment cup will
serve the purpose), a suitable round-nosed block
on the concave side of the disc, and compress
as necessary between the jaws of the vice. To
decrease the doming compress the disc in the
vice. Should there be a tendency, owing to a
thin leg joint, for the spring disc to become
engaged in the thread clearance cannelure in
the stud, the cannelure can be filled with waxed
thread coated over with heel-ball.

After the correct adjustment has been obtained
it should be seen that the handles when home to
the nut in their freed position are not liable to
become bent by striking the ground when the
mounting is swung down on the ground with the
legs hinged back as in "elementary gun drill."
Should the free movement be excessive it can be
reduced by filing back the shoulder of the stud
against which the nut seats, and fitting a washer
of the same diameter as the nut between the
shoulder and the nut. When the movement is
insufficient it can be increased by filing back the
inner face of the nut. On no account should the
outer face of the clamping handles be filed ; the
amount of adjustment required to make any appreciable difference would reduce the length of thread

engagement and consequently the life of the handle.

(x) *Adjustment of clamping nut of rear leg.*—When the vice pin is incorrectly located adjustment can be made by changing the starting position on the screw thread of the stud or exchanging handles with those from other mountings, making and fitting a washer or by reducing the face of the nut. In the case of the last two methods it may be necessary to reduce one end or the other of the cannelure for the crosspin stop, or the outer end of the joint pin, care being taken to see that the end wall of the pin is not weakened.

Should it be found that the adjustment required is greater than that which is possible by such means, an additional keyway may be cut in the leg joint or a new key fitted to the joint pin.

The angular distance of the new keyway or key from the original should not be less than 60°.

(xi) *Re-painting.*—Will be carried out, where necessary, in accordance with Appendix II.

Mounting, Overbank M.G., Mk. I
(War Reserve only)

This mounting was introduced for use during the Great War, and a number are held in store for issue in emergency.

The mounting is constructed on the parallel motion principle, and is provided for use in conjunction with the service Mk. IV tripod mounting, in order that the gun, when mounted, may be raised or lowered at will within a limit of vertical movement of about 7 inches, and fired in any position within that limit. The mounting is connected to the tripod mounting by means of the crosshead and elevating joint pins of the latter mounting ; corresponding joint pins are chained to the Overbank mounting for the connection of the gun.

The general features of the mounting are as follows :—

(i) A bronze connecting link. To the front end of this are pivoted, one each side—

(ii) A pair of bronze tripod links in the upper end of which the crosshead joint of the gun engages. In the rear end of the connecting link is pivoted—

(iii) A bronze elevating link on the upper end of which the elevating joint pin of the gun engages—

(iv) A stay tube, pivoted between the tripod links near their upper end and extended downwards through the middle of the joint of the elevating link and within a pair of clamp dogs which can be clamped up by a clamping handle placed on the left side of the connecting link.

The lower end of the tripod links forms the bearing which engage in the crosshead joint of the tripod. The elevating joint is formed at the rear end of the connecting link.

A list of maintenance parts is given in Section C1 of Vocabulary of Army Ordnance Stores.

Mounting, Trench, M.G., Mk. I
(War Reserve only)

This also was used in the Great War and a number are held in store for emergency.

As its name implies, it is intended for use in a trench or emplacement, and is designed to enable the gun to fire through a small aperture and yet have an extensive traverse.

The traversing pivot is situated immediately below the muzzle of the gun, and the traversing arm, which carries the crosshead of a Mk. IV tripod mounting to which the gun is mounted, swings about this pivot upon a quadrant-shaped frame called the traversing arc. The arm carries a clamp by which it can be secured to the arc at any required angle of traverse. The frame is provided with four pointed angle-iron legs, which can be driven into the ground, and carries round its rear arc a brass strip graduated with five-degree divisions. Two adjustable stops are provided for limiting traverse as required. In order to steady the mounting when firing, the frame is fitted with three ground plates, which can be loaded with sand bags, one across the front, and two at the rear end of, and tangential to, the graduated arc.

A list of maintenance parts is given in Section C1 of Vocabulary of Army Ordnance Stores.

PART IV

BICYCLES

Drawing Nos. S.A.I.D. 2270, 2271, 2272, 2273

Section 1.—General Information

The following two patterns of bicycle only are in use :—

Mk. IV—with coaster hub and front brake.

Mk. IV*—with free-wheel hub and front and rear hand-applied brakes.

The Mk. IV* bicycles are obsolescent, but will be used whilst they remain serviceable.

Weight about 43 lb.

1. For use in peace bicycles are issued from store less the following accessories, which are held on charge and demanded separately.

Bicycles so issued are designated Mk. IV B and Mk. IV* B respectively.

Bag, tool.	Lamp, front.
Bell.	Outfit.†
Can, oil.	Pump.
Carriers, kit, Mk. II, front.	Reflector, rear.
Clips, rifle, butt.	Screwdriver.
Clips, rifle, fore-end, Mk. II*.	Spanners (2).

† Supplied under local arrangements.

2. When issued on mobilization the bicycles are complete in all respects (*see* Vocabulary of Army Ordnance Stores, Section C2); when so issued they are designated Mk. IV A, and Mk. IV* A respectively.

3. The Mk. IV* pattern is fitted either with Mk. II or Mk. III rear kit carrier, whereas the Mk. IV is fitted either with the Mk. II or Mk. IV rear kit carrier.

4. Instructions for the general care of bicycles by the user and the extent of adjustment which he is authorized to carry out are contained in the "Handbook on Military (Pedal) Bicycles" issued with each bicycle.

(270)—G

5. The identification number of each bicycle is stamped on the right side of the seat lug of the frame. It has also been stamped on the handle-bar lug, but this will be ignored.

6. The frame is known as 24-inch. Frame sizes are measured from centre of bottom bracket to top of seat lug.

7. The gear is 67 in both marks of bicycle. The gear is found by multiplying the number of inches in the diameter of the back wheel by the number of teeth on the bottom bracket chain wheel, and dividing the product by the number of teeth on the back hub chain wheel. Thus $\dfrac{28 \times 48}{20} = 67$.

8. The chain consists of 114 links ; the pitch is $\frac{1}{2}$ inch and the spacing for chain wheels $\frac{3}{16}$ inch wide.

The " chain line " is the distance from the centre of the chain links to the centre line of the bicycle. This should always be $1\frac{3}{4}$ inches, and the assembling should be so done that this measurement is observed in the distance of the centre of the teeth on both chain wheels from the centre line of the machine.

9. The coaster hub in the Mk. IV bicycle is of the positive drive type with provision for free-wheeling and for back-pedalling brake action (*see* description and figure in Section 4).

10. Tyre covers are of two types and sizes :—

    Mk. I—woven canvas, $28 \times 1\frac{5}{8}$.
    Mk. II—cord fabric, $28 \times 1\frac{3}{4}$.

Both types have beaded edges.

The covers are interchangeable on rims, and the inner tubes, which correspond in mark and size respectively with the covers, are interchangeable in the covers.

11. The following sizes and quantities of balls are employed in each bicycle :—

Marks IV and IV*	Size	Quantity
Ball-head	$\frac{1}{8}$-in.	60
Bottom bracket	$\frac{1}{4}$-in.	22
Pedals (cone end)	$\frac{3}{16}$-in.	9
,, (crank end)	$\frac{3}{16}$-in.	10
Hub, front	$\frac{3}{16}$-in.	20

Mark IV

	Size	
Hub, back, coaster	$\frac{1}{4}$-in.	$\begin{cases} 7 & \text{Cage No. 2.} \\ 9 \\ 9 \end{cases}$ Cage No. 1.

Mk. IV*

	Size	
Hub, back, free-wheel	$\frac{1}{4}$ in.	$\begin{cases} 7 & \text{Cage No. 2.} \\ 9 & \text{Cage No. 1.} \\ 9 & \text{Loose.} \end{cases}$

12. The screw threads are to the Cycle Engineers' Institute Standard throughout. Details as follows : —

Diameter	Threads to the inch	Names of parts
·080·in. (14 gauge)	62	Spokes.
·154-in.	40	Nuts and bolts for chains.
·1875-in.	32	Chain adjusters.
·266-in.	26	Cotters for bottom brackets.
·3125-in.	26	Front hub spindles ; handle-bar clip screw ; seat lug screws No. 2 ; and cone end of pedal pins.
·375-in.	26	Back hub spindles.
·5625-in.	20	Pedal pins, crank end (left and right).
·9675-in	30	Ball-head stem inside.
1·2900-in.	24	Hub lock nut (left-hand).
1·3700-in.	24	Bottom bracket cups and hub chain wheels.

Note.—For particulars of stocks and dies, *see* Appendix VII.

Section 2.—Stripping and Assembling Mks. IV and IV* Bicycles

Note.—The paragraphs are arranged in a convenient order for the complete stripping of the bicycle.

To Strip

1. *Ball-head and front wheel.*—Remove the parts in the following order :—

(i) Slacken nuts from adjusting bolt and washers ; remove nuts and washers from shoe lugs ; remove brake shoes.

(ii) Slacken clip nut and remove handle-bar.

(iii) Nuts and washers from front hub ; front mudguard.

(iv) Front wheel by forcing out forks sufficiently with two screwdrivers to clear shoulder of cones ; the wheel then drops clear.

(v) To remove forks from the ball-head, when necessary, unscrew top nut, remove washer and insert screwdriver between the top lug and the socket ring ; hold the socket ring and clip together and at the same time keep the forks up to the ball-head to prevent the balls from falling out of the bottom ring. Carefully remove forks with balls in position.

2. *Chain.*—Locate the bolt and nut between teeth of chain wheel, and detach them with a thin spanner and screwdriver.

3. *Rear wheel* (*No.* 3 *or* 4).—Remove :—

  (i) Footstep, nut, washer, mudguard and rear carrying stays. Also nut and clip screw from brake plate of No. 3 wheel.

  (ii) Wheel and chain adjusters from frame.

4. *Rear mudguard.*—Remove nuts, washers and mudguard with leather washers and bolts.

5. *Front carrier.*—Remove clip screws and carrier from frame.

6. *Rear carrier.*—Remove nut, washer bolt and carrier from frame.

7. *Saddle and seat pillar.*—Slacken clip nuts and remove saddle from the pillar, slacken seat lug nut and remove pillar.

8. *Bottom bracket.*—Remove :—

  (i) Cotter nuts and washers, support cranks with a metal block, drive out cotters with copper hammer and remove cranks.

  (ii) Locking pin nuts and pins.

  (iii) Lift cup with thin spanner, pressing spindle upward at the same time to keep the balls in the cup, remove spindle, then cup and balls from right side.

9. *Pedals.*

  (i) Remove pins from cranks (the plain crank has L.H. and the wheel crank has R.H. screw threads) and grip singly in vice on flats.

  (ii) Unscrew cap, apply thin spanner to the cone and at the same time loosen the lock nut with the thick spanner ; remove lock nut and cone from pin, balls and pin.

  (iii) Remove bar nuts and tap end plates lightly to remove from centres. Bars with rubbers are now free.

  (iv) Press bar and rubber on end of open jaw of vice, then grip plain part of bar and remove rubber.

10. *Front hub.*—Unscrew adjustable cone, place the palm of the hand on the end of the body and draw spindle outward ; at the same time shake the hub to enable the balls to drop into the hand.

11. *Coaster hub for Mk. IV bicycle* (*see* Fig. 1 in Section 4). Remove :—

  (i) Plain collar and adjustable cone.

  (ii) Chain wheel with lock nut and No. 2 cage—Turn the chain wheel round once and draw outward.

(iii) No. 1 cage from clutch cup.

(iv) Spindle with attachments.

> *To strip spindle.*—Remove clutch nut, grip spindle firmly and withdraw brake clutch with inner split collar ; remove spindle and outer split collar from brake plate ; tap brake plate sharply on bench to remove lever.
>
> When it is necessary to remove the chain wheel or to examine the inside bearing of the driving screw, grip the flats on the latter in a vice and tap the lock nut (L.H. thread) round clockwise with punch and remove with No. 2 cage. On no account should the chain wheel be held in a vice and the wheel rim used as a lever to unscrew the lock nut.

12. *Free-wheel hub* (Mk. IV* bicycle).—Remove :—

(i) Cone and loose balls from left side.

(ii) Right-hand cone, using spanner if necessary.

(iii) Turn chain wheel round one turn anti-clockwise and remove with driving screw, lock nut and No. 2 cage.

(iv) Cage No. 1 from clutch cup.

(v) Clutch cup by tapping round anti-clockwise with punch and hammer.

(vi) Withdraw spindle with clutch nut and washer. To remove lock nut (L.H. thread), No. 2 cage and chain wheel from driving screw, hold the latter by the flats in a vice and tap lock nut round, anti-clockwise, with punch and hammer.

13. *Front brake from handle-bar and fork* (when necessary).— Remove :—

(i) Lever screw and lever from handle-bar.

(ii) Screws from clip ; joint screw, rod joint with rod and bolt from tube.

(iii) Lug stirrup screws, stirrup with tube from hangers.

(iv) Slacken lamp bracket screws, and slide off lamp bracket.

(v) Slacken clip screws, slide the clip off the forks, detach hanger screws and hangers from clips.

14. *Rear brake* (Mk. IV* bicycle).—Remove :—

(i) Adjusting rod and lever with clip screws and clip from handle-bar stem.

(ii) Adjusting bolt, joint screw and tube.

(iii) Joint screws and bottom rod.

(iv) Nut and bolt from bell crank clip lever.

(v) Clip from frame—force ends open sufficiently to clear.

(vi) Bell crank lever axis bolt, and lever from clip.

(vii) Hanger screws, and stirrup with rod, from rocking lever.

(viii) Clip nuts, clip with screws, and rocking lever with bush, from frame.

(ix) Back fork clip nuts, clips and hangers from chain stays ; hanger screws and axis bolt.

15. *Tyres from wheels.*—Remove cap, air plug and lock nut from valve. Press the body of the valve up slightly into the cover, remove the small flap of the cover, detach the inner tube and then the cover from rim. The small flap of the cover is on the left side of both wheels.

To Assemble

Note.—All bearings should be oiled during assembly.

Order of assembly :—

1. *Tyres to wheels.*—*See* Handbook supplied with each bicycle.

2. (a) *Free-wheel hub* (Mk. IV* bicycle).—Assemble in reverse order of stripping, giving especial attention to the following details :—

(i) Shoulder of chain wheel must abut on face of driving screw.

(ii) Plain side of No. 1 ball cage in clutch cup must be next to cone.

(iii) Ensure that driving screw engages clutch nut.

(iv) See that the full complement of nine $\frac{1}{4}$-inch balls is inserted in the cup on the left side and that the cone is adjusted to permit of a slight amount of play for free operation.

(b) *Coaster hub* (Mk. IV bicycle).—Before assembly, coat the brake band with red mineral jelly. Assemble in reverse order of stripping, giving special attention to the following details :—

(i) When replacing the brake clutch on the spindle see that the stud is located in the slot of the lever.

(ii) When replacing the spindle, with its assembled details, in the body of the hub, the wheel should be horizontal and the enlarged part of the hub upward.

(iii) Plain side of No. 1 cage in the clutch cup must be next to the cone.

(iv) When adjusting bearings by means of the cone on the right side, allow a slight amount of play for free operation.

3. *Front hub.*—Place the spindle with fixed cone into the body of the hub and insert ten $\frac{3}{16}$-inch balls into the cup. Hold the spindle in position, reverse the wheel and insert a similar quantity of the $\frac{3}{16}$-inch balls into the other cup, then screw on the adjustable cone and adjust.

4. *Pedals.*—Assemble in reverse order of stripping, attending especially to the following details :—

    (i) When assembling the screwed end plate to the pedal centre see that the lubricator cover is at about 45° to a line drawn through the rubber bar centres.

    (ii) When assembling bars with rubbers to the end plates see that one of the flat surfaces of each bar lies parallel with the tread.

    (iii) Ten $\frac{3}{16}$-inch balls are required in the plain or crank end and nine similar balls in the screwed or outer end.

5. *Bottom bracket.*—Assemble in reverse order of stripping, but see that the cup in the right side is allowed to project about one turn out from the side of the bracket, and that it is there secured by the locking pin and nut. Care must be taken when assembling locking pins and nuts to avoid excessive tightening of the nuts, which causes damage to cups. The number of $\frac{1}{4}$-inch balls in each side should be eleven. The cotters must be assembled in opposite directions on the two cranks, so that the plain end of the cotter is to the front when the pedal end of the crank, to which it is fitted, is upward.

6. *Saddle and seat pillar.*—See that the cantle of the saddle is slightly raised and the saddle well secured.

7. *Front carrier.*

8. *Rear mudguard* (fit stays to spindle during item 10).

9. *Rear brake fittings* to chain stays.

10. *Rear wheel.*—Assemble in reverse order of stripping, seeing that the plain collar is assembled to the spindle on the left side of the hub in the No. 3 wheel, and that the flat portion of the chain adjuster is outermost.

11. *Rear Carrier.*

12. *Chain.*—The screwed portion of the end plate should be on the inside. When adjusting the chain by means of the chain adjusters, see that the wheel is central in the forks, and that this is maintained when the washers, nut and footstep are tightened. A slight amount of slack must be allowed in the chain to allow of free running. See that the rear wheel is correctly adjusted for free running, that the brake plate of

No. 3 wheel is tightly screwed to the chain stay clip, and that the footstep and nut are tightly screwed home.

13. *Ball-head and front wheel.*—Assemble in reverse order of stripping. When the front brake fittings have been removed from the forks they must be replaced before the wheel is assembled.

The top of the brake clips on the forks should be fixed at $2\frac{3}{4}$ inches from the lower edge of the bottom crown plate.

When the forks have been removed from the ball-head see that the correct quantity of $\frac{1}{8}$-inch balls (30) are placed in the bottom ring of the forks and the same quantity in the clip under the socket ring at the top.

When placing the wheel into the forks see that the adjustable cone is on the left side.

14. *Rear brake.*—Complete the assembly in reverse order of stripping. The lever with its attachments should be fitted to the handle-bar stem about one inch from the lug.

The brake tube should be parallel with the ball-head tube and the bell crank lever clip about $\frac{1}{4}$ inch from the bottom lug. The closed end of the brake shoes must be at the bottom, and the brake pads about $\frac{1}{8}$ inch clear of the rim in their free position.

After assembly, test brake for efficiency.

15. *Front brake.*—Complete the assembly in reverse order of stripping, seeing that the closed end of the brake shoes is at the front, and the pads about $\frac{1}{8}$ inch clear of the rim in their free position.

After assembly, test brake for efficiency.

Finally ensure that all nuts are properly tightened and that the bicycle is fit to ride.

Section 3.—Examination.

The bicycle should be examined methodically part by part, each component or group of components being taken in order, and particular attention paid to the points enumerated below.

1. Check number on seat lug of frame and mark of bicycle (IV or IV*) with record and history sheet ; and see that the corps mark or title of unit is marked on bicycles in use.

2. First look over generally to see that the bicycle is free from serious damage, then proceed to examine in detail.

3. *Ball-head.*—Test for adjustment of bearings, condition of front forks ; handle-bar, including security of handles.

4. *Frame.*—Examine to see that it is free from fracture, especially at the joints.

5. *Wheels.*—Turn bicycle upside down. Examine for true spinning, rigidity of spokes, and alignment of bearings, engagement of cones of front wheel in forks, and condition of hub chain wheel. Should alignment be in error examine for cause, which may be due to dished wheels, front forks or stem bent, frame twisted or bent, or chain stay tubes bent.

6. *Bottom bracket.*—Condition, alignment and fit of cranks, chain wheel, chain and pedals, free running and adjustment of bearings and chain.

7. *Backstays.*—Condition and alignment.

8. *Mudguards.*—Condition and security.

9. *Front brakes.*—Condition, security of the parts and adjustment ; see that the shoes are assembled in the right direction and that the pads are not worn down too close to the shoes.

10. *Rear brake* (Mk. IV* bicycle).—As for front brake.

11. *Tyres.*—Condition and security on rims and condition of valves.

12. *Carriers.*—Correctness of pattern, according to mark of bicycle, condition and security.

13. *Enamelling.*—Condition. Where chipped so as to expose metal, the part should be painted with the Service air drying enamel after removing any rust present.

14. *Lubricators.*—See that all oil holes are clear, that the lubricators are secure and caps, where provided, are in working order.

15. Finally see that saddle, seat pillar, and handle-bars are well secured, that the accessories and tools are in serviceable condition, and that the bicycle generally when found serviceable from the foregoing examination is fit to ride.

Note.—(*a*) Should any of the bearings give signs of undue friction or excessive play which cannot be readily adjusted they should be stripped for examination in detail.

(*b*) Special attention should be given during examination to see that the parts are of Service pattern.

Section 4.—Repairs and Adjustments

1. *Chain.*

(i) *Cleaning.*—To clean a very dirty chain, take off, soak in paraffin for a few hours, work the links about until quite free and clean, and hang it up to drain. Then immerse in hot tallow at a simmering heat for about one hour. Wipe off the superfluous grease when cold.   Too much grease on a chain causes it to gather grit.

To fix the chain, bring the ends together over the bottom bracket chain wheel ; the teeth will then keep the chain in position while the bolt is inserted.

(ii) *Adjustment.*—Slacken the spindle nut and footstep, and regulate chain adjusters as necessary.   Before securing the wheel by tightening the nut and footstep, see that the hub is at right-angles to the centre line of the machine.   This should be finally tested by revolving the wheel and observing that the rim maintains a central position between the chain stays.   The chain should be adjusted so that there is a little play or back-lash between the chain wheels when the crank is moved slightly by hand. It is essential that the chain wheels should run in correct line.   If the examination of the teeth shows that one side is more worn than the other, the alignment of the wheels should be attended to at once.

2. *Bearings.*—The instructions given for the adjustment of bearings in the Handbook issued with each bicycle should be followed.

When bearings, cups, balls, etc., are scored or roughened by wear, usually due to want of care in cleaning or oiling, the defective part or parts must be exchanged.

Bearings of bicycles issued to units from store may be found filled with mineral jelly.   This must be removed and the bearings oiled before the bicycles are taken into use.

3. *Wheel repairs.*—Instructions for wheel building (para. 8) serve for any repairs which may be necessary.   Complete wheel building will be undertaken only at R.A.O.C. Workshops, but regimental and corps armourers are required to remedy slightly bent rims and replace defective or missing spokes.

Whenever it is necessary to correct a bent rim, care should be taken to avoid short kinks and to first loosen those spokes which restrict the movement of the rim in the direction in which setting is required.

The usual method of setting employed is to place the wheel horizontally on a bench, support the rim where necessary on wood blocks, and force by hand in the direction required.

4. *Setting frames, front forks, spindles, etc.*
(i) *Tube of frames.*—When slightly bent these can usually be set by gripping the sides of the bottom bracket

between lead clams in a strong vice, and forcing the tube or tubes in the direction required.

When the bend or distortion is more serious it may be necessary in some cases to apply heat to the tube, but whenever this is done care must be taken to avoid loosening the brazed joints.

After setting, the alignment of the top, bottom and seat tubes should be checked by means of a straight-edge applied to the faces of the bottom bracket.

(ii) *Chain stays.*—A distance of 4¾ inches should be maintained between the fork ends when setting.

(iii) *Backstays.*—To set, fix in vice at bridge portion.

(iv) *Front forks.*—When setting has been carried out, alignment should be tested by two straight-edges, one in the hub spindle jaws and the other across the crown. When correct the straight-edges should lie parallel.

(v) *Handle-bars.*—These can be set by means of a suitable mandril inserted in the end of the tube, the mandril being held in the vice.

(vi) *Hub spindles and pedal pins.*—Place between centres of wheel trueing stand, or lathe, and set with the copper hammer on a vice or suitable block.

(vii) *Bottom bracket chain wheel.*—When slightly bent, the wheel can be set by pressure applied when in its assembled position. When badly bent, it should be removed and set in a vice or on a suitable block.

(viii) *Cranks.*—Straighten on a suitable block, protecting the surfaces of the crank as necessary. As the crank is hardened (toughened) care must be taken to avoid fracture. The straight-edge should be used for testing alignment.

5. *Coaster hub.*—Fig. 1 and a brief description are included for the ready identification and location of the parts. Repair is usually limited to the replacement of damaged or excessively worn parts.

The driving screw E is screwed to the chain wheel I, and locked by the nut M (L.H. thread) ; the clutch nut D operates on the driving screw E ; it is roughened at the cone, where it engages the brake clutch C, and has teeth on the face at the opposite end to engage the clutch cup F.

The forward drive and braking are both effected through the clutch cup F, clutch nut D and the clutch brake C. On the forward drive, D is brought into close engagement with F and free from C. When braking, *i.e.* back-pedalling, the chain wheel is turned slightly in the reverse direction, so D is disengaged from F and brought into engagement with C, thereby causing the brake band A to expand on to the body B. When

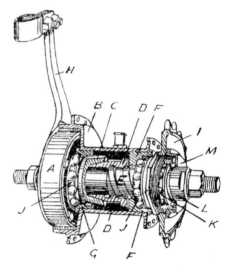

A.   Brake band with phosphor bronze ring.
B.   Body.
C.   Brake clutch.
D.   Clutch nut.
E.   Driving screw.
F.   Clutch cup (R.H. thread).
G.   Plain cup (L.H. thread).
H.   Brake plate.
I.   Chain wheel.
J.   No. 1 cage.
K.   No. 2 cage.
L.   Adjustable cone.
M.   Lock nut.

Fig. 1.

free-wheeling, D is out of engagement with both F and C, consequently the hub rotates freely and on the ball bearings at J.

Should it be necessary to fit new brake bands to the brake plate, it is desirable, in order to avoid damage to the studs in the plate, to employ a tool of the type illustrated in Fig. 2. The tool can be made by armourers.

6. *Inner tubes of tyres.*—To make a fresh joint, coat the ends internally and externally, over a length of about two inches, with rubber solution and allow to get tacky, then, before joining, dip the ends in mineral naphtha; this will allow the one end of the tube to slide easily into the other. After the naphtha has evaporated the joint can be made secure.

7. *Valves of inner tubes.*—To refix in the tube after detachment, remove the supporting tab from the tube and pass the body of the valve into the tube. Select the new location for the valve, and cut a fresh aperture, which should not be larger than the screwed portion of the body; insert the body through the aperture and retain it in position by affixing another supporting tab having an aperture of similar size to

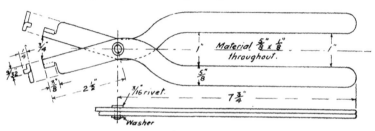

Fig 2.

that in the tube to ensure a good fit around the body. Repair the original aperture in the tube and assemble the lock nut and valve.

8. *Wheel building.*

Hubs.—The holes in the hub flanges are countersunk alternately inside and outside.

Rims.—The holes in the rims are drilled obliquely, so that the holes are directed towards the hub flanges and not towards the hub centre. As the spokes in the finished wheel proceed from the rim alternately to the right and left flanges, the rim holes are likewise arranged alternately in direction. Under these conditions the nipples can seat correctly without causing any undue lateral strain to the rim or spokes.

Spokes.—The spokes which have their heads on the outside of the flange when the wheel is built up are called inside spokes, and vice versa.

Assembling front wheel.—The hubs and rims are drilled

ready for use. The spokes are supplied cut to length and screwed. Lay the rim on a bench, take the hub, and, in either of the two flanges, put eight inside spokes into the eight holes which are countersunk on the outside, letting them hang loosely downwards. Now gather them up and bring them into the position shown in Fig. 3. Take one of the spokes and pass it through one of the holes in the rim which points upward, put a washer on, and screw on the nipple about six turns. Now take the remaining spokes in rotation and put them into the rim at every fourth hole, so that between each two spokes there is one unoccupied hole in the flange of the hub and three in the rim. Place a washer and nipple on each spoke and screw all the nipples down the same distance. Now look carefully over the rim to see that all the spokes are in their proper places.

Next, turn the hub and rim upside down and manipulate the hub so that the spokes lie radially, or in other words, so

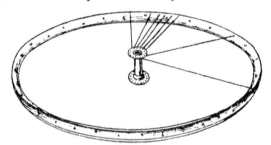

Fig. 3.

that any two opposite spokes are in alignment and form a diametrical line across the rim. Put a spoke in one of the holes of the top flange which are countersunk on the outside, and without disturbing the hub and spokes already assembled lay this spoke radially so that its outer end rests on the rim, as in Fig. 4. It will be noticed that this spoke A lies between two others 1 and 2, and that it is immediately over a hole in the rim. Pass this spoke either to the right or left, so that it crosses the three spokes numbered 2, 3, 4 in one direction, and 1, 8, 7 in the other. Spoke A is now again between two spokes, 4 and 5 or 6 and 7, as the case may be. Place in the same relative position to these two as it was previously in relation to 1 and 2. Pass spoke A, turning the hub if necessary, through the hole, which will be found immediately underneath it or opposite it, and secure it with a washer and nipple. Assemble the remaining seven inside spokes, missing one hole in the flange and three in the rim. Look over the wheel and see that the same relation between the spokes is maintained throughout, and that the nipples are all screwed down the same distance. Now deal with the outside spokes. These can all be put in the flange before the lacing is begun or they can be put in and laced one at a time, whichever is the more convenient. They must be passed through the flange from the opposite side of the wheel and brought up outside. Before trying to put the spoke in the rim see that the head of it is in the right position against the inside of the flange.

Lay the spoke midway between those on either side of it, in its own flange. If the wheel is now held vertically, and looked

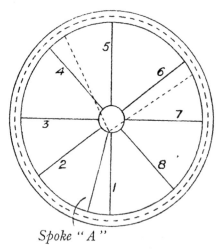

Spoke " A "

Fig. 4.

at from the side, it will be seen that all the spokes in this flange are tangential in one direction of rotation, whereas those in the opposite flange are tangential in the opposite direction. Take the outside spoke, now being dealt with, and pass it over three spokes so that it is in the same direction of rotation as the spokes in the opposite flange. It will now be found that it is in the proximity of two unoccupied holes, and bearing in mind that adjacent spokes on the rim proceed to opposite flanges, it will be easy to determine which is the correct hole of these two. As a check it should be noted that the rim hole points in the correct direction. The remaining outside spokes in this flange can now be correctly positioned and secured. The wheel must now be turned over again, and the same system followed out for the outside spokes in the other flange. If the crossing of three is kept in mind it will be almost impossible to lace these wrongly.

All the nipples can now be screwed home a proportionate distance until a slight tension is perceptible on the spokes, after which the wheel can be put in the trueing stand and finished, care being taken that it is kept central and true and that the spokes are properly tensioned.

Assembling rear wheel.—Hubs, back, coaster, and hubs, back, free-wheel. The foregoing instructions, with the following exceptions, equally apply.

There are ten inside and ten outside spokes to each flange, whereas in the front wheel there are only eight ; this necessitates the crossing of four spokes in each case instead of three.

Coaster hub.—The holes for the spoke heads in the right flange are on a circle of smaller diameter than those on the left, and, in addition, each pair of holes is joined by a slot enlarged in the centre so as to admit of the spoke head being passed through. In the finished wheel the heads of one inside and one outside spoke will rest at opposite ends of the opening formed by each pair of holes and their connecting slot.

First assemble the ten inside spokes in the left flange as in the plain hub. Now put the outside spokes in the same flange, commencing with one spoke passed through the flange from the inside of the hub ; cross it over four and put it into the middle one of the three unoccupied holes in the rim. Proceed in the same way with the other nine outside spokes. Screw home all the nipples so as to bring the flange roughly in the same plane as the rim. The object is to ensure that when the spokes are being put in the right flange they are brought slightly under tension with a few turns of the nipples, as otherwise they would be continually falling out while the lacing was being done. Now place the wheel with the left flange and assembled spokes downward.

Select any two of these spokes which are in alignment with or in prolongation of one another, and mark the left flange at the position of their heads.

Note the slot and pair of holes in the right flange situated between these two marks and place the head of an inside spoke therein in position. Being an inside spoke its direction of rotation is the same as that of the outside spokes in the opposite flange, from which it is easy to determine at which end of the slot the head must lie, and in which direction the spoke must be turned. Place this spoke at right-angles to the two spokes in the left flange selected earlier.   It will be found that its screwed end is over an unoccupied hole.   The spoke must be turned and secured in the fourth unoccupied hole from this. Position and secure the remaining inside spokes.   The outside spokes can now be put in, remembering that their heads must be inside, and that each outside spoke must cross four of the inside spokes in the same flange.   The wheel must then be finished in the trueing stand.

APPENDICES

APPENDIX I

Browning Mixture and Process

(See Part I, Chapter III.)

Mixture

The following quantity is sufficient for 50 rifles. One-third of this quantity will be sufficient for 50 bayonets and scabbards :—

Rain or soft water	..	..	..	12	oz.
Blue stone ..	..	..	..	..	$\frac{1}{16}$,,
Nitric acid ..	..	..	..	..	$1\frac{1}{4}$,,
Tincture of steel	..	..	..	..	$3\frac{1}{2}$,,
Spirits of wine	..	..	..	..	2 ,,
,, ,, nitre	..	..	..	..	3 ,,

Note.—For the first coat only, take 2 oz. of the mixture and add $\frac{1}{4}$ oz. of nitric acid.

The above-mentioned ingredients will be mixed by the armourer in the order shown, directly they are received. They must not be kept in separate bottles, as danger from fire is likely to arise from the nitric acid if it is spilt before being mixed with the other ingredients.

If the armourer has a larger quantity of ingredients than he actually requires for the arms he has to brown, he will at once return the surplus to the quartermaster's store.

Ingredients for browning mixture should be measured by fluid measure as follows :—

> 60 minims = 1 dram.
> 8 drams   = 1oz.
> 20 oz.   = 1 pint.

Process

1st *Day.*

Boil components in strong soda water for $\frac{1}{2}$ hour ($1\frac{1}{2}$ lb. of soda to one gallon of water) to remove the grease. Wipe down with clean wet cloths to remove soda (inside of barrels to be wiped out with rod and wet jute). When barrels and components are cold, coat with the mixture, rubbing the first coat well in. Stand in a dry place for 3 to 4 hours, then again coat cold with the mixture, and stand in the drying room for the night.

2nd Day.

Boil components in clean water for 20 minutes and, when cold, scratch off. Coat cold with the mixture and stand them in a dry place for 3 to 4 hours. Then again coat cold and stand them in the drying room for the night.

3rd Day.

Repeat as for the 2nd Day.

4th Day.

Boil in clean water for 20 minutes. When cold, scratch off and oil.

Note.—Materials for less than one quart of the mixture will not be supplied to home stations, nor for less than a gallon to stations abroad.

APPENDIX II

Painting of Machine Guns, Mountings, etc.

Parts to be painted and materials and time allowed for cleaning and painting. (*See* Part I, Chapter III.)

" Paint, khaki colour, special, for machine guns " will be used for painting machine guns, mountings and metal boxes, and ordinary " service colour " paint for painting wood boxes and chests.

Note.—For allowances of material and for time allowed for cleaning and painting, *see* Equipment Regulations, Part I.

Description of guns, mountings, etc.	Parts to be painted.
Guns, machine, Hotchkiss ·303-in. (a)	Barrel (including spare) and hand-guard.
Guns, machine, Lewis ·303-in. ..	Radiator casings and exposed surfaces of trigger guard.
Guns, machine, Vickers ·303-in. ..	Barrel casing and exposed surfaces of feed block when latter is of gunmetal.
Holders, A A. Hotchkiss ·303-in. M.G. .. .. Holders, A.A. Lewis ·303-in. M.G	All over, except gun bearings and frictional surfaces.

(*a*) *See* Section 6, Chapter I, Part III.

Descriptions of gun mountings, etc.	Parts to be painted.
Magazines, Lewis ·303-in. M.G., Mk. I	Externally only.
Mounts, field, Lewis ·303-in. M.G., Mk. III	All over.
Mountings, tripod, A.A. Lewis or Hotchkiss ·303-in. M.G.	All over, except lower frictional surfaces of tubular post.
Mountings, tripod ·303-in. M.G., Mk. IV (b)	All over, excepting gun and joint pin bearing surfaces, screw threads of elevating gear, and stems of joint pins.
Mountings, tripod, Hotchkiss ·303-in. M.G.	All over, excepting gun bearings and frictional surfaces.
Boxes, belt, Vickers ·303-in. M.G. (metal)	Externally (and internally where necessary).
Boxes, carrier, magazine, Lewis ·303-in. M.G. (metal)	Externally (and internally where necessary).
Boxes, strips, Hotchkiss ·303-in. M.G. (wood)	Externally.
Box, battalion spares, Lewis ·303-in. M.G.	Externally.
Chests, Vickers or Lewis ·303-in. M.G. (wood)	Externally.

(b) *See* also Appendix III.

APPENDIX III

Polishing of Mountings, tripod ·303-inch M.G. Mk. IV, held by units of the Regular Army for peace use.

The following parts and surfaces only will be polished :—

Chains.	All over.
Crosshead.	The prominent top surfaces only.
Handles, jamming front legs.	Handle portion only.
Legs.	The flange of shoe and up to 1 inch above the flange only.
Nut, jamming, rear leg.	Including the handle.
Pins, joint, crosshead ⎱ ,, ,, elevating ⎰	Handles only.
Screw, clamp, checking traverse.	Handle portion only.
Wheel, elevating.	The outer rim where graduated.

Mountings not actually in use, and those held in Store, will not be polished.

Care must be taken to see that the number and other markings on the crosshead are not obliterated, nor damage done to the graduations of the elevating wheel " B " by excessive polishing.

Authorization has been given for local provision of the materials required for the polishing.

APPENDIX IV

Instructions for packing Small Arms in Chests Nos. 1 to 12

(*See* Part I, Chapter IV.)

20 *Rifles*, *No*. 1, *in Chest*, *S.A.*, *No*. 1, *Mk. II*.—See that the supports are screwed in the correct position as required for packing rifles with long, short, normal or bantam butts. When rifles with long, normal and short butts are packed, the $2\frac{1}{4}$-inch width of the supports will face the ends of the chest, but when bantam butts are packed the $1\frac{1}{2}$-inch width will do so.

Remove all loose fittings with the exception of boards " A " and " B," and No. 1 bottom-bridged battens. The battens should be placed in the fillets nearest to the centre of the chest. Ten rifles will then be laid in the chest (the fore-ends in the grooves in the battens, and the butts resting on the battens at the opposite end).

No. 1 butt slips are then placed between the butts of the rifles as follows :—

      For long butts —grooved side to muzzle.
      ,, normal ,,   —plain side to muzzle.
      ,, short   ,,   —plain side to muzzle, and with the $\frac{1}{2}$-inch No. 1 butt strip behind the butt.
      ,, bantam ,,   —grooved side to muzzle.

The No. 1 middle-bridged battens are then placed over the butts of the rifles, and the second layer of rifles laid in the chest. The remaining fittings are then placed in their respective positions. If desired, rifles with normal, long and short butts can be packed together, provided they are in even numbers.

This is effected by placing rifles with the same length of butt in the top layer over the same length in the bottom layer.

Smaller quantities of rifles can be packed as follows :—

10 Rifles in Chest, S.A., No. 2, Mk. II
 8   ,,   ,,   ,,   No. 3 ,,
 6   ,,   ,,   ,,   No. 4 ,,
 4   ,,   ,,   ,,   No. 5 Mk. II*
 2   ,,   ,,   ,,   No. 6 ,,

The method of packing is similar to that described for the first layer in Chest, S.A., No. 1, Mk. II.

Rifles, No. 3, Mk. I* (T) with telescopic sight will be packed in modified Chests, S.A., Nos. 5 and 6, Mk. II*, as follows :—

Chest, S.A., No. 6.—The bayonets and scabbards will be placed in the bottom of the chest. One arm chest board and one end support will be removed, the board being screwed down over the bayonets and scabbards, and the end support screwed to the bottom of the chest for retention.

To allow clearance for the telescope locking bolt on the rear fitting of the rifles, it is necessary to make a cavity in each side of the chest large enough to clear the locking bolt in all positions (*see* Fig. 1).

The telescope cases will be wrapped in soft material to prevent movement and will be placed alongside the backsights of the rifles.

Finally, the remainder of the fittings will be replaced in their usual positions and the lid screwed on.

When packing one rifle only, the loose butt slip will be nailed to the chest to assist in holding the rifle rigid.

Chest, S.A., No. 5.—The foregoing instructions apply to this chest also, excepting that the centre fittings are placed at one end of the chest.

When packing three rifles only, the loose butt slip will be nailed to the chest.

24 *Swords, Cavalry, No.* 1, *Mk. I*, in Chest, S.A., No.* 8, *Mk. I.*—The swords are packed in three layers, eight in each layer.

1*st layer.*—Three at one end of chest held in position by a No. 8 " A " bridged batten, and five at the other end held in position by a No. 8 " B " bridged batten. To prevent any forward movement of the extra two swords in No. 8 " B " bridged batten, a No. 8 " C " plain batten is placed in fillets in front of the hilts.

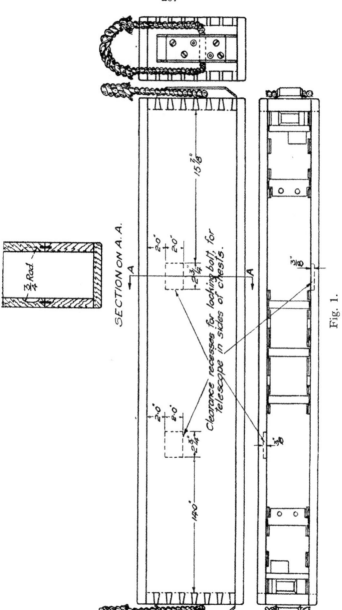

Fig. 1.

2nd layer.—Similar to 1st layer with No. 8 " A " and " B " bridged battens reversed.

3rd layer.—Similar to 1st layer. Two No. 8 " A " plain battens are placed on the No. 8 " A " and " B " bridged battens, and a No. 8 " B " plain batten, over swords, in fillets in front of hilts.

200 *Bayonets, No.* 1, *Mk. I, in Chest, S.A., No.* 9, *Mk. II.*—The bayonets are packed in layers of twenty-five—twelve in No. 9 " A " rack and thirteen in No. 9 " B " rack. They are in two compartments, each compartment holding four layers. No. 9 plain battens are used for holding the fittings down.

200 *Scabbards, bayonet, No. I, Mk. II, in Chest, S.A., No.* 10, *Mk. I.*—The scabbards are packed in layers of ten, on No. 10 " A " plain battens. They are in two compartments, each compartment holding ten layers of ten. No. 10 " B " plain battens are placed over the upper layer next the lid.

20 *Barrels with bodies in Chest, S.A., No.* 11, *Mk. I.*—These are packed in four layers, five in each layer in No. 11 " A " and " B " bridged battens. No. 11 battens are placed over the upper layer next the lid.

20 *Lances in Chest, S.A., No.* 12, *Mk. I.*—The lances are packed in five layers, four in each layer. They are placed in the chest as follows :—

1st layer.—Reverse the lances alternatively when placing them in the fittings, *i.e.* one head to end of case then one shoe to the same end, and so on.

2nd layer.—The shoe end is placed in first over the head of the lance below, then continue as in first layer.

The other layers follow in similar order.

Pistols, revolver, No. 1, are packed each in a cardboard box, the lid of which is secured by string. These boxes are packed in any suitable S.A. case.

APPENDIX V

List of fittings in Chests, S.A., Nos. 1 to 7

(See Part I, Chapter IV.)

Detail (Dimensions in inches)	No. 1, Mk. II	No. 2, Mk. II and No. 7	No. 3, Mk. II	No. 4, Mk. II	No. 5, Mk. II* and Mk. II	No. 6, Mk. II* and Mk. II
Battens—						
bridged, top—						
No. 1 $(19\frac{1}{8} \times 5\frac{5}{8} \times \frac{7}{8})$ ..	2	2	—	—	—	—
No. 3 $(15\frac{1}{2} \times 5\frac{5}{8} \times \frac{7}{8})$ ..	—	—	2	—	—	—
No. 4 $(11\frac{7}{8} \times 5\frac{5}{8} \times \frac{7}{8})$ ..	—	—	—	2	—	—
No. 5 $(8\frac{1}{4} \times 5\frac{5}{8} \times \frac{7}{8})$ ..	—	—	—	—	2	—
No. 6 $(4\frac{5}{8} \times 5\frac{5}{8} \times \frac{7}{8})$ ..	—	—	—	—	—	2
bridged, middle—						
No. 1 $(19\frac{1}{8} \times 5\frac{7}{16} \times \frac{7}{8})$ ..	2	—	—	—	—	—
bridged, bottom—						
No. 1 $(19\frac{1}{8} \times 2\frac{11}{16} \times \frac{7}{8})$ ..	2	2	—	—	—	—
No. 3 $(15\frac{1}{2} \times 2\frac{11}{16} \times \frac{7}{8})$ ..	—	—	2	—	—	—
No. 4 $(11\frac{7}{8} \times 2\frac{11}{16} \times \frac{7}{8})$ ..	—	—	—	2	—	—
No. 5 $(8\frac{1}{4} \times 2\frac{11}{16} \times \frac{7}{8})$ ..	—	—	—	—	2	—
No. 6 $(4\frac{5}{8} \times 2\frac{11}{16} \times \frac{7}{8})$ ..	—	—	—	—	—	2
plain—						
No. 1 $(19\frac{1}{4} \times \frac{7}{8} \times \frac{7}{8})$ ..	1	1	—	—	—	—
No. 3 $(15\frac{1}{2} \times \frac{7}{8} \times \frac{7}{8})$ ..	—	—	1	—	—	—
No. 4 $(11\frac{7}{8} \times \frac{7}{8} \times \frac{7}{8})$ ..	—	—	—	1	—	—
No. 5 $(8\frac{1}{4} \times \frac{7}{8} \times \frac{7}{8})$ ..	—	—	—	—	1	—
No. 6 $(4\frac{5}{8} \times \frac{7}{8} \times \frac{7}{8})$ ..	—	—	—	—	—	1
Bearers—						
No. 1 $(13 \times 2\frac{1}{2} \times \frac{3}{8})$ ..	2	2	2	2	2	2
Boards—						
No. 1						
" A " $(19\frac{1}{8} \times 6\frac{1}{4} \times \frac{5}{8})$ ..	2	—	—	—	—	—
" B " $(19\frac{1}{8} \times 8\frac{7}{8} \times \frac{5}{8})$ ..	2	2	—	—	—	—
No. 3 $(15\frac{1}{2} \times 8\frac{7}{8} \times \frac{5}{8})$ ..	—	—	2	—	—	—
No. 4 $(11\frac{7}{8} \times 8\frac{7}{8} \times \frac{5}{8})$ ..	—	—	—	2	—	—
No. 5 $(8\frac{1}{4} \times 8\frac{7}{8} \times \frac{5}{8})$ ..	—	—	—	—	2	—
No. 6 $(4\frac{5}{8} \times 8\frac{7}{8} \times \frac{5}{8})$ ..	—	—	—	—	—	2
Fillets—						
No. 1 " A " $(15\frac{1}{4} \times 1\frac{1}{4} \times \frac{3}{8})$	8	—	—	—	—	—
No. 2 " A " $(9\frac{7}{8} \times 1\frac{1}{4} \times \frac{3}{8})$	—	8	8	8	8	8
No. 1 " B " $(15\frac{1}{4} \times 1 \times \frac{3}{8})$	8	—	—	—	—	—
No. 2 " B " $(9\frac{7}{8} \times 1 \times \frac{3}{8})$	—	12	12	12	12	12
No. 1 " C " $(14\frac{1}{2} \times 1 \times \frac{5}{8})$	4	—	—	—	—	—
No. 1 " D " $(2\frac{5}{16} \times 1 \times \frac{3}{4})$	8	8	8	8	8	8
No. 1 " E " $(2\frac{5}{16} \times 2 \times \frac{3}{8})$	4	4	4	4	4	4

Detail (Dimensions in inches)	Pattern of Chest and No. of fittings.					
	No. I, Mk. II	No. 2, Mk. II. and No. 7	No. 3, Mk. II	No. 4, Mk. II	No. 5, Mk. II* and Mk. II	No. 6, Mk. II* and Mk. II
Racks—						
No. 1 " A " ($19\frac{1}{8} \times 2\frac{7}{16} \times \frac{7}{8}$)	2	2	—	—	—	—
No. 3 " A " ($15\frac{1}{2} \times 2\frac{7}{16} \times \frac{7}{8}$)	—	—	2	—	—	—
No. 4 " A " ($11\frac{7}{8} \times 2\frac{7}{16} \times \frac{7}{8}$)	—	—	—	2	—	—
No. 5 " A " ($8\frac{1}{4} \times 2\frac{7}{16} \times \frac{7}{8}$)	—	—	—	—	2	—
No. 6 " A " ($4\frac{5}{8} \times 2\frac{7}{16} \times \frac{7}{8}$)	—	—	—	—	—	2
No. 1 " B " ($19\frac{1}{8} \times 1\frac{1}{2} \times \frac{7}{8}$)	2	2	—	—	—	—
No. 3 " B " ($15\frac{1}{2} \times 1\frac{1}{2} \times \frac{7}{8}$)	—	—	2	—	—	—
No. 4 " B " ($11\frac{7}{8} \times 1\frac{1}{2} \times \frac{7}{8}$)	—	—	—	2	—	—
No. 5 " B " ($8\frac{1}{4} \times \frac{1}{2} \times \frac{7}{8}$)	—	—	—	—	2	—
No. 6 " B " ($4\frac{5}{8} \times 1\frac{1}{2} \times \frac{7}{8}$)	—	—	—	—	—	2
No. 1 " C " ($19\frac{1}{8} \times 2\frac{3}{4} \times \frac{7}{8}$)	1	1	—	—	—	—
No. 3 " C " ($15\frac{1}{2} \times 2\frac{3}{4} \times \frac{7}{8}$)	—	—	1	—	—	—
No. 4 " C " ($11\frac{7}{8} \times 2\frac{3}{4} \times \frac{7}{8}$)	—	—	—	1	—	—
No. 5 " C " ($8\frac{1}{4} \times 2\frac{3}{4} \times \frac{7}{8}$)	—	—	—	—	1	—
No. 6 " C " ($4\frac{5}{8} \times 2\frac{3}{4} \times \frac{7}{8}$)	—	—	—	—	—	1
Supports—						
No. 1 ($15\frac{1}{8} \times 2\frac{1}{4} \times 1\frac{1}{2}$) ..	4	—	—	—	—	—
No. 2 ($9\frac{7}{8} \times 2\frac{1}{4} \times 1\frac{1}{2}$) ..	—	4	4	2	2	2
Slips, butt—						
No. 1 ($15\frac{1}{8} \times 2 \times 1\frac{5}{16}$) ..	10	—	—	—	—	—
No. 2 ($9\frac{7}{8} \times 2 \times 1\frac{5}{16}$) ..	—	10	8	6	4	2
Strips, butt—						
No. 1 ($15\frac{1}{8} \times 1\frac{1}{2} \times \frac{1}{2}$) ..	10	—	—	—	—	—
No. 2 ($9\frac{7}{8} \times 1\frac{1}{2} \times \frac{1}{2}$) ..	—	10	8	6	4	2

APPENDIX VI

Plates, Screw, and Taps, S.A.

The plates are lettered " A " to " F," and the holes in plates numbered 1 to 13 (two per plate, except " F," which has three).

The taps are numbered 1 to 13.

The following table shows which holes in the plates and which taps are suitable for the screws and holes in the various arms.

Screws, etc.	Plate	Tap No.	Diameter, inch	Threads to the inch
Screw, stop, backsight, No. 3	} A	1	·084	57
,, cut-off, No. 1		2	·114	49
Screw, bolt, stop, No. 3		} 3	·126	42
,, extractor, No. 1				
,, guard, trigger, back, No. 1	} B			
,, spring, sight, back, No. 1		4	·144	37
,, ,, ,, No. 3				
,, striker, No. 1				
Screw, cap, backsight, No. 1				
,, ejector, No. 1				
,, grip; Bayonets, Nos. 1 and 3				
,, spring, bolt, locking, No. 1				
,, ,, trap, butt-plate, No. 1				
,, cap, nose, No. 3	} C	5	·1656	37
,, sight, dial, fixing; Rifle, No. 3				
,, sight, dial, pivot; Rifle, No. 3				
,, spring, trap, butt-plate, No. 3				
Nuts, grip; Bayonets, Nos. 1 and 3				
Screw, sear, No. 1		6	·1745	50
Bolts; Bayonets, No. 1		} 7	·181	26½
,, ,, No. 3				
Nuts, bolt; Bayonets, Nos. 1 and 3				
Screw, band, inner, No. 1				
,. cap, nose, back, No. 1	} D			
,. ,, ,, front, No. 1				
,, catch, slide, backsight, No. 1		8	·1875	33
,, protector, No. 1				
,, swivel				
Nut, bolt, tie, No. 3				
Bolt, tie, No. 3				
Tools and gauges, armourers various		9	·203	26½
Screw, guard, trigger, front, No. 1	} E			
,, ,, ,, No. 3		} 10	·25	30
,, ,, ,, back, No. 3				
Screw, axis, backsight, No. 3		11	·096	56
,, cap, handguard, No. 1				
Nuts, backsight, No. 3				
Screw, windgauge, R.S.M.L.E., Mk. I	} F	12	·125	20
† ,, ,, backsight, No. 1		13	·17	46

* Obsolete.   † Obsolescent.

APPENDIX VII

Stocks and Dies, Bicycle

Component parts of the bicycle for which the dies and taps supplied are suitable. (*See* Part IV, Section 1.)

Note.—One pair of dies and two taps (one taper and one plug) are provided for each size.

Component	Taps	Dies	Threads to the inch
Bottom bracket—			
Cotters	} ·266	·266	26 R.H.
Nuts, cotter			
Hubs, front—			
Spindle			
Nuts			
Pedals—			
Pins (left and right)			
Nuts, locking			
Frames, bicycle—			
Screws, seat lug	} ·3125	·3125	26 R.H.
Nuts, seat lug			
Ball-head—			
Screws, clip			
Nuts, clip			
Clips, rifle, bicycle—			
Butt, Mk. II			
Nuts			
Hubs, back, coaster—			
Spindles			
Hubs, back, free-wheel—			
Spindles	·375		
Hubs, back, coaster and free-wheel—			
Nuts, spindle			
Pedals—			
Pins, left		·5625	20 L.H.
Pins, right		·5625	20 R.H.
Bottom brackets—			
Cranks, chain wheel	·5625 R.H.		
Cranks, plain	·5625 L.H.		
*Dies, spoke		No. 14 gauge (·08-in.)	62 R H.

* Separately demandable; does not constitute part of the set of stocks and dies, bicycle.

APPENDIX VIII

Special gauges, components special to Examiners and special tools (N.I.V.) supplied to Commands at home and to authorized stations overseas for use of the R.A.O.C. in the examination of small arms and machine guns in the hands of troops. (*See* Part I, Chapter II.)

Item to be gauged	Description of gauge, etc.	Reg. No. of gauge	Remarks
	Gauges for Rifles, No. 1, Mks. III and III*		
Barrel	Plug, large cone (tapped at end) ..	42	Not to enter beyond ·10 inch. Also for M.G. barrels.
Bolt	Eccentricity of striker	2115	Used with armourers' gauge, ·064-inch acc.
Rifle assembled ..	Bolt-head dummy ·639	—	Spare part length. When the rifle bolt, with this gauge dummy inserted, turns over the ·074-inch gauge, the rifle will be exchanged.
Bayonet No. 1, Mk. I, and No. 3.	Test, curve	2113	With the × mark on the blade on the outer (convex) side from the curve, insert the point in the block and bend the blade once only to conform to the curve. The blade must not be over-stressed, so causing the middle portion to be bent outward from the curve of the test. The blade to be examined for straightness before and after test.
	Gauges for Rifle No. 2		
Arms assembled ..	Slip, distance from face of bolt to face of barrel ·008 reject	—	If this gauge slip enters without pressure, the rifle will be exchanged.

Item to be gauged	Description of gauge, etc.	Reg. No. of gauge	Remarks
Cylinder	*Gauges for Pistol, Revolver, No. 1, Mk. VI* Plug, compound, diameters ·441 and ·3105 (used with Reg. No. 100C).	100	For testing concentricity of chambers with bore.
	Handle, screwed (used with Reg. No. 100).	100A	Ditto.
	Cartridges, dummy, 6 (used with Reg. No. 100).	100C	Ditto.
Blade	*Gauges for Swords, Cavalry, No. 1, Mk. I*, and No. 2, Mk. II* Test, box	—	First examine blade for straightness, then spring down once in test from left to right to shorten 3½ inches (× on convex side), and again examine for straightness. When testing No. 2 swords the steel block on the outside of the box is to be removed.
Block, breech (Hotchkiss) Bolt (Lewis) .. .. Extractor (Vickers) ..	*Gauges for all ·303-inch Machine Guns* Plug, plain, diameter of firing pin or striker hole ·088 High	915	
Barrel	Plug, plain, diameter ·306 (tapped at end) ..	Nil	This gauge should not enter barrels held for mobilization.
Gun	*Gauges for Guns, Machine, Vickers, ·303-in.* Level, spirit	4741	For testing alignment of barrel and breech casings.
Muzzle-attachment (ball)	Plug, long, special, diameter ·303 in. .. Sleeve (for use with No. 985)	985 989	For testing alignment of bullet exit hole in front cone from bore of barrel.
	Plug, plain, diameter of hole in gland ·64 in. rej.	S	

Barrel	Plate, grooved, diameter at muzzle bearing ·627-in. rej.	4700	This is not applicable to the portion in front of the bearing.
Extractor	Plate, profile and depth of bullet groove ·058 in.	932	For cartridge seating of gib. (Represents minimum rim of cartridge.)
	Cartridge head, ·058 in.	202	·253 portion for tumbler and trigger axis holes.
Casing, lock	Plug, double-ended, diameter of tumbler and trigger axis pin holes, ·253 reject and ·303 reject.	923	·303 portion for the larger tumbler axis hole.
Lock, assembled ..	Plate, grooved, length overall 4·445 H., 4·438 L.	4794	
	Plate, protrusion of firing pin ·065 H., ·058 L.	4703	

Components Special for Examiners

			For comparison with doubtful components, upon assembly. The selected components are correctly adjusted for the following points:—
	Lever, extractor, right, No. 2	—	For radial and angular bents.
	Lever, extractor, left, No. 2	—	For radial and angular bents.
	Pin, firing	—	For height and length of bent (High) and height from point to shoulder (Low).
	Sear (with spring)	—	For height and length of bent (High).
	Tumbler	—	For height of bent (High) and set of tail in relation to head.
	Trigger	—	For height and length of bent (High).

Gauges for Guns, Machine, Lewis ·303-in, Mk. I

Rod, piston	Plate grooved, diameter of head ·745 acc., ·741 rej.	2707	
Rod, piston	Length of radiator, gas cylinder and piston rod (in 3 pieces).	2720	Rod, piston, 22·285 High, 22·225 Low.
Cylinder, gas			Cylinder, gas, 19·59 Low.
Radiator			Radiator 23·71 High.

Item to be gauged	Description of gauge, etc.	Reg. No. of gauge	Remarks
Cover body (assembled gun).	Plate wing, distance from magazine post to pawls 3·9 and to edge of cover 4·05.	2686	For protrusion of pawls and minimum distance of radial edge of body cover.
	Slip, taper, height and angle of tongue for cartridge guide seating, from body.	2677	This is to check distortion. The tongue can be set as necessary to suit the gauge.
Cylinder, gas	Plug flat, diameter of bore at front end ·751 High.	2693	
Body	Locking piece, modified (used with No. 2891)	2892	For testing wear in body affecting cartridge head space.
	Bolt, modified, minimum length 3·661 (used with Nos. 2891 and 2892).	2957	These gauges are for use either in conjunction or separately, as the case may be.
	Breech end of barrel, modified (used with No. 2892).	2891	
	Components Special for Examiners		For comparison with doubtful components, upon assembly. The selected components are correctly adjusted for the following points:—
	Arm, feed	—	For cartridge stop from underside, and position of studs in relation to hole for magazine post and groove for actuating stud.
	Chamber, gas	—	For maximum wear (overturn) of thread in barrel band and gas cylinder.
	Handle, cocking	—	For minimum thickness of shank and depth of flange, ·155 × 20.
	Sear	—	For length of tail and height of bent in relation to tail and axis hole.
	Pawl, stop, magazine, No. 1, left, Mk. I* ..	—	From stop to acting face.
	Pawl, stop, magazine, No. 2, right, Mk. I* ..	—	Ditto.
	Pawl, feed arm	—	Ditto.

Gauges for Gun, Machine, Hotchkiss .303-in.

Item	Gauge	No.	Remarks
Piston	Plug flat, diameter of piston cup .7895 High	3010	For use during modification.
Barrel	Plate grooved, diameter of gas nozzle .779 Low	3004	
Regulator, gas	Plug flat, diameter of gas cylinder .611 High Plate grooved, diameter of flanges .606 High, .604 Low	3038	
Gun, assembled, Mk. I*	Plate, profile and position of stop pawl, No. 2 feed spring, from guide.	3013 3043	

Components Special for Examiners

For comparison with doubtful components upon assembly. The selected components are correctly adjusted for the following points:—

Item		No.	Remarks
Sear		—	For height of bent in relation to stop.
Trigger		—	For underside of hook, and bevel at tail end in relation to stop.
Feed piece (modified) ..		—	For acting face and height of lever in relation to actuating arm.
Pin, firing		—	Maximum length from driving face to point.
Piston		—	For stop and alignment of gas cup.
Spring, recoil (slave) ..		—	For use when recoil springs are not available.

Gauges for Mountings, Tripod, .303-in. M.G., Mk. IV and Vickers .303-in. M.G.

Item	Gauge	No.	Remarks
Crosshead of gun and mounting.	Plug plain, diameter of crosshead joint pin hole .565 reject.	962	May pass through the left bush but not through the right bush of mounting.
Elevating gear and gun	Plug, double-ended, diameter of elevating joint pin hole .445 rej. and .45 rej.	970	*Elevating gear.*—.445 plug is not to pass through. *Gun.*—.445 plug is not to pass through left side. .45 plug is not to pass through right side.

Item to be gauged	Description of gauge, etc.	Reg. No. of gauge	Remarks
Crosshead	*Gauges for Mounting Tripod ·303-in. M.G., Mk. IV*		
	Plug plain, diameter of crosshead joint pin hole ·567 in. rej.	2514	Left bush only.
	Plate grooved, diameter of crosshead joint pin ·556 Low, diameter of elevating joint pin ·436 Low and width between crossheads 2·36 Low.	2553	The gun and mounting bearings of the joint pins will be gauged separately. If the low limit gauge is not "kept off" the greater part of the circumference, for at least half the length of any one of those bearings, the pin should be sentenced "Unserviceable."
	Tools for Guns, Machine, Vickers ·303-in. Mk. I		
	Straight-edge, 8-in.	—	For general purposes.
	Die for thread of muzzle end of barrel	—	For removing burrs, etc.
	Tap, ·875 × 24 threads, for gland hole in barrel casing	—	Ditto.
	Tap, ·625 × 20 threads, for cup muzzle attachment.	—	For removing fouling.
	Tool removing steam tube	—	
	Tools for Guns, Machine, Lewis ·303-in. Mk. I		
	Die for thread of muzzle end of barrel	—	Left-hand thread.
	Tap, ·622 × 20 threads per inch for barrel mouthpiece	—	For removing burrs, fouling, etc.

APPENDIX IX

List of General Drawings supplied apart from these Instructions

Drawing No.	*Designation, etc.*
A.I.D.1711	Guns, machine, Lewis, ·303-inch. (Instructions to guide fitting of Eliminator, Flash, Mk. I.)
S.A.I.D.	
2053	Pistol, revolver, No. 1, Mks. III, IV, V, VI. (General Arrangement and Components.)
2058	Rifles, No. 3, Mk. I* (F) and Mk. 1* (T). (General Arrangement and Stock.)
2059	Rifles, No. 3, Mk. 1* (F) and Mk. I* (T). (Components.)
2062	Gun, machine, Vickers, ·303-inch Mk. I. (General Arrangements and Components.)
2063	Gun, machine, Lewis, ·303-inch, Mk. I. (General Arrangements and Components.)
2064	Gun, machine, Hotchkiss, ·303-inch, Mk. I*, Nos. 1 and 2.
2081	Mountings, tripod, ·303-inch M.G. Mk. IV. (General Arrangement and details.)
,,	Mountings, tripod, Hotchkiss ·303-inch M.G. Mk. II* and II**. (General Arrangement and details.)
,,	Mount, field, Lewis ·303-inch M.G. Mk. III. (General Arrangement and details.)
2267	Rifles, No. 1, Mk. III and III* and No. 2, Mk. IV*. (General Arrangements.)
2268	Rifles, No. 1, Mk. III and III* and No. 2, Mk. IV*. (Components.)
2269	Rifles, No. 1, Mk. III and III* and No. 2, Mk. IV*. (Components.)
2270	Bicycle, Mk. IV. (General Arrangement.)
2271 2272 2273	Bicycle, Mk. IV. (Components and Accessories.)
2474	Bayonets, Dirks, Swords and Scabbards.
2530	Pistol, Signal, No. 1, Mk. III*.
D.D.(E).871	Mountings, tripod, ·303-inch M.G. Mk. IV. Instructions to guide local adjustment and repair of.
D.D(E).1000	Mounting, tripod, Mk. IV : Wheel elevating " B " (Instructions for modification of wheel " A.")

Printed under the authority of HIS MAJESTY'S STATIONERY OFFICE by William Clowes and Sons, Ltd., London and Beccles.

(270) Wt. 17758—9623/1368. 4,500. 8/31. W. C. & S., Ltd. **Gp. 310.**

Printed in Great Britain
by Amazon